The Nonprofit Sector in the Mixed Economy

The Nonprofit Sector
in the Mixed Economy

Edited by Avner Ben-Ner and Benedetto Gui

Ann Arbor

THE UNIVERSITY OF MICHIGAN PRESS

Copyright © by the University of Michigan 1993
All rights reserved
Published in the United States of America by
The University of Michigan Press
Manufactured in the United States of America

1996 1995 1994 1993 4 3 2 1

A CIP catalogue record for this book is available from the British Library.

Library of Congress Cataloging-in-Publication Data

The Nonprofit sector in the mixed economy / edited by Avner Ben-Ner
  and Benedetto Gui.
     p.   cm.
    Includes bibliographical references and index.
    ISBN 0-472-10429-2 (alk. paper)
    1. Nonprofit organizations. 2. Mixed economy. I. Ben-Ner,
  Avener. II. Gui, Benedetto.
  HD2769. 15.N663 1993
  338.7'4—dc20   93-19165
                                         CIP

Preface

Interest in nonprofit organizations is growing among scholars, practitioners, and policymakers. The number of scholars doing research and teaching on the nonprofit sector, the number of research and teaching centers dedicated to it, and the number of books and journals focusing on the topic of nonprofit organizations have all grown significantly in recent years. This book seeks to contribute to the literature on nonprofit organizations by explicitly recognizing and emphasizing the role and behavior of the nonprofit sector in the *mixed economy*, along with the for-profit and government sectors.

The book's twelve chapters present a picture of the nonprofit sector and its relationship with other sectors of the mixed economy, and theoretically and empirically analyze various aspects of this relationship. Although the focus of the book is nonprofit organizations, it everywhere recognizes its numerous interactions with for-profit and government organizations.

The book offers, among other things, (a) new perspectives on the role of nonprofit organizations via-à-vis for-profit firms and government organizations, (b) a theoretical reevaluation of the relationship between government expenditures and private contributions and a critique of the econometric studies of the "crowd-in" and "crowd-out" issues, (c) new results on the Pareto efficiency of philanthropy, (d) a new analysis of the relationship between government expenditures and competition between nonprofit organizations and for-profit firms, using data from the 1980s, (e) an empirical test of the relationship between consumer informedness and the search for signal of trustworthiness in the type of organization of nursing homes, and (f) a comparative empirical investigation of financial vulnerability. Additionally, the book offers comprehensive statistical information on key variables in nonprofit organizations in comparison with for-profit firms and government organizations in several countries. Important policy issues are examined throughout the book.

Most chapters in this volume are authored by economists. However, they were written also to be accessible to other social scientists and practitioners interested in nonprofit organizations as well as public policy, comparative organizations, industrial organization, public economics, organization theory, and organizational economics.

This book is the result of the collective effort of its contributors, as well as of the numerous scholars who commented on individual chapters and the entire volume. We thank Celia Coelho-Kamath for help in compiling the index; De Boeck Universite of Brussels for granting the right to reproduce, with minor changes, articles (all but the first and last chapters included in this volume) that were published in the *Annals of Public and Cooperative Economics* 62, no. 4 (1991), copyright DeBoeck-Wesmael, S.A.; and the Italian Ministry for University and Research for its financial support.

Contents

INTRODUCTION

by

Avern BEN-NER and Benedetto GUI

Market economic systems are often referred to as "capitalist" to indicate that they rely for production and distribution on firms in which profits are appropriated by "capitalists," the private providers of equity capital. The recognition that a significant share of economic activity takes place in governmental organizations has led to the widespread adoption of the label "mixed economies." The use of this label in the title of this book is additionally motivated by the existence of a large (and in many places growing) population of private nongovernmental organizations that do not seek to maximize profits to be distributed among proprietors (if they have any), or whose owners are not "capitalists" interested only in returns to their investments, or whose owners are primarily interested in the product they obtain from their organization, even if they do receive monetary dividends. Such organizations, often referred to collectively as the "third sector," include nonprofit organizations—organizations that do not distribute profits as monetary compensation to their owners—as well as a wide array of cooperatives (consumer, producer, agricultural, credit), and organizations in which important ownership rights are vested in employees.

While the term "nonprofit organization" is gaining broad acceptance among academics and even practitioners outside the United States, it is mainly in the United States that it has a well-defined legal meaning. In other countries nonprofit organizations are variously identified as voluntary associations, foundations, civic associations, charities, mutual organizations, nongovernmental organizations, and other terms.[1] Under a variety of names, nonprofit

---

1   The term *nonprofit organization* does not have a commonly understood meaning in several languages, where the English term is used in academic

organizations are important economic actors and becoming more so, especially in health care, education, social welfare, culture, recreation, personal services, and research. In these industries nonprofit organizations often compete directly with for-profit firms and government organizations, engaging in complex market transactions and employing a large number of workers (in many industries employing more workers than the average for-profit firm). And while the nonprofit sector's share in total employment is usually below 10% (with its largest share being in the U.S.), the rate of growth of the nonprofit sector has exceeded that of the for-profit and government sectors in many countries during the 1980s.

Economists have traditionally focused their attention on for-profit firms, and to a much lesser extent on government-owned firms. Third sector organizations were commonly viewed as noneconomic phenomena, worthy of study by political scientists and sociologists, but outside the economists' research domain. It is only during the last two decades that academic economists have started expressing interest in third sector organizations. This interest has coincided with a growing uneasiness among economists in regarding firms as just "black boxes" that respond to market stimuli, and with the expansion in the scope of what economists regard as legitimate objects of economic inquiry. Together these developments have generated a considerable quantity of research on issues of internal organization and organizational diversity and this type of research is now increasingly recognized under the banner of "organizational economics." Among the early precursors of the organizational economics literature, one may count institutional economics, transaction costs economics, grants economics, and club theory. Since the early 1970s worker-managed firms and worker cooperatives have attracted considerable attention (see Bonin, Jones and Putterman, forthcoming, for a survey of the literature). Other types of cooperatives have also been investigated (e.g., Carson, 1977, Heflebower, 1980), though to a much lesser extent.

The economics literature on nonprofit organizations also has roots in the early 1970s; Clarkson (1972), Nelson and Krashinsky (1973), Newhouse (1970), Pauly and Redisch (1973), and Weisbrod

---

writing. The term *third sector* has moderate recognition among English-speaking academics; the French use the term *economie sociale* (social economy), whereas the Germans prefer *Gemeinwirtschaft,* which evokes the notion of "community" (in contrast with the less intimate "society").

(1975) were among the forerunners. Many of these early contributions concentrated on issues that characterize the industries in which these organizations operate (hospitals and day-care for children in particular), while recognizing the different nature of nonprofit organizations. Later work, much of it represented in a volume edited by Rose-Ackerman (1986), focused on *sui generis* traits of the nonprofit form of organization which supersede the particulars of the industries in which they operate. The approach that underlies these contributions recognizes that the behavior of an organization is determined by both the nature of the product and the market in which it is sold and the nature of ownership in the organization and the identity of those who control it. For many organizational economists the commonalities between nonprofit organizations operating in different industries present a more captivating subject of research than the commonalities between for-profit and nonprofit organizations engendered by their belonging to the same industry. Inquiry that is motivated thus is comparative by nature. The papers in this book subscribe (at least implicitly) to this view, examining nonprofit organizations as a special form of organization, and comparing them with for-profit and government organizations.

Though the mere existence of nonprofit organizations in market economies, together with their economic importance, provides the general motivation for the study of these organizations, three themes appear to be of particular interest to both scholars and policymakers. First, the existence of organizations that are constituted voluntarily (but *not* for the pursuit of profit to be appropriated as returns to private investment) raises the question of the economic rationality of these ventures. If, as most scholars of nonprofit organizations believe, such organizations do express economic rationality, then understanding their existence and operation may throw further light on the market economic system. Second, it is important to know whether and in what direction nonprofit organization behavior departs from that of for-profit and government organizations, and how they interact with other types of organizations. Third, since nonprofit organizations depend on transfers of resources from private and public supporters, understanding their behavior, the motives for donative behavior, and the effects of public policy are significant issues for donors and governments, as well as for nonprofit organizations.

The papers collected in this book view nonprofit organizations as economic phenomena and investigate various aspects of these three themes. The papers throw new light on the nature of nonprofit organizations and their institutional setting in specific country contexts, and delineate the varying boundaries of the nonprofit sector in the mixed economy. After discussing some definitional issues below, we outline the contributions of these papers in the context of the existing literature according to the three themes mentioned above.

Identifying Nonprofit Organizations

Differing theoretical perspectives as well as legal and social traditions around the world provide alternative definitions for what we call here nonprofit organizations. A type of organization may be defined according to various criteria, including: the organization's objectives, the identity of its owners, the identity of its beneficiaries, and the major constraints that the organization faces. The first criterion had been used to define the conventional capitalist ("for-profit," "profit-maximizing") firm in the "black box" tradition. This criterion has not been used to identify nonprofit organizations, because their (unobservable) objectives are deemed to be too diverse to be useful for definitional purposes. (This is not to say that a set of consistent objectives cannot be attributed to nonprofit organizations; see discussion below.)

The ownership criterion has come to be used more frequently with the advent of organizational economics, where the first question that is typically asked about an organization is "who are its principals?" The principals are commonly identified with the owners, who have at least one of the following rights: to control the organization, to dispose of its returns, and to transfer the previous two rights (see, for example, Grossman and Hart, 1986, Hansmann, 1988, Ben-Ner and Jones, 1992, and Montias, Ben-Ner, and Neuberger, forthcoming). Whereas the identity of the owners is clearest in the case of capitalist firms, in the case of nonprofit organizations the situation is much more complex. In the first chapter, Ben-Ner and Van Hoomissen adopt this approach to defining nonprofit organizations. They partition the universe of organizations according to the relationship of owners to the organization: whether they provide inputs (such as investors and workers) and are therefore interested in the benefits that accrue to these inputs as supply-side stakeholders, or have an interest in the organization's output (such as consumers, donors, and sponsors) and are therefore interested in its quantity, quality and price as demand-side stakeholders. Demand-side stakeholder-controlled organizations and supply-side stakeholder-controlled organizations differ along many dimensions, including the ways in which ownership rights are defined and exercised. Demand-side stakeholder-controlled organizations include nonprofit organizations (such as traditional charities and nonprofit hospitals), as well as clubs, chambers of commerce, consumer cooperatives, and firms formed through backward vertical integration (by purchasing a supplier of inputs).[2]

The identity of beneficiaries is the criterion that is most widely used in the legal definition of nonprofit organizations, as the chapters on individual countries in this book indicate. The law commonly requires that a nonprofit organization (by this or other names) benefit the public through the provision of public goods or some positive externality. The law sometimes allows the members of the organization to benefit from its operation (even exclusively), and so chambers of commerce, professional and business associations, and consumer cooperatives are embraced by this definition. Nonetheless, these organizations typically enjoy fewer tax benefits than do "public-benefit" nonprofit organizations. However, the exact meaning of public benefit is elusive. Gui's definition straddles two criteria: the identity of controllers or owners ("the dominant category") and the identity of beneficiaries. He defines public benefit organizations as organizations in which the category of controllers does not substantially overlap with the category of beneficiaries, thus distinguishing them from mutual benefit organizations (e.g., clubs, consumer cooperatives).

The most widely used definition in the academic literature is probably due to Hansmann (1980), who builds on American legal practice. This definition suggests that nonprofit organizations are private organizations that constrain themselves to not distribute profits to shareholders, officers or employees and, therefore, to reinvest profits into the organization, to produce larger quantities or better quality, or to reduce prices. This constraint is believed to shield nonprofit organizations' customers and donors from the negative effects of the profit motive.

The undisputed core of the nonprofit sector contains organizations which comply with all three definitions. In many countries this includes the majority of organizations operating in the fields of education and research, health services, and social welfare (see James, 1987). Relatively few organizations (e.g., clubs, membership organi-

---

2   Montias, Ben-Ner, and Neuberger (forthcoming) refer to nonprofit organizations as "user-oriented organizations" and divide them into two categories: stakeholder organizations, where the controllers are also the users of the organization's output, and fiduciary organizations, where the majority of users are not controllers.

zations, consumer cooperatives) are nonprofit organizations according to the most expansive definition (control by demand-side stakeholders) but not according to the public benefit and nondistribution-of-profit constraint criteria. At the same time, all definitions exclude from the nonprofit sector essentially the same classes of organizations, especially employee-owned firms and other related third-sector organizations.

On the Formation and Role of Nonprofit Organizations in Market Economies

Are nonprofit organizations a political creation due primarily to favorable tax treatment, or historical accidents perpetuated by organizational inertia, or "organic" organizational forms engendered by the operation of the market economy? The question concerning the place of nonprofit organizations in the market economic system has been addressed repeatedly in the literature[3] and is revisited in this book.

Although favorable tax treatment and other advantages conferred by government on nonprofit organizations undoubtedly enhance their presence (Hansmann, 1987b), only few scholars (e.g., Clark, 1980) claim that their existence is due to positive governmental action. In fact, nonprofit organizations in the United States existed before such advantages were granted to them (Hall, 1987); indeed, they preceded governments in many parts of the world (Salamon, 1987). Theories of nonprofit organizations begin with the (mostly implicit) assumption that the for-profit sector is the dominant sector in the economy, the government is the main corrective to failures of the for-profit sector, and the nonprofit sector represents the residual corrective to both market and government failures. These theories therefore predict that nonprofit organizations will not arise in perfectly competitive markets.[4]

---

3   See the surveys by James and Rose-Ackerman (1986), Gui (1987), Hansmann (1987a), Holtmann (1988), and DiMaggio and Anheier (1990).

4   This approach should be contrasted with one that considers the evolution of an economy in which initially all forms of organization compete with each other, or even an economy where the nonprofit form dominates. At a seminar expounding on the theory that nonprofit organizations come into existence as a response to market failure, E. Charles Lindblom commented that it is only because of rabbit failure that knights ride horses (the seminar took place in the early 1980s at Yale University's Program on Non-Profit

There are three well-known classes of explanations for the existence of nonprofit organizations. According to the "inadequate public provision" (government failure) argument nonprofit organizations complement governmental provision of public and mixed ("collective") goods. Nonprofit organizations do so for the benefit of high-demand citizens who, at the going tax rate, are under-satisfied with the quantity, quality, or variety of these goods, which, due to the nature of the democratic political process, are aimed to satisfy the demand of median voters (Weisbrod, 1975 and 1988; see also James, 1987).

The "contract failure" argument focuses on the market failure that occurs in the case of hard-to-evaluate services. For-profit firms have an incentive to take advantage of their superior information relative to customers and donors who cannot write and enforce detailed contracts economically. Nonprofit organizations are more trustworthy because they have different incentives (Arrow, 1963, Nelson and Krashinsky, 1973, Hansmann, 1980, and Easley and O'Hara, 1983). In particular, the nondistribution-of-profit constraint is often regarded as a protection for uninformed customers and donors against providers of hard-to-evaluate services. The constraint is a signal to consumers and donors that the organization does not have incentive to take advantage of them (Hansmann, 1980).

The "consumer control" argument states that market failures (including the one just discussed) or government failure cannot be satisfactorily addressed by nonprofit organizations unless some persons take determined action to create these organizations, thus ensuring consumer or donor control. Such control is needed in order to bring the firm's choices more closely in line with the preferences of consumers and donors (rather than management) and to elicit their cooperation in revealing preferences and making contributions (Ben-Ner, 1986, Hansmann, 1980).

These three classes of arguments have not been entirely separated from each other (Hansmann, 1987a and Weisbrod, 1988), and they are being increasingly integrated into a more general theory of the nonprofit sector in the mixed economy. Ben-Ner and Van Hoomissen's and Gui's papers make such integrative attempts.

Ben-Ner and Van Hoomissen recognize several market and government failures that may cause dissatisfaction among individuals or

---

Organizations). Note that the existence of purely redistributive motives on the part of donors does not explain the existence of nonprofit organizations—as suggested below, the explanations rely, in the end, on some market imperfections, such as those due to asymmetric information.

organizations (private and government) interested in the provision of some goods and services for their own use or that of others (whom they sponsor or help defray the costs of their consumption with donations). However, it is insufficient to demonstrate the existence of demand for an alternative organizational form; one must also show how this form arises. Extending the consumer-control argument, the authors suggest that the initiative for forming a nonprofit organization may come from demand-side stakeholders, or from professional administrators who see a potential demand for their services or an opportunity to pursue their ideals, and seek to establish a coalition from among latent demand-side stakeholders.[5] The nonprofit organization can be therefore viewed as backward vertical integration by demand-side stakeholders: those who demand an alternative form of organization are also those who supply it. Controlling stakeholders are the limited "owners" of the organization: they exercise control but may not have the right to sell it, and their return rights may be exercised primarily through lower prices or higher quality for the products of their organization rather than through monetary returns to stock.[6]

Gui characterizes for-profit firms as "mutual benefit" organizations where investors constitute both the "dominant" (controllers) and the "beneficiary" categories; for example, a capitalist firm is controlled by investors for their own benefit, and a worker cooperative is controlled by workers who benefit themselves. The categories of controllers and beneficiaries represent separate groups in "public-benefit" organizations; for example, donors or trustees control nonprofit hospitals for the benefit of buyers, job creation enterprises do so for the benefit of workers and investment funds and trusts do so for the benefit of investors. Gui finds that the emergence of all third

---

5   Because the existence of a nonprofit organization is predicated on demand-side stakeholders' revelation of preferences and voluntary price discrimination, any nonprofit entrepreneur must cooperate with key high-demand stakeholders and de facto make them controlling stakeholders.

6   Ben-Ner and Van Hoomissen regard the nondistribution-of-profit constraint primarily as a method of distribution of a firm's returns when shares in the organization's equity cannot be issued without risking transformation into a for-profit firm. They consider this constraint less as a signal of trust-worthiness of the organization because managers may satisfy this constraint while pursuing their own goals. Because stakeholder-controlled organizations provide primarily nonrival services, controlling and noncontrolling stakeholders enjoy the same service, which provides the latter group with a direct signal of trustworthiness of the organization.

sector organizations is induced by similar market failures: market power, asymmetric information, and unsatisfactory for-profit provision of public goods. His approach associates, on the one hand, the incentive effects of the nondistribution constraint (as stressed by the contract failure argument) with the assignment of the beneficiary position to a category threatened with exploitation (the public benefit case), and, on the other hand, the incentive effects of control with the assignment of the dominant position also to that category (the mutual benefit case).

It is extremely difficult to carry out direct empirical tests of theories that explain the existence of nonprofit organizations, particularly with traditional economic data.[7] However, there have been a few empirical studies that bear on the implications of such theories. The "inadequate public provision" argument implies that demographic and economic heterogeneity will positively affect the prevalence of nonprofit organizations. Indeed, Lee and Weisbrod (1977) find a positive correlation between demographic and economic proxies for heterogeneity and the ratio of nonprofit organization to government hospitals. Similar results were obtained by Feigenbaum (1980), James (1986) and Ben-Ner and Van Hoomissen (1992a).

Surveys designed to ascertain consumer perception of organizations' trustworthiness confirm moderately the predictions of the "contract failure" argument (see Permut, 1981, and Hansmann's reply). Weisbrod and Schlesinger (1986) also find significantly fewer complaints (an indirect measure of service quality) in Wisconsin nonprofit nursing homes than in for-profit homes (see also Weisbrod, 1988).

The paper by Holtmann and Ullmann in this volume examines empirically the effects of asymmetric information between providers and consumers or their sponsors (demand-side stakeholders) on the latter's choice of for-profit over nonprofit nursing homes. The authors hypothesize that if nonprofit organizations really provide consumer protection then, since consumers differ in their ability to monitor sellers' performance, in equilibrium stakeholders with the least ability to monitor performance will select nonprofit providers. Using data on U.S. nursing homes, the authors identify a list of indicators of the patient's need for protection (a concept that combines limited access to information and acute need for good treatment), which includes the degree of disability, the lack of either a spouse or a child who might

---

7   The literature on nonprofit organizations shares this deficiency with the literature on employee-owned firms; see Bonin, Jones, and Putterman (forthcoming).

help monitor the quality of care, and lack of mental health. The results of their econometric analysis confirm that for-profit homes serve better-informed patients than do nonprofit homes. This effect is sustained after controlling for the level of fees.

However, Holtmann and Ullmann suggest several alternative explanations to their results. First, the type of organization from which stakeholders make their purchases could arise from providers' willingness to serve them, besides stakeholder choices. For example, the authors suggest that religious nonprofit organizations may be less reluctant than for-profit firms to accept patients that require intense care. Second, demographic factors and other kinds of heterogeneity among demand-side stakeholders also affect the *supply* of nonprofit services. One reason, provided by Young (1983), is entrepreneurial sorting: those who are not primarily motivated by monetary gain may prefer to associate with nonprofit organizations. James (1987) suggests that starting and supporting nonprofit organizations is a way for ambitious individuals to gain prestige (possibly to be spent in the political arena). In addition, religious and political groups find in nonprofit organizations (especially in health care and education) a convenient tool for proselytizing and improving society's goodwill toward them. Gui also regards the emergence of mutual-benefit organizations as responses by members of the dominant category who seek to remedy a particular market failure, whereas Ben-Ner and Van Hoomissen place such supply considerations at the center stage of their theory.

There has been very little empirical work seeking to examine the role of supply-side factors in the emergence and operation of nonprofit organizations (for indirect attempts, see Schiff and Weisbrod, in this volume, and Ben-Ner and Van Hoomissen, 1992a). Studies of boards of directors (see discussion by DiMaggio and Anheier, 1990) reveal the role of high-demand stakeholders in the founding and control of nonprofit organizations, but the design of these studies is such that they throw only limited light on the theories of economists. Moreover, there seem to be no comparative studies of the ways in which nonprofit organizations and for-profit firms are controlled, and of the role of various groups such as shareholders, demand-side stakeholders, boards of directors, and employees.

The Behavior of Nonprofit Organizations

The behavior of an organization comprises a myriad of actions undertaken in order to promote its objectives, given the organization's environment and its chosen internal structure. These actions include: the determination of organizational objectives, the choice of inputs (including investment) and outputs and reaction to their prices, the choice of financial strategy, employment practices, the choice of monitoring techniques and reward structures, and more. The arguments that are postulated in the literature to enter the objective function of nonprofit organizations include quantity and quality of service provided, the budget, the income of the dominant class of professionals (e.g., the physicians in a hospital), prestige derived from technical excellence (see the survey by James and Rose-Ackerman, 1986, and Steinberg, 1986). These objectives can be derived from the objectives of management, professionals, or controlling demand-side stakeholders and are affected by the extent of the agency problems between the latter group and the former groups and the ways in which these problems are handled (Montias, Ben-Ner, and Neuberger, forthcoming).

Many of these maximands entail different choices of inputs and outputs than profit maximization would, given the same market environment. In perfectly competitive markets with no externalities and with symmetric information nonprofit behavior is suboptimal relative to for-profit behavior; this is the case, for example, for quality maximands which lead to excessive quality relative to consumer demand. However, the discussion in the previous subsection indicated that there is no reason to expect the emergence of nonprofit organizations in perfectly competitive markets. When market imperfections of various kinds enter the picture, the input and output choices of nonprofit organizations may be superior relative to those of for-profit firms. For example, nonprofit behavior may be socially desirable if the preferred product is actually (or expected to be) undersupplied by for-profit firms. This has been shown to be the case in models of multiproduct nonprofit organizations, under the assumption that managers derive utility from supplying some products that constitute the mission of their organizations and disutility from supplying other products, such as commercial activities needed to generate income of support of the mission.

Schiff and Weisbrod in this volume adopt an objective function of this sort to explore nonprofit organizations' choice of revenue sources (sales, government support, and private donations). The additional assumption that private donors react negatively to the expansion of commercial activity by the nonprofit organization they support generates an interesting trade-off between sources of income. On the one hand, greater commercial activity generates additional profits that permit the firm to cross-subsidize its service, thus increasing the manager's utility. On the other hand, commercial activity has two negative effects on utility: one direct (the manager dislikes commercial activity) and the other indirect (via reduced donation income). Assuming that the manager's equilibrium choice is disturbed by a reduction in the exogenous government support, as occurred in the United States during the 1980s, Schiff and Weisbrod's theoretical predictions are that the mission activity will diminish, but by less than the government cutbacks; the commercial activity will increase; donations will decrease; and exit of nonprofit organizations will occur. These predictions are confirmed by the authors' econometric analysis of United States tax data.

Nonprofit organizations' commercial activities raise another important behavioral issue, that of competition between nonprofit organizations and for-profit firms. Conventional economic wisdom suggests that in long-run equilibrium one form of organization will predominate, that is, either nonprofit organizations will be outcompeted by more cost-efficient for-profit competitors, or, if nonprofit organizations enjoy tax benefits and efficiency or other advantages, the opposite will occur. However, the two sectors do coexist; Schiff and Weisbrod provide an explanation for how this can happen. Both the assumption that nonprofit organization managers dislike commercial activity, and the complementarities in either production or consumption between mission and commercial products, are sufficient to insure long-run survival of both types of organization. This coexistence result serves as a basis for the authors' policy recommendations. They advocate direct and specific forms for supporting the production of mission goods instead of the tax-exemption regime presently enjoyed by United States nonprofit organizations (which subsidizes both mission and "related" commercial activities).

Competition with for-profit firms is also the starting point of Chang and Tuckman. These authors focus on nonprofit organizations' survivability, which represents the ultimate measure of their ability to compete and therefore of their performance. Chang and Tuckman develop survivability measures that do not require the use of output data. They focus chiefly on financial vulnerability—an organization's inability to absorb a financial shock without cutting its programs— which is measured according to four criteria: revenue diversification, and the ratios of equity, profit, and administrative costs to revenue. These measures are intended to capture the amplitude of wealth and income margins available to an organization. Chang and Tuckman compute survivability using mid-1980s U.S. data and find that about 40% of nonprofit organizations in the sample are vulnerable with respect to at least one of the four criteria, but only extremely few (0.16%) are vulnerable with respect to all four criteria. However, vulnerability does not seem to translate into much firm exit, as only about 3% of nonprofit organizations go out of business each year, even during a period of government cutbacks.[8] In order to reconcile the discrepancy between vulnerability and exit rates, the authors suggest that weak nonprofit organizations might have survived by engaging in strategies such as those predicted by Schiff and Weisbrod: cutting services and increasing commercial activities to cross-subsidize mission services.

Donations and Government Support

Private monetary contributions (donations) constitute roughly 15% of the revenue of nonprofit organizations in the United States, though for most organizations other than hospitals the percentage is much higher (see next section). Moreover, nonprofit organizations are the beneficiaries of free labor from volunteers. In contrast, government and especially for-profits receive very little by way of private donations.[9] Hence, donative behavior has always been an important subject for investigation in the literature on nonprofit organizations[10] and is of increasing interest to scholars of public economics who focus on the "voluntary provision of public goods."

---

8   This rate is higher than the average 1% annual attrition rate of for-profit firms. However, much higher failure rates for for-profit firms are presented elsewhere (e.g., Ben-Ner [1988] and Dunne, Roberts, and Samuelson [1989]).

9   Preston (1988) reports that the average U.S. for-profit day-care center receives in donations less than 7% of the amount received by the average nonprofit center. According to a 1985 Gallup Poll, 78.4% of all volunteer hours go to the nonprofit sector, 4% to the for-profit sector, and the remainder to government, mainly local (see Steinberg, 1990, and his sources).

10   See, for example, James (1983), who focuses on cross-subsidization of products preferred by nonprofit organization managers using donations intended to support other products; Rose-Ackerman (1986), who sees the need to rely on private donations, rather than public funds, as a constraint on nonprofit organization managers pursuing their own preferences as to product variety; Preston (1988), who views donations as the force driving non-profit organizations to choose product varieties with greater ratios of social to private benefits.

Donations represent a puzzle for traditional economic approaches because the inclusion of, for example, the welfare of the poor into agents' utility function does not imply that they will make voluntary donations. Recipients' welfare is a public good, and therefore utility maximization given others' behavior dictates free-riding, letting others bear the cost, yet benefiting nonetheless from the relief of poverty.[11] The likelihood of voluntary contributions is greater the smaller the number of agents interested in the effects of the donations, but even with few agents the amounts fall below the Pareto-efficient levels (see, for example, Sugden, 1982).

Various proposals have been put forth to solve the puzzle of voluntary contributions. These include, among others, Margolis's (1982) notion of a "fair share" of one's resources that individuals would allocate to the welfare of the "group" they feel part of, as well as Sugden's (1984) "theory of reciprocity," where one commits to give no less than the others (but no more than one thinks everybody should contribute, along Kantian lines). Kaufman (in this volume) discusses donations in the context of utility maximization. He assumes that giving by others is not a substitute for one's own giving. The existence of such "competitive" (or "self-serving") philanthropic preferences, supported in empirical studies of giving behavior, overcomes the result of free-riding, and can, under certain conditions, generate Pareto-optimal outcomes without recourse to public intervention (see also Hollander, 1990). This also bears on the solicitation strategies of nonprofit organizations, which, Kaufman suggests, should identify the nature of donors' preferences in order to save fundraising costs and/or increase donative revenue.

Donations are also the subject of Steinberg's paper, but from a different perspective. Steinberg considers the alleged discouraging effect that government spending may exert on voluntary donations. After briefly reporting the claims emerging from the theoretical debate, the author surveys the empirical works that attempt to identify and measure such "crowding out" effects. The paper examines several interesting aspects of the question, including: the

---

11   Donations need not be always motivated by concern for others. As Hansmann (1982), Ben-Ner (1986) and Ben-Ner and Van Hoomissen (in this volume) suggest, high-demand consumers may want to pay higher prices than other consumers in order to ensure the provision of appropriate quantity or quality of a collective good which they consume. However, this does not alter the problem of free ridership.

variety of forms of government financial support to nonprofit organizations, each possibly causing a "crowdout" effect of a different magnitude; the crowdout (or, possibly, "crowdin") effect of federal spending on local government spending, adding to donation crowdout; and the variety of types of donations, such as volunteer work and bequests. Steinberg's analysis suggests that great caution must be exercised in the interpretation of empirical results. The same holds true for the specification of equations and estimation procedures, which the author also discusses in detail. In addition to the comprehensive tables summarizing empirical findings, Steinberg also provides an overall evaluation of the crowdout effect, that appears to be statistically significant, but considerably smaller than the often claimed value of 100%—an important conclusion for policy makers.

The Nonprofit Sector in Mixed Economies: Country Studies

An increasing number of studies of the nonprofit sector in various countries reveals that it plays a significant role in most market economies (see, for example, James, 1989, and Anheier and Seibel, 1990). Everywhere, one finds that information pertaining to this sector is limited in comparison with information about the for-profit sector. Nonetheless, the available data make it clear that (1) nonprofit organizations account for large shares (often a majority), in education, health, social welfare and cultural services, but not anything of significance outside service industries, (2) nonprofit organizations compete with both for-profit firms and government organizations, (3) they rely on voluntary donations in money, kind and time, and (4) although they face differing legal environments, the policy issues with which nonprofit organizations have to contend with are similar in different countries. Furthermore, because the trend toward a greater service industry role and privatization of government services continues worldwide, the share of the nonprofit sector in total economic activity is growing in many countries, with consequent growing attention to the sector by policy makers.

The four country studies included in this book—by Anheier (on West Germany), Borzaga (on Italy), Ben-Ner and Van Hoomissen (on New York State in the U.S.) and Knapp and Kendall (on England and Wales in the U.K.)—confirm these observations. Statistical information about the nonprofit sector in the four developed countries covered here is only partially available, the coverage is inconsistent, and the nonprofit sector is sometimes not distinguishable from other sectors.[12] Without a drastic change in the collection and presentation of statistical information in all the countries discussed here (and in other volumes), detailed comparisons of the nonprofit sector in different countries will remain fraught with difficulties if not outright impossible.

The nonprofit sectors of these four countries share important similarities but also exhibit significant differences. The differences stem from the influence of different national, social, political, and legal legacies. A few general observations may be made on the basis of the available data. First, in all four countries, nonprofit organizations are prominent in social welfare services. For example, in West Germany, 73% of employees working in day care for children are in the nonprofit sector, compared with 17.5% in the public sector and 9.4% in the for-profit sector, whereas in New York the comparable figures are 76.5%, 0.0%, and 23.5%, respectively. The nonprofit sector provides a large share of educational services, though only in the United States does it also have an important presence in higher education. In the United States, the nonprofit sector is a major player in culture, art and recreation; in the other countries examined in this book, government is more heavily involved in these activities. The nonprofit sector is quite active in health services across all four countries, although it is again in the United States that the share of government is smaller and that of the nonprofit sector is larger. Nonprofit organizations are essentially absent in non-service industries. These observations on the industrial concentration of the nonprofit sector indicate, among other things, that (a) to the extent that nonprofit organizations represent correctives to market and government failures, they either cannot do so outside the service industries, or such failures in, for example, manufacturing, are not as grave, and (b) the extent of such failures and/or the ability of nonprofit organizations to compensate for them differ across countries. Various chapters of this book attempt to explain these phenomena.

Second, the industries in which the nonprofit sector operates are arenas for competition among all three sectors. For example, an examination of Table 4a by Anheier, and of Tables 1 and 2 in the last

---

12   Information is particularly poor for Italy, and the chapter by Borzaga represents the first publication in English of some key aspects of the Italian nonprofit sector.

chapter by Ben-Ner and Van Hoomissen reveals that the service industries segment of these two developed market economies is actually mixed, with organizations in all three sectors offering similar services in direct competition with each other. The coexistence of sectors (rather than the domination by only one sector) in an industry is an important topic which contributors to this book have helped clarify.

Third, nonprofit organizations rely on donations by individuals for roughly 15% of their revenues (no information is presented for West Germany). Individuals also donate time, where the value of such time may exceed their donations of money (see Knapp and Kendall for the U.K.; for the U.S., see Weisbrod, 1988, and Steinberg, 1990). Knapp and Kendall provide detailed information about various sources of additional income in nonprofit organizations (see Borzaga and Ben-Ner and Van Hoomissen, in this volume). Program revenues (income generated directly by the service for fee) account for more than half of total income generated by nonprofit organizations in the United Kingdom and the United States. Government support by way of grants constitutes a small proportion of income (one-tenth is a useful benchmark figure), but the role of government in supporting nonprofit organizations is reflected in many other ways as Steinberg and Knapp and Kendall show.

The legal and public policy environment in the four countries surveyed here differs considerably. However, there are also strong common elements, including the requirement of "public benefit" as a condition for the receipt of diverse tax benefits (though, as an official U.K. government commission, quoted by Knapp and Kendall, commented, "It is not possible to define precisely what amounts to actual benefit or what forms a sufficient section of the public; cases must largely be considered on their merits"). As noted in the country studies and other chapters in this book, public policy affects the operation of nonprofit organizations in myriad ways. Knapp and Kendall point out four key policy issues whose relevance extends beyond the United Kingdom. First, the role of law is pivotal in generating trust among donors regarding the uses of their contributions, and government must enhance its supervision of nonprofit organizations.[13] Second, many individuals appear to be uninformed about the mechanisms of giving, in terms of the costs of both fund raising and

---

[13]   We may add here that the law should also encourage improved control by nonprofit organizations' stakeholders (Ben-Ner and Van Hoomissen, 1992b).

giving (accounting for income tax benefits). Government policy should be directed at improving awareness of these factors (help individuals make rational giving decisions). Third, there is an apparent trend towards replacing grants to nonprofit organizations with contracts for specific services. Although this may improve accountability by nonprofit organizations towards government, it may also reduce their autonomy and their pursuit of their original mission. Fourth, there is an ongoing attempt to replace support for nonprofit providers with support granted to clients (often in form of vouchers). Although vouchers do increase consumer choice, such choice might be undesirable in markets where consumers are asymmetrically informed. Information problems are intrinsic to many services provided by the nonprofit sector. These policy issues are relevant to the nonprofit sector in other mixed economies as well.

Future Research

The study of nonprofit organizations has matured lately: several journals are now devoted to publishing research on nonprofit organizations,[14] many books on nonprofit organizations are being published, several research and teaching centers have been established,[15] and funding of research specifically on nonprofit organ-

---

14   *Nonprofit Management and Leadership, Nonprofit and Voluntary Sector Quarterly,* and *Voluntas* are multidisciplinary journals devoted entirely to publication on nonprofit organizations, with a substantial presence of economic papers (the last two journals were launched in the early 1990s, a time when the first journal changed its name to include the adjective "nonprofit"). Since the late 1980s, *Annals of Public and Cooperative Economics* has included the nonprofit sector in its purview, in addition to the public and cooperative sectors.

15   In the United States, in addition to the Program on Non-Profit Organizations at Yale University, which has been in existence since the late 1970s, there is a Center on Philanthropy at Indiana University, the Mandel Center for Nonprofit Organizations at Case Western Reserve University, the Center for the Study of Nonprofit Organizations at New York University, the Center on Nonprofit Organizations at the University of San Francisco, as well as many teaching programs either dedicated entirely to nonprofit organizations, or in which nonprofit organizations are central to the curriculum. Research and teaching on nonprofit organizations is also increasing in other countries; for example, in the United Kingdom is the Center for Voluntary Studies at the London School of Economics. A professional organization, the Association for Research on Nonprofit Organizations and Voluntary Action, organizes annual

izations has been formalized. The economics of nonprofit organizations is approaching the stage of "normal science." Thus fundamental theoretical questions have been raised and addressed, and, although these are not answered, there is now a sufficient common understanding of central issues to provide guidance for theoretical and empirical research. While it is too soon to pronounce *the* dominant paradigm, it is certainly the case that demand-side considerations with respect to the existence of the nonprofit sector are widely accepted and empirical work is broadly supportive of these conclusions. This situation is reflected in the present book: the theoretical papers build on extant contributions rather than try to supplant them, and the empirical contributions are aimed at throwing light on theory or examining information previously unavailable.

However, as a relatively new field, the economics of nonprofit organizations still suffers from major gaps in the understanding of its subject matter. In particular, little is known about the economic dimensions of nonprofit organizations' internal organization, productivity, and efficiency, etc., relative to for-profit firms and government organizations. Many of these gaps are related to the question of ownership and control of nonprofit organizations, which remain poorly understood. The nature of ownership and control in nonprofit organizations has important implications for agency problems and the way they are addressed. For example, some authors argue that the agency problems between principals and agents may be more acute in nonprofit organizations than in for-profit firms (e.g., Jensen and Warner, 1988, and Montias, Ben-Ner, and Neuberger, forthcoming), in part because ownership is ill-defined. And while there are known cases of mergers and takeovers among nonprofit organizations, the market for takeovers most likely functions poorly for nonprofit organizations. With public subsidies, uncertain entry of competitors, and a weak or nonexistent takeover market, who will make sure that managers pursue the mission of the organization for which they are responsible? Who sets the mission of the organization? What is the role of the board of directors or trustees? The legal authorities in charge of nonprofit organizations examine, at least in principle, the activities of nonprofit organizations in more detail than they do those of for-profit firms, but on whose behalf? And while the law (at least in the U.S.) prescribes stricter fiduciary requirements for nonprofit in comparison to for-profit directors, whose behalf are they acting upon? Is it the public at large, the current users of an

---

conferences on nonprofit organizations, and other organizations are in the process of being established.

organization's services, or those who make donations? Are nonprofit organizations operated efficiently? How is efficiency defined in nonprofit organizations? Is there a life-cycle pattern common to nonprofit organizations? This host of questions has remained essentially unanswered (even the issue of efficiency of production in the much-discussed health care industry has been understudied) and is in need of theoretical answers and empirical insights.

Examination of questions of this sort by organizational economists typically starts with the establishment of core facts: who are the players in an organization, what are their objectives, what are their endowments and what are the actions in which they may engage in pursuit of their objectives? Once these basic facts are known, the relationship between the players can be examined by applying, for example, the tools of agency or bargaining theory. It is then that propositions about organizational behavior can be developed and tested empirically. However, at the moment there is no clear understanding of the identity of the key players in nonprofit organizations, or of their rights, obligations, and motives. Consider a comparison of a nonprofit with a for-profit hospital (or day care center, or museum, or theater). Who appoints their respective boards of directors? Are those who appoint them the "owners" in both cases? Are the interests of these "owners" equally invested in the two organizations and will they pursue them with equal vigor? Will the latitude afforded nonprofit managers cause them to be more lax in maximizing the objective function of their organization relative to their for-profit counterparts? Or will their professional commitment, the nondistribution-of-profit constraint, and the needs for survival in a competitive environment make them behave "just right"?[16]

It therefore appears that supply-side analyses provide the greatest expected returns to research on nonprofit organizations. Who are the players that provide the crucial entrepreneurial inputs required for the entry of new nonprofit organizations? Who are the players that ensure the organizations' effective operation? What is the role of corporate law and public policy in ensuring that the entrepreneurial and managerial functions are carried out properly? How do nonprofit organizations' operations compare with other types of organizations? The answers to these questions are necessary to understand and improve the behavior of nonprofit organizations, in both mixed market economies and in the transition economies of Eastern Europe and

---

16   Some of these issues are examined by Ben-Ner and Van Hoomissen (1992b).

the former Soviet Union (see Gui, forthcoming). Demand-side theories have amply established the existence of a welfare-enhancing niche for nonprofit organizations in the mixed economy. It is time now for concerted research on the supply-side of these organizations.

REFERENCES

ANHEIER H.K. and SEIBEL, W., 1990, eds., *The Third Sector: Nonprofit Organizations in Comparative and International Perspectives,* de Gruyter, Berlin and New York.

ARROW K.J., 1963, "Uncertainty and the Welfare Economics of Medical Care," *The American Economic Review* 53(5), 941–73.

BEN-NER A., 1986, "Nonprofit Organizations: Why Do They Exist in Market Economies?," in S. Rose-Ackerman (ed.) *The Economics of Nonprofit Institutions: Studies in Structure and Policy,* Oxford University Press, Oxford.

BEN-NER A., 1988, "Comparative Empirical Observations on Worker-Owned and Capitalist Firms," in *International Journal of Industrial Organization,* 6, 7–31.

BEN-NER A. and JONES D.C., 1992, "A New Conceptual Framework for the Analysis of the Impact of Employee Participation, Profit Sharing and Ownership on Firm Performance," Industrial Relations Center, University of Minnesota, and Department of Economics, Hamilton College.

BEN-NER A. and VAN HOOMISSEN T., 1992a, "An Empirical Investigation of the Joint Determination of the Size of For-Profit, Nonprofit and Government Sectors," *Annals of Public and Cooperative Economics,* 63, 469–94.

BEN-NER A. and VAN HOOMISSEN T., 1992b, "The Governance of Nonprofit Organizations: Law and Public Policy," Industrial Relations Center, University of Minnesota.

BONIN J., JONES D.C. and PUTTERMAN L., forthcoming, "Theoretical and Empirical Studies of Producer Cooperatives: Will the Twain Ever Meet?," in *Journal of Economic Literature.*

CARSON R., 1977, "A Theory of Cooperatives," in *Canadian Journal of Economics,* 10, 565–89.

CLARK, R., 1980, "Does the Nonprofit Form Fit the Hospital Industry?" in *Harvard Law Review,* 93, 1416–89.

CLARKSON K., 1972, "Some Implications of Property Rights in Hospital Management," in *Journal of Law and Economics,* 15, 363–84.

DIMAGGIO P.J. and ANHEIER H.K., 1990, "The Sociology of Nonprofit Organizations and Sectors," *Annual Review of Sociology,* 16, 137–59.

DUNNE T., ROBERTS M.J. and SAMUELSON L., 1989, "The Growth and Failure of U.S. Manufacturing Plants," *Quarterly Journal of Economics,* 104, 671–98.

EASLEY D. and O'HARA M., 1983, "The Economic Role of Nonprofit Firms," *Bell Journal of Economics,* 14, 531–38.

FEIGENBAUM S., 1980, "The Case of Income Redistribution: A Theory of Government and Private Provision of Collective Goods," in *Public Finance Quarterly,* 8, 3–22.

GROSSMAN S. and HART O., 1986, "The Costs and Benefits of Ownership: A Theory of Vertical and Lateral Integration," in *Journal of Political Economy,* 94, 691–719.

GUI B., 1987, "Productive Private Nonprofit Organizations: A Conceptual Framework," in *Annals of Public and Cooperative Economics,* 58(4), 415–35.

GUI B., forthcoming, "On the 'Third Sector' in Central and Eastern European Post-Soviet Type Economies," in T. Clarke (ed.) *International Privatisation: Strategies and Practices,* de Gruyter, Berlin.

HALL P.D., 1987, "A Historical Overview of the Private Nonprofit Sector," in W. W. Powell (ed.) *The Nonprofit Sector: A Research Handbook,* Yale University Press, New Haven.

HANSMANN H., 1980, "The Role of Nonprofit Enterprise," in *Yale Law Journal,* 89, 835–98.

HANSMANN H., 1987a, "Economic Theories of Nonprofit Organization," in W. W. Powell (ed.) *The Nonprofit Sector: A Research Handbook,* Yale University Press, New Haven.

HANSMANN H., 1987b, "The Effect of Tax Exemption and Other Factors on the Market Share of Nonprofit versus For-Profit Firms," in *National Tax Journal,* 60, 71–72.

HANSMANN H., 1988, "The Ownership of the Firm," in *Journal of Law, Economics, and Organization,* 4, 267–304.

HEFLEBOWER R.B., 1980, *Cooperatives and Mutuals in the Market System,* University of Wisconsin Press, Madison, WI.

HOLLANDER H., 1990, "A Social Exchange Approach to Voluntary Cooperation," in *American Economic Review,* 80, 1157–67.

HOLTMANN A., 1988, "Theories of Nonprofit Organizations," in *Journal of Economic Surveys,* 2:29–45.

JAMES E., 1983, "How Nonprofits Grow," *Journal of Policy Analysis and Management,* 2, 350–66.

JAMES E., 1986, "The Private Nonprofit Provision of Education: A Theoretical Model and Application to Japan," in *Journal of Comparative Economics,* 10, 255–76.

JAMES E., 1987, "The Nonprofit Sector in Comparative Perspective," in W. W. Powell (ed.) *The Nonprofit Sector: A Research Handbook,* Yale University Press, New Haven.

JAMES E., ed., 1989, *The Nonprofit Sector in International Perspective,* Oxford University Press, New York.

JAMES E. and ROSE-ACKERMAN S., eds., 1986, *The Nonprofit Enterprise in Market Economics,* Fundamentals of Pure and Applied Economics, n. 9, Harwood Academic Publishers, Chur, Switzerland.

JENSEN M.C. and WARNER J.B., 1988, "The Distribution of Power Among Corporate Managers, Shareholders, and Directors," in *Journal of Financial Economics,* 20, 3–4.

LEE A.J. and WEISBROD B.A., 1977, "Collective Goods and the Voluntary Sector: The Case of the Hospital Industry," in B. A. Weisbrod (ed.) *The Voluntary Nonprofit Sector,* Heath, Lexington, MA.

MARGOLIS H., 1982, *Selfishness, Altruism and Rationality,* Cambridge University Press, Cambridge.

MONTIAS J.M., BEN-NER A. and NEUBERGER E., 1993, in J. Lesourne and H. Sonnenschein (eds.) *Comparative Economics,* Fundamentals of Pure and Applied Economics, Harwood Academic Publishers, London and New York.

NELSON R.R. and KRASHINSKY M., 1987, "Two Major Issues of Public Policy: Public Subsidy and the Organization of Supply," in R. Nelson and D. Young (eds.) *Public Policy for Day Care of Young Children,* D.C. Heath, Lexington, MA.

NEWHOUSE J., 1970, "Toward an Economic Theory of Non-profit Institutions: An Economic Model of a Hospital," *American Economic Review,* 60, 64–73.

PAULY M. and REDISCH M., 1973, "The Not-for-Profit Hospital as a Physician's Cooperative," in *American Economic Review,* 63, 87–99.

PERMUT S., 1981, "Consumer Perceptions of Nonprofit Enterprise: A Comment on Hansmann," in *Yale Law Journal,* 91, 1623–32.

PRESTON A., 1988, "The Effects of Property Rights on Labor Costs of Nonprofit Firms: An Application to the Day Care Industry," in *The Journal of Industrial Economics,* 36, 337–50.

ROSE-ACKERMAN S., ed., 1986, *The Economics of Nonprofit Institutions: Studies in Structure and Policy,* Oxford University Press, Oxford.

SALAMON L.M., 1987, *Of Market Failure, Voluntary Failure, and Third-Party Government: Toward a Theory of Government-Nonprofit Relations in the Modern Welfare State,* Oxford University Press, Oxford.

STEINBERG R., 1986, "The Revealed Objective Functions of Nonprofit Firms," in *Rand Journal of Economics,* 17(4), 508–26.

STEINBERG R., 1990, "Labor Economics and the Nonprofit Sector: A Literature Review," in *Nonprofit and Voluntary Sector Quarterly,* 19, 151–70.

SUGDEN R., 1982, "On the Economics of Philanthropy," in *Economic Journal,* 92, 341–50.

SUGDEN R., 1984, "Reciprocity: The Supply of Public Goods through Voluntary Contributions," in *Economic Journal,* 94, 772–87.

WEISBROD B.A., 1975, "Toward a Theory of the Voluntary Nonprofit Sector in a Three-Sector Economy," in E. Phelps (ed.) *Altruism, Morality and Economic Theory,* Russell Sage Foundation, New York.

WEISBROD B.A., 1988, *The Nonprofit Economy,* Harvard University Press, Cambridge, MA.

WEISBROD B.A. and SCHLESINGER M., 1986, "Public, Private, Nonprofit Ownership and the Response to Asymmetric Information: The Case of Nursing Homes," in S. Rose-Ackerman (ed.) *The Economics of Nonprofit Institutions: Studies in Structure and Policy,* Oxford University Press, New York and Oxford.

YOUNG D., 1983, *If Not for Profit, for What?,* Heath, Lexington, MA.

PART 1
General

NONPROFIT ORGANIZATIONS IN THE MIXED ECONOMY
A Demand and Supply Analysis

by

Avner BEN-NER*

Industrial Relations Center

University of Minnesota

and

Theresa VAN HOOMISSEN*

Humphrey Institute for Public Affairs

University of Minnesota

Introduction

Nonprofit organizations occupy an important niche in many market economies. For example, in the United States the nonprofit sector employs nearly one-tenth of the workforce while the government and for-profit sectors employ approximately fifteen and seventy-five percent, respectively. Nonprofit organizations operate almost exclusively in service industries, where they often coexist with for-profit and government organizations. The weight of the nonprofit sector in services varies from predominance in museums and social services to insignificance in professional and personal services (see Table 1 for data on New York State). The geographical incidence of the nonprofit sector also varies greatly, even when controlling for industry (see Ben-Ner and Van Hoomissen, 1989 and 1990).

* We acknowledge helpful comments on earlier drafts by Dennis Ahlburg, Benedetto Gui, Henry Hansmann, Estelle James, Egon Neuberger, Richard Steinberg and anonymous referees.

These facts suggest the broad hypothesis that the relative prevalence of nonprofit organizations depends on the nature of an industry's output, industrial organization characteristics, and economic, demographic, political and other locality-specific attributes. This paper advances a theory that explains broadly the place of the nonprofit sector in the mixed economy, building on the literature on nonprofit organizations and on organizational economics. While accepting the important role researchers commonly accord to the demand for provision of services by nonprofit organizations, we suggest that conditions of organizational supply also play a critical role in the formation and existence of nonprofit organizations. Hence the confluence of demand *and* supply factors determines the incidence of nonprofit organizations relative to other organizational forms. The most important supply factor is the ability of some demand-side stakeholders (consumers, sponsors, or donors) to ensure that the nonprofit organizations of interest to them perform according to their wishes within economic feasibility constraints. Stakeholder control is key to the ability of nonprofit organizations to correct market and government failures, hence we characterize them as (demand-side) stakeholder controlled organizations. Control by stakeholders, which is typically incomplete, is supported by the prohibition on the distribution of profits and other provisions regarding organizational structure.

The paper is structured as follows. In the next section we examine the term "nonprofit organization" and develop a conceptual framework for the analysis of organizational choice in the mixed economy. In section 2 we develop a theory of demand for nonprofit provision, identifying circumstances in which some stakeholders demand a different organizational form than the for-profit or government forms. In section 3 we elaborate on the supply of nonprofit organizations, focusing on the costs of forming and operating such organizations. The concept of nonprofit ownership, the role of the nondistribution-of-profit constraint, and the open books policy of nonprofit organizations are discussed in section 4. In section 5 we discuss the confluence of demand and supply for nonprofit organizations. Factors affecting the incidence of nonprofit organizations are analyzed in section 6, focusing on the interaction between product characteristics, attributes of stakeholders, and market size. A summary and conclusions are offered in the last section.

1   Theoretical Issues and Preambles

Nonprofit organizations have been characterized in various ways. For example, Hall (1987), writing from an historical perspective, defines nonprofit organizations as "a body of individuals who associate for any of three purposes: (1) to perform public tasks that have been delegated to them by the state; (2) to perform public tasks for which there is a demand that neither the state nor for-profit organizations are willing to fulfill; or (3) to influence the direction of policy in the state, the for-profit sector, or other nonprofit organizations". Economists posit that nonprofit organizations perform activities that the for-profit and/or the government sectors do not do well, and, accordingly, view nonprofit organizations as correctives to certain market and government failures[1]. Hansmann (1980) focuses additionally on the legal form of incorporation, noting that all nonprofits assume a nondistribution-of-profit constraint: all profit earned must be used to enhance production or reduce prices and cannot be distributed to administrators, employees or owners.

We expand on these views by adding supply considerations, and arrive at a different characterization of nonprofit organizations. We regard such organizations, *at their inception,* as coalitions of individuals who associate to provide themselves and others with goods or services that are not adequately supplied by either for-profit or government organizations. When inadequate provision stems not from economic infeasibility but from market or government failures, nonprofit organizations may correct these failures at their roots. They do so not (necessarily or primarily) through the benevolence of nonprofit entrepreneurs or managers, but through demand-side stakeholder (consumer, donor, or sponsor) control. Stakeholder control in nonprofit organizations eliminates, in principle, any problems of asymmetric information between two parties to a transaction, and stakeholders may safely reveal their demands and make contributions without fear of exploitation. However, stakeholder control can materialize only if certain conditions are met, and if the organization is structured in a way which facilitates exercise of such control. Thus the demand for nonprofit provision by stakeholders can be met only if some stakeholders engage also in nonprofit supply.

---

1   See Nelson and Krashinsky (1973), Weisbrod (1975 and 1988), Hansmann (1980), Ben-Ner (1986), Gui (1987), Preston (1988), and reviews by James and Rose-Ackerman (1986), Hansmann (1987), and Holtmann (1988).

Our investigation of the problem of the existence of nonprofit organizations in the mixed economy is guided by ideas in organizational economics on the choice of organizational forms[2]. The basic paradigm can be summarized in four propositions. First, every economic transaction generates both a unity and a conflict of interest between various organizational stakeholders[3]. Second, control over a transaction affords controllers a direct way to advance their interests. Third, the benefits from control and the cost of exercising it depend on characteristics of individuals and goods. Fourth, if it can be freely exchanged, control will be acquired by those for whom its net value is greatest.

The theory laid out in the remainder of the paper is based on the paradigm described above. First, there is a conflict of interest between demand- and supply-side stakeholders. Second, the nonprofit form is a potential means of control by demand-side stakeholders. Third, a nonprofit organization will be formed if some demand-side stakeholders find that the benefits of control outweigh its costs and if this net benefit is greater than the net benefit achieved by purchasing elsewhere. Fourth, nonprofits will be established by those demand-side stakeholders for whom the net value of control is largest.

We use the term "demand" in the remainder of the paper to include *all* willingness and ability to pay, even when it is purely altruistic. Thus, individuals might demand housing for the homeless and education for the handicapped even if no one in their household is either homeless or handicapped. Rather than truly expand the economic definition of demand to include such interdependent preferences – which would entail recasting key concepts in the literature on market failure – we simply append altruistic demand to traditional demand and add a potential market failure: insufficient provision of *charitable* goods. We define charitable goods as goods which do not

---

2   See, for example, Williamson (1985), Hansmann (1988), Grossman and Hart (1986), Ben-Ner (1991), Hart and Moore (1990), and Van Hoomissen (1991).

3   Organizational stakeholders may be classified according to their position in the supply-of-resources—demand-for-output dichotomy, and the specific supply or demand role they fulfill. Supply-side stakeholders supply resources; they may be workers, managers, providers of equity or debt, banks, parent organizations, the state, or suppliers. Demand-side stakeholders use or have an interest in the organizational output; they may be clients, customers, donors, the state or sponsors. (Hybrid stakeholders provide more than one type of input or are on both the demand and supply sides).

benefit the payer (or his/her household) directly but rather benefit a third party. Charitable goods, like public goods, have benefits which are nonexcludable and nonrival to individuals with similar preferences (housing for the homeless, for example, directly benefits anyone who is concerned about homelessness).

Demand-side stakeholders include individuals, organizations, or public bodies that either 1) pay for and consume a good (traditional consumers), or 2) sponsor the consumption of a good by someone else. Thus, demand-side stakeholders include, in addition to traditional consumers, the parents of children in day care, family members of nursing home residents, donors to charitable or public causes, local governments that contract out the provision of certain services, theater-goers, corporate foundations that make grants to local arts groups, and so forth. They do not include, however, those individuals or organizations that are only the beneficiaries of a good made available to them by others . This distinction is based on the *potential for action,* which is an important determinant in the choice of organizational form. Note that organizations – ranging from IBM to local sanitation departments to the United States Department of Housing and Urban Development to Lions Clubs to churches – are at times demand-side stakeholders. For presentational ease, the term stakeholders (without qualifier) will henceforth refer to demand-side stakeholders only.

Our theory of organizational choice is summarized schematically in Figure 1[4]. A convenient conceptual starting point (the *status quo)* is a market economy in which the for-profit sector is the key provider of goods and services, and the government and the nonprofit sectors react to failures originating in that sector. In the presence of market failure (due, for example, to public goods, externalities and asymmetric information) some stakeholders cannot get in the for-profit sector the quantity or quality they are willing and able to buy. Such stakeholders must choose among three alternatives: 1) do nothing (which results in no change in the level or nature of provision of the good or service); 2) form a coalition to lobby the government to correct the market failure via regulation, direct provision, or contracting out; or 3) form a coalition to arrange for the provision of the good to

---

4   Van Hoomissen (1991) analyzes in detail the issue of organizational choice. Many branches down the government trunk in Figure 1 – including government regulation, tax incentives, and the contracting-out decision – are discussed more completely there.

Figure 1: The Choice of Organizational Form

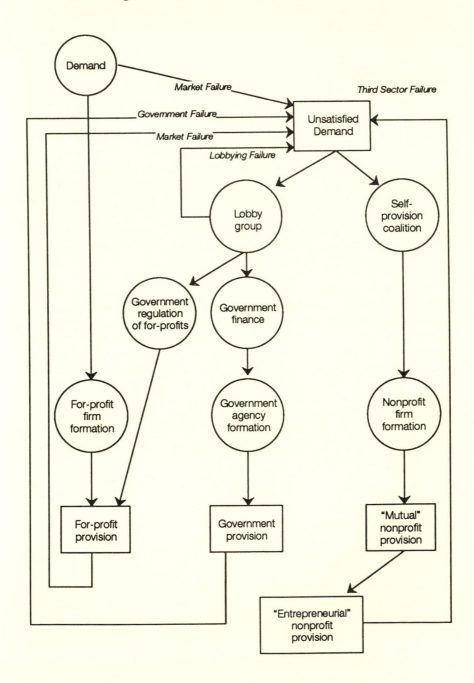

themselves. This paper examines situations in which the third option is chosen and the resulting organization adopts a nondistribution constraint. This option represents the nonprofit solution.

2   The Demand for Nonprofit Organizations

There is an inherent conflict of interest between demand- and supply-side stakeholders: demand-side stakeholders want more quality and quantity for a lower price while supply-side stakeholders want the opposite. Market failure exacerbates this conflict, generating a demand for alternative organizational forms. A combination of three major sources of market failure is particularly relevant to nonprofit demand: the existence of public goods and charitable goods, which we examine in terms of the underlying issues of rivalry and excludability in consumption, and asymmetric information. In many cases, government responds imperfectly to market failure, an inadequacy which is sometimes termed "government failure".

Most goods can be described according to the degree to which they are rival and excludable. The degree of excludability depends mainly on the cost of excluding nonpayers, and the degree of rivalry depends primarily on the extent to which crowding affects the quality of provision. Pure private goods are excludable and rival, pure public goods are nonexcludable and nonrival, club goods, commonly referred to as a subset of public goods, are excludable but nonrival, whereas other goods, such as air, also regarded as public goods, are nonexcludable but rival. Some goods, like a research paper, are "mixed": they are excludable but have some consumption aspects which are entirely rival (the paper copy) and some which are nonrival (the research results).

Both nonrivalry and nonexcludability play a role in the failure of markets to adequately supply public and charitable goods. For-profit firms do not adequately provide nonexcludable goods because they cannot force payment from those who wish to "free ride". Nonrival goods must be provided until marginal cost equals vertically summed marginal benefits in order for maximum net social benefit to be achieved, whereas unhindered markets will only provide a good until marginal cost equals horizontally summed marginal benefits. Optimal provision of nonrival goods, in fact, requires perfect price discrimination: each consumer must pay the value of his/her own marginal benefit at the quantity provided.

Asymmetric information may favor either stakeholders or sellers. In both cases, however, the market fails to provide goods at the same (optimal) level that they would be provided if there were no asymmetric information or, alternatively, if the conflict of interest between the parties did not exist.

There are three major situations in which asymmetric information arises to the disadvantage of stakeholders (Nelson and Krashinsky, 1973, Hansmann, 1980): (a) when there is a lag between the time of purchase and the time when the good can be evaluated, (b) when the stakeholder (payer) and the consumer (beneficiary) of the good are different entities (individuals or organizations), and (c) when the good is complex and its precise characteristics are difficult to evaluate by stakeholders. With several important exceptions, stakeholders in these situations fear that their lack of information about quality or quantity will be exploited by for-profit firms in order to enhance profit[5].

In the case of reverse asymmetric information, stakeholders fear revealing their demand schedules because the information could be used to their detriment by a for-profit firm.

Next we focus on the nature of goods to characterize the circumstances under which demand for nonprofit organizations will arise[6]. We demonstrate that two categories of goods[7], "trust" and

---

5   One important exception arises when firms stand to gain by establishing a reputation. A second important exception occurs when vigilant government supervision prevents firms from taking advantage of stakeholder ignorance. See Van Hoomissen (1988) for a discussion of strategies of profit-seeking firms facing imperfectly informed consumers.

6   Excludability, rivalry, and asymmetric information are not strictly intrinsic attributes of goods, but are affected by the variable circumstances under which they are transacted. One could reasonably define day care for young children provided under conditions of complete and asymmetric information as two different goods. While recognizing this, for the sake of simplicity we will mostly refer to excludability and rivalry as if they were attributes of goods, while treating asymmetric information as an attribute of both goods and transactions.

7   We are using Weisbrod's (1988) terminology, although our definitions do, in some ways, differ. For example, in Weisbrod's definition, trust goods include all goods with an asymmetric information problem for consumers, while we require also significant nonrivalry aspects.

"collective" goods, can potentially be provided more advantageously by demand-side stakeholders themselves. Asymmetric information and nonrivalry are common to both categories; asymmetric information drives stakeholders to search for a different organizational form, whereas nonrivalry makes the nonprofit form acceptable.

2.1 Trust Goods

We define trust goods as club goods and mixed goods for which there is an asymmetric information problem to the disadvantage of stakeholders. As noted above, in the presence of asymmetric information to their disadvantage, stakeholders suspect that for-profit firms will deceive them about quantity or quality in order to enhance profit. Thus, for trust goods, demand exists for a different organizational form, one in which profit is not the dominant motive, because it is the profit motive which gives the firm incentive to deceive.

Stakeholders of trust goods might look more favorably on an organization which is not-for-profit (i.e., adopts a nondistribution constraint), but some suspicion regarding the organization's incentives would undoubtedly remain. The not-for-profit status indicates only that the organization does not directly distribute profit, and stakeholders recognize that the incentive to deceive can arise out of other motivations as well. The organization's managers may, for example, seek to expand their salaries, perquisites, status, or power, may want to hold onto their jobs, or may wish to pursue their own preferences regarding the product of the organization.

One type of organization that will arouse more interest is one controlled by stakeholders. Because trust goods have nonrival aspects, noncontrolling stakeholders consume the same unit(s) simultaneously with controlling stakeholders; the latter can deceive others only if they are willing to "punish" themselves as well[8]. If the good were rival, controlling stakeholders could exploit others by providing them a different, relatively inferior quality-quantity-price combination, much as a for-profit firm could. Thus, stakeholder control signals trustworthiness for nonrival goods but not for rival goods[9]. We thus

---

8   See Olson's (1971) discussion of the closely related concept of "jointness in supply".

9   Nonrivalry can, to a certain extent, be intentionally produced. For example, an agricultural purchasing cooperative which sells fertilizer to its stakeholders members may dispense from a single and observable storage facility, from which both members and nonmembers (noncontrolling

conclude that in the case of trust goods, a demand for stakeholder-controlled organizations exists.

To illustrate some of the points made above, consider as an example a couple seeking day care for their young child[10]. They have difficulty evaluating the care provided at different centers and think it is possible that for-profit firms claim to provide higher quality care than they actually provide. They seek such indirect signals as reputation and the effectiveness of government supervision but, in their area, these signals are weak. They choose a parent-controlled nonprofit day care over others because the people on the managing committee are similar to themselves, and have also enrolled their own children. The nonprofit status of the organization further indicates lack of financial interests that may come at the expense of quality of care. An alternative scenario, considered in section 3, would have the parents join with others in similar circumstances to start a new center that then appeals to outsiders because of the parent-control. In either case, controlling parents need not be very vigil about the actions of their associates because of the nonrival nature of day care).[11]

The market for automobile repair provides a useful counter example. Stakeholders (automobile owners) often have difficulty evaluating the quality of repairs provided by repair shops and know

---

stakeholders) partake. This purposefully induced nonrivalry generates trust for noncontrollers since they are assured that the organization does not treat them differently from members and therefore does not take advantage of them. Heflebower (1980) suggests that fertilizer purchasing cooperatives came into existence because of the uncertainty regarding the quality of fertilizers sold by for-profit firms. Similarly, the famous Rochdale cooperative was founded by the local community to combat the phenomenon of adulterated flour sold by for-profit merchants. The opportunities for producing nonrivalry in rival goods seem, however, limited.

10   We use this example because it has been frequently used in the literature on nonprofit organizations to illustrate the kind of asymmetric information discussed here; see, for example, Nelson and Krashinsky (1973), Hansmann (1980), and Rose-Ackerman (1986). Day care for children also possesses important collective good attributes, discussed later.

11   See Nelson and Krashinsky (1973) for a detailed examination of the day care industry and a similar view concerning both the important role of parents and the secondary role of the nondistribution-of-profit constraint. For a view that attributes trustworthiness entirely to the nondistribution-of-profit constraint, see Hansmann (1980).

that some for-profit shops claim to provide services that they do not actually provide. In this case, however, a consumer-controlled nonprofit shop will not signal trustworthiness because the service is not nonrival: controlling stakeholders could provide quality care for their own cars and still cheat other customers. A nondistribution constraint will not imbue trust because controlling stakeholders can use amplified revenues and reduced costs to provide themselves with cheaper repair services. Thus, despite the significant asymmetric information problem, nonprofit automobile repair shops will not form, ultimately, because car repair is rival. Stakeholders must therefore either depend on reputation or participate actively in the control of a repair shop. For most stakeholders, the control option is probably costlier than the expected losses from patronizing a for-profit shop.

2.2 Collective Goods

We define collective goods to include pure public goods, charitable goods, and mixed goods with a large and expensive-to-produce nonrival component. These goods have in common not only nonrivalry, but also the necessity of voluntary price discrimination (donations) if they are to be provided by nongovernmental entities. Pure public and charitable goods must be paid for by way of donation because they are nonexcludable. Mixed goods with a large and expensive-to produce nonrival component require donations by high-demand stakeholders because nondiscriminating for-profit provision leaves them undersatisfied (quantity rationed)[12]. A for-profit firm that knew the demand of individual stakeholders or was otherwise able to price-discriminate (i.e., charge a higher price to high-demanders) would not ration by quantity[13].

---

12   Hansmann (1980) was first to recognize a potential role for nonprofits in this situation.

13   The intuition behind the necessity of donations for mixed goods with a large and expensive-to-produce nonrival component can be illustrated with a simple example. Opera is a mixed good because it is entirely excludable but has consumption aspects which are entirely rival (e.g., the seat at a performance) and others which are entirely nonrival (e.g., the mounting of a "production", including the nonrival directing, acting, costume and scenery). Each opera production is also very expensive to produce. Suppose there is a community with L low-demand stakeholders and H high-demand stakeholders of opera and a single for-profit provider. It is easy to show that the profit-maximizing price and quantity will leave high-demanders with excess demand if H is small enough relative to L and if the cost C of a production is high enough. Suppose the firm chooses a price P and production

The state of being quantity rationed signals high-demand stakeholders that their welfare could be increased by identifying themselves to the firm, voluntarily revealing their willingness to pay, and submitting to price discrimination. Stakeholders of pure public and charitable goods, who are also undersatisfied by for-profit provision, could do the same. The for-profit firm, however, has incentive to take advantage of the revealed information, charge inflated prices, and extract most of the consumer surplus. Thus, unless the firm consents to reveal its private cost information (accounts or audits) and make monitorable and enforceable contractual agreements on the basis of both demand *and* cost information, stakeholders will not reveal their preferences to a for-profit firm (Ben-Ner and Van Hoomissen, 1991b)[14].

In the absence of such arrangements, stakeholders of collective goods may seek an organization to which they can safely reveal demand information. A stakeholder controlled organization meets this requirement to a considerable extent. Since collective goods are nonrival, stakeholder control also indicates to noncontrolling stakeholders that the firm is operated so as to meet the unsatisfied demand of like-minded people. We thus conclude that there exists a demand for stakeholder-controlled organizations that provide collective goods.

Stakeholder controlled organizations are an instance of vertical integration between demand- and supply-side stakeholders, serving

---

quantity Q such that high-demanders want more productions but low-demanders are satisfied. (This implies that the price-quantity point is in the inelastic region on the demand curve of a typical low-demander so that increasing the price to low-demanders reduces total revenue; this is an outcome of profit-maximizing behavior. See Ben-Ner and Van Hoomissen [1991b] for details.) Consider now the circumstances in which it will not be profitable for the firm to change P or Q to satisfy high-demanders. First, note that increasing Q by one unit (staging an additional production) without increasing price will increase revenue by only H*P since low-demanders do not want more at price P. Thus, if H is small enough and C is high enough, this move will reduce profit. Second, note that increasing P (without changing Q) reduces revenue from the L low-demanders and increases revenue from the H high-demanders. Again, this will reduce profit if H is small relative to L. In sum, it will be profit-maximizing for the firm to quantity-ration high-demanders when H is small relative to L and C is high.

14   Such demand revelation may occur if one of the stakeholders is very large (e.g., the federal government or a large corporation).

as a low-cost substitute for information verification and judicial enforcement of contracts between stakeholders and sellers. High-demand stakeholders that patronize such an organization receive a superior quality-quantity-price package, although they may (voluntarily) pay more than others. This higher price may be paid through donations or through contractually specified payments, as in the case of local governments contracting out social services[15]. Only a few stakeholders-a subset of those with higher demand-need to participate in control[16].

2.3 Government Failure

Since governments often provide goods in an attempt to correct some market failure in the provision of public goods, their services are frequently nonrival. While government agencies determine service levels according to different criteria than for-profit firms, the outcome may resemble that which occurs in for-profit provision. Just as for-profit providers of nonrival goods may find it profitable to target the demand of 'average' stakeholders, government bodies may find it politically expedient to respond to the median voter's demand and set tax rates and service levels which leave some residents undersatisfied (Weisbrod, 1975). High-demand stakeholders may seek an alternative source to supply their unsatisfied demand. Since some market failure prevented provision by for-profit firms in the first place, the unsatisfied demand translates into a demand for nonprofit organizations when the goods in question belong to the trust or collective goods categories.

---

15   Like other stakeholders, government decision-makers may be in a difficult position to judge the quality or quantity provided by a private for-profit contractor or may be a high-demand buyer of a nonrival good or service that is underprovided by for-profit firms (e.g., social services). For this reason, government agencies are also a source of demand for the nonprofit form. In some cases, an agency may choose to act as a controlling stakeholder of a nonprofit organization rather than provide the service itself or interact on the market with for-profit firms.

16   This view, which applies equally to trust goods, is related to the 'voice' interpretation of nonprofit organizations (versus 'exit' in for-profit firms) by Nelson and Krashinsky (1973) and Friedman (1984, chapter 15), as well as to Williamson's (1985) interpretation of upstream vertical integration.

2.4 Summary of Demand Considerations

We have shown that demand for an alternative to for-profit and government provision exists for trust and collective goods, and that an organization which is stakeholder controlled may satisfy that demand. We call such firms "nonprofit organizations", although discussion of the nondistribution-of-profit constraint is postponed until section 4.

Most *goods* (in the narrow sense of the term) are rival; *services*, however, range from almost purely rival to almost purely nonrival. Services such as automobile repair and financial and legal services are essentially rival, hospital care is only somewhat rival, and day care and theater are primarily nonrival. Many nonrival services are afflicted by asymmetric information problems, suggesting a trust aspect, and many are additionally designed such that multiple consumers use the same high-cost facilities and enjoy the same quality of service, suggesting a collective aspect. Such "composite goods" include, for example, day care for children. Day care is significantly nonrival because the same physical facility and quality of service are provided to all children. And, because the nonrival aspect is produced at a relatively high cost, some parents may be willing to pay more for better day care (i.e., in accord with their preferences) than they could find on the for-profit market. This service also has trust aspects derived from the inability of parents to observe the exact care provided to their children.

3   The Supply of Nonprofit Organizations

The existence of demand for nonprofit organizations is insufficient to explain their existence. In the for-profit sector, entrepreneurs form new firms and satisfy existing demand because they hope to make a profit. Potential profit obviously cannot entice anyone to form a nonprofit organization. A nonprofit organization will be formed only if there is a group of stakeholders who value the expected flow of net benefits from a self-run organization more than the benefits they can derive from alternative sources and who choose not to free-ride on each other's demand revelation, contributions and control activities. The supply of nonprofit organizations is thus affected by the costs involved in their formation and operation. These entail:

– identifying and assembling a group of stakeholders willing to participate in forming and controlling an organization without receiving any direct monetary gain for that activity;

- determining that there is sufficient demand to allow for the provision of the good[17] at a price and quantity that makes the operation of the organization worthwhile to the founding body;

- assembling inputs to produce the good;

- developing and maintaining a control mechanism to ensure that stakeholder interests are pursued by the organization;

- recruiting managers whose values and personal objectives are expected to cause only limited agency problems;

- identifying and convincing high-demanders (of collective goods) that it is to their benefit to reveal their demands and provide financial support; and

- designing mechanisms to discourage some stakeholders from free-riding on the control activities of others.

Stakeholders may start the process of formation of a nonprofit organization directly by seeking out and establishing a "seed" group, indirectly through the representatives of other organizations, or with the assistance of a "nonprofit entrepreneur" who helps facilitate the establishment of a seed group. Thus, the initiative for the formation of a nonprofit organization may come from stakeholders aware of their own demand for the nonprofit form or from input providers who seek to market their inputs to a potential nonprofit organization, but in both cases demand-side stakeholders must play an active role in order for nonprofit supply to emerge.

Direct stakeholder action is the most transparent process of creation of nonprofit supply: a group of stakeholders with unsatisfied demand establish first an organizing body and then a supply organization. For example, parents of young children in a neighborhood that are unsatisfied with existing child care (or its absence) may seek each other out and consider forming a day care center, or one household may raise the issue at a meeting of their local church, community center, or cultural association. After preliminary discussions on the likely success of such an organization, a management board will be formed from among interested parents and representatives of any organization which has chosen to facilitate the parents' activities. The

---

17   We now again use the term "good" in the broad sense that includes services.

board will then consider the organization's feasibility in more detail, assessing interest among additional parents and perhaps hiring a consultant to provide expertise in setting up the organization and finding an administrator. The administrator will work under the direction of the board to complete the key entrepreneurial functions. Capital funds may come from interested parents, an organization whose members are interested in the services of the day care center, or a local government body committed to supporting activities that involve externalities. Once the center is in operation, the role of the board will be to determine organizational standards, policies, and long term goals, and to oversee paid administrators charged with day-to-day management. As in the for-profit sector, hired administrators may seek to free themselves from control by the board and/or affect the board's composition. Often administrators become more powerful as the organization ages and members of the founding body move on, especially if an adequate mechanism for passing on the baton has not been developed. By definition, the founding body will consist of people who have chosen not to free-ride on the control activities of others, and if a group of like-minded people does not exist among the organization's stakeholders, a control gap will develop which is often filled, by default, by hired administrators.

Often the initiative for the formation of a nonprofit organization comes from the leadership of an organization with which stakeholders are associated. Organizations such as community centers, cultural associations, churches, fraternal or political clubs, and support groups often seek to enable beneficial collective action on behalf of their members, and can assume an entrepreneurial role when demand by their members is noted. When the problem of free ridership is particularly grave, such organizations may be the primary nonprofit supply mechanism. Although direct government provision of public goods is a solution to the problem of free ridership (through compulsory taxation), political constraints and other considerations noted earlier sometimes prevent the use of this tool. In such cases, a government unit may seek to facilitate nongovernmental provision by supplying some of the entrepreneurial input and providing some financial assistance to form a new stakeholder-controlled organization, often appointing government representatives to the board of directors on behalf of the public (the free-riding stakeholders).

Another source of nonprofit initiative comes from such input suppliers as professional administrators and staff people. Because of their day-to-day immersion in a trust or collective goods industry, these professionals may be aware of the existence of unsatisfied demand (i.e., nonprofit demand) and see some potential gain to themselves from facilitating the formation of a coalition of interested parties. With this in mind, they may approach interested individuals or organizations, suggesting actions which would ultimately lead to the formation of a nonprofit organization. The motivation of such individuals may be employment, the desire to work in a particular field, and/or a purely altruistic desire to promote a valued cause (making them demand-side stakeholders). Because of the market failure associated with trust and collective goods industries, these individuals could not, even if they wanted, establish a for-profit firm.

When stakeholders are geographically dispersed, nonprofit entrepreneurs – as facilitators of the confluence of demand and supply – may be indispensable. Many national organizations (such as Mothers Against Drunk Driving and the Sierra Club) were formed by future administrators who surmised that there was enough demand to sustain these organizations. These nonprofit entrepreneurs were themselves stakeholders (had a demand for action on the issues the organization subsequently pursued), but additionally saw the potential organization as a source of desirable employment. Given the potential rewards, they proceeded to find and bring together a group of stakeholders to establish an organization, taking the risk that the organization would not succeed and their time and resources would be wasted. Once such a group was established, the remainder of the process of formation and operation was similar to the scenario developed for the parent-initiated day care center[18].

---

18   The Guthrie Theater in Minneapolis is yet another example of a nonprofit organization established at the initiation of input suppliers. In the early 1960s, the stage director and playwright Sir Tyrone Guthrie toured the United States in search of a community to support his theater. In the Twin Cities of Minneapolis and Saint Paul he found an "hospitable" environment: its residents were cultured, there was little professional theater, the community was relatively close knit with a strong civic spirit, and there were individuals and companies willing to support the local arts. Given this, he approached various community leaders, garnering interest and support for his theater, eventually establishing the nonprofit Guthrie Theater. In our framework, we view Tyrone Guthrie as a professional seeking desirable employment (as well as, of course, being a stakeholder of his type of theater). His search for an hospitable environment was in fact a search for unsatisfied high demanders in a community capable of exerting pressure to reduce free-ridership in the revelation of demand and the payment of donations. The

4   Ownership Shares, the Nondistribution-of-Profit Constraint, and Open Books

Nonprofit organizations are distinguished from both for-profit and government organizations by a unique combination of characteristics. We have discussed thus far two of these characteristics, stakeholder control and the type of goods nonprofit organizations provide (trust and collective). This section considers three additional characteristics: the lack of ownership shares, the nondistribution-of-profit constraint, and the "open books" policy.

4.1   Ownership Shares

Ownership of an organization can be defined as the possession of two rights: the right to control – i.e., to determine organizational objectives – and the right to returns – i.e., to dispose of any financial or physical returns resulting from the organization's activities. In the for-profit sector, these rights are divided into ownership shares, representing proportional rights to control and, returns. Sometimes these shares can be purchased and sold on an open market but if founders wish they can write into the organization's bylaws restrictions designed to keep ownership in certain hands.

Despite appearances to the contrary, nonprofit organizations are also "owned": they have objectives that are somehow fashioned and their financial and physical returns are disposed of. Instead of being embedded in shares, these rights are typically associated with one's voluntary status as a stakeholder. The absence of shares (in particular, transferable ones) in many nonprofit organizations, we posit, is primarily *a device adopted by founders to ensure the maintenance of stakeholder-control by preventing the concentration of control and return rights.* That is, founders write into the organization's bylaws (extreme) restrictions on the transferability of shares in order to keep ownership in the hands of stakeholders as a group, because they recognize that otherwise the organization may cease to be a solution

---

Twin Cities fit this description in many ways. Many other nonprofit arts organizations were formed under similar circumstances (for a recent example, compare the role of Harry Parker in the Dallas Museum of Arts with that of Tyrone Guthrie), yet many others were initiated by high-demand stakeholders (for example, New York's Metropolitan Opera and the Goodspeed Theater in Connecticut).

to the market or government failure that generated it[19]. Thus, in nonprofit organizations, the rights to control and returns are vested permanently in demand-side stakeholders generally via the absence of ownership shares. Control responsibilities are, nonetheless *delegated* (not turned over) to a minority subset of these stakeholders, either explicitly or implicitly.

4.2 The Nondistribution-of-Profit Constraint

The nondistribution-of-profit constraint (NDPC) adopted by many nonprofit organizations goes hand in hand with invisible, non-transferable ownership shares: given that demand-side stakeholders as a group are the organization's owners, the NDPC serves mainly as a distribution rule, assuring that organizational returns are not distributed to the controlling subset only[20]. Again, the organization's founders adopt this rule to ensure the organization's continued existence[21].

An organization that wishes to signal trustworthiness to its customers (in order to enhance sales and, thereby, viability) will

---

19   See also Ben-Ner (1986). Ellman (1982, p. 1036) states that "[e]asily negotiable, dividend-issuing equity shares, therefore, would be inappropriate [in nonprofit organizations] since they would have no purpose but to facilitate ownership by the very class of persons the organization was formed to avoid".
20   See also Gui (1990). The implied net revenue of the nonprofit organization often is not distributed equally among controlling and noncontrolling stakeholders. As we show in Ben-Ner and Van Hoomissen (1991b), the objectives of the organization, determined by controlling stakeholders, will generally tilt the distribution of net revenue in their favor.
21   The arguments regarding ownership shares and the nondistribution constraint here are essentially supply-side: founders adopt them in order to ensure the organization's continued existence. Still, this is only a supply-side concern because nonprofit demand depends on stakeholder control, and thus, as before, demand- and supply-side concerns are not entirely separable because the organization is supply oriented but controlled by demanders. Fama and Jensen (1983) argue similarly that the absence of transferable shares is a tool to prevent the development of an agency problem between donors and managers. Although they do not take the argument to its conclusion, the presumption must be that "donors" are the principals in the organization's actions (and so the organization is "donor-controlled") and the absence of transferable shares is a tool they devise to keep control in their own hands. The idea that founders impose an organizational structure that restricts future changes in the nature of the organization is also advanced by Moe (1990) in the context of government agencies.

sometimes adopt an NDPC because it suggests to buyers that the organization uses all its revenues to either improve service or reduce prices rather than pad the owner's bank account (Nelson and Krashinsky, 1973 and Hansmann, 1980). As a signal of trustworthiness, however, the NDPC is weak and imperfect because non-controlling stakeholders suspect that it can be circumvented and that managers have enough room within the constraint to pursue their own preferences. Hence an NDPC can play only a limited demand-side role, one that cannot substitute for stakeholder control.

An NDPC can also serve to discipline hired managers. In the for-profit sector, the market for the shares limits the extent that managers can pursue nonprofit goals because such behavior invites takeover by outsiders who will replace "bad" managers with better ones. Additionally, managers of for-profit firms often have a stake in the organization (through share ownership or profit-sharing schemes) which serves to align their interests with those of owners. In the nonprofit sector it is difficult to design incentive schemes that align managerial and stakeholder interests, especially because stakeholder interests are multidimensional and complex. In the presence of this agency problem, controlling stakeholders may employ the nondistribution constraint to limit self-aggrandizement by managers (Fama and Jensen, 1983, and Easley and O'Hara, 1983). Controlling stakeholders may also seek compliance with their goals by hiring "believers", managers who support the goals of the organization (Young, 1986).

A government certified and enforced NDPC can serve several additional purposes. It can indicate reduced incentive for firm misbehavior to potential buyers, and reduces monitoring costs associated with hired managers. Adoption of the NDPC, along with a charitable, public benefit or educational mission, also confers a number of tax and related financial advantages in the United States, giving stakeholder-controlled organizations yet another incentive to adopt it. These advantages include income tax exemption, unemployment insurance exemption, lower postal rates, and exemption from local property taxes in many states[22]. These benefits could not encourage for-profit owners – whose goal is to maximize shareholder returns – to adopt the NDPC.

---

22   See Simon (1987) for a comprehensive discussion of public policy towards the nonprofit sector.

These two government policies – subsidization via tax exemption and enforcement of the NDPC – deserve a brief comment. Policy makers, while recognizing the existence of market failure and wishing to promote the provision of undersupplied goods, who look favorably on solutions that do not require government provision, designing policies to encourage nonprofit formation, provision, and longevity[23]. Tax and other subsidies help overcome the problems of collective action by reducing startup and operation costs. Tax exemption is probably the politically most expedient method for the government to subsidize nonprofit organizations.

As time passes after the inception of a nonprofit organization, members of the founding body often move away, and control over hired administrators diminishes. As this happens, the internal agency problem intensifies and the trust noncontrolling stakeholders have in the organization – conditional on stakeholder control – weakens. For this reason the nondistribution constraint, as a support to stakeholder control and discipliner of hired managers, takes on more importance as time passes[24].

The nondistribution-of-profit constraint has negative qualities as well. Importantly, it imposes an inflexibility on the organization, forcing stakeholders to adjust prices, quantities and qualities to absorb any profit, although they may prefer to distribute it for uses outside the organization. Stakeholders will not adopt the NDPC if its net effect is to reduce stakeholder welfare. Consumer and agricultural purchasing cooperatives, for example, are essentially nonprofit organizations that do not adopt the NDPC.

4.3   Open Books

Another important feature found in most nonprofit organizations is their policy of making financial and managerial information public. This policy, like the NDPC, is directly related to the "invisible" ownership shares that are a hallmark of the nonprofit form. Since access to information is a prerogative of ownership (being a prerequisite for control) and since stakeholders are *de facto* owners in nonprofit organizations, an open books policy is a simple device to give owners access to internal information. Because the stakeholder

---

23   Hall (1987) suggests that in the United States, policy toward nonprofits grew out of philosophical opposition to big government combined with a desire to promote a private-sector alternative to socialism.
24   For a related analysis, see Ben-Ner (1987).

population may be unstable over time, and because direct stakeholder control can weaken as the organization ages, an open books policy which is enshrined in an organization's statutes ensures that stakeholders will always have the ability to audit the organization's activities. Thus this policy is yet another means of supporting stakeholder control. Additionally, this policy strengthens demand-side trust in the organization because it makes it more difficult for managers to employ asymmetric information in their own interest and against the interests of stakeholders[25].

5   The Confluence of Nonprofit Demand and Supply

The critical difference between nonprofit organizations and for-profit firms is that there must be a confluence between the demand for the organizational form and the ability to provide it in order for a nonprofit organization to be formed. Nonprofit organizations, as described here, are an instance of vertical integration by demand-side stakeholders. Although the process of nonprofit formation can be facilitated by individuals other than stakeholders, demand-side stakeholders must play an active role in forming and operating a nonprofit organization, because demand will not materialize unless the organization is stakeholder controlled. Nonprofit organizations will thus come into existence only if there are stakeholders who value the expected flow of net benefits from a self-run organization more than the benefits they can derive from alternative sources.

Stakeholders have varying demand incentives to be involved in the control and operation of an organization, and bear different costs in carrying out such activities. As a result, not all stakeholders will be actively involved in control and in the extreme, there may not be enough controlling stakeholders for a nonprofit organization to exist. In other cases, only a small minority of stakeholders will participate in control.

---

25   In their analysis of day care centers, Nelson and Krashinsky (1973:63) write: "However, while the not-for-profit legal form seems helpful in assuring trustworthy day care centers, it certainly is not foolproof. (In fact, directors of nonprofit centers can be as selfish and neglectful of children in their pursuit of power and status as their profit-seeking counterparts.) Neither is the not-for-profit organizational form absolutely necessary. What *is* most important is that day care centers be open to detailed observation by both parents and citizen groups. Day care centers must operate in a *fish bowl*, which private enterprise generally has been reluctant to do".

Stakeholders with relatively large demand have more to lose from control contrary to their preferences and so have more incentive to be involved in controlling and auditing hired managers. Even if such stakeholders are very few, other, trust seeking, stakeholders may benefit from the organization's operation relative to a for-profit firm. Some stakeholders that are neither quantity rationed nor trust seeking may benefit from a quantity-quality-price combination not available elsewhere. The fact that the ratio of controlling to noncontrolling stakeholders is low does not change the fundamental nature of the nonprofit as a stakeholder-controlled organization: the organization still exists because of a nonrivalry and/or asymmetric information problem which is solved, partly, by stakeholder control. The delegation of important decision making power to salaried managers also does not change the nature of the firm.

6   Determinants of the Incidence of Nonprofits

Having established that demand for nonprofit organizations exists only for trust and collective goods, we now extend the analysis to examine the major demand and supply factors that affect the existence of nonprofit organizations in particular industries and geographical areas. These factors can be classified into three interdependent categories: market size, stakeholder characteristics, and product attributes.

6.1 Market Size

Market size has opposite effects on the demand for nonprofits in trust and collective services. The larger a market – i.e., the larger is market demand relative to the minimum efficient scale of production – the more likely it is that diverse tastes can be satisfied in the for-profit sector because larger markets can bear more firms and thus more variants of a good. Consequently, the larger the market for a collective good, the fewer quantity-rationed high-demand stakeholders there will be and the lower will be the demand for the nonprofit form of organization.

For trust goods, a larger market size compounds the asymmetric information problem. With more firms, stakeholders must gather more information in order to be informed and firms must work harder to build a reputation. Stakeholders of this type of service must spend considerable effort to determine which firms are trustworthy, and a large market enables firms to exploit the rational choice some stakeholders make to search less than exhaustively. This will induce demand for more trust-worthy stakeholder controlled nonprofit organizations.

6.2 Stakeholder Characteristics

Four characteristics of the population from amongst which stakeholders emerge play an important role in determining the inci-dence of the nonprofit sector: income and its distribution, education, demand heterogeneity, and social cohesion.

High income and better educated stakeholders are more capable of choosing a reliable for-profit provider of trust services because they have access to more reliable references and information sources. Poorer and less educated stakeholders are therefore more likely to rely on the nonprofit form for the provision of trust goods. For collec-tive goods, income has a reverse effect. For many goods, high income coincides with high demand, and high demand stakeholders are the primary source of demand for nonprofit organizations in collective goods. Hence for collective goods demand for the nonprofit form is likely to be positively associated with income. In terms of ability to supply nonprofit organizations, better education and higher income are likely to reduce the costs associated with forming and controlling a nonprofit organization. Hence demand and supply considerations suggest that income and education will be positively associated with nonprofit provision of collective goods, and inconclusively and weakly with that of trust goods.

Demand heterogeneity affects the price and quantity combina-tion set by for-profit firms and the tax and service package provided by governments in the market for collective services. The more homo-geneous stakeholders are in their willingness-to-pay, the less likely it is that there will be dissatisfaction with for-profit or government provision of collective goods. Conversely, demand heterogeneity en-hances demand for nonprofit provision of collective goods. As for trust goods, there appears to be no connection between demand heteroge-neity and nonprofit demand. Demand heterogeneity depends on the distribution of income, and on social, cultural and religious differences that generate preference heterogeneity. Hence income inequality and social and cultural diversity in a particular geographic area are likely to enhance the demand for nonprofit organizations in collective services[26].

---

26   Weisbrod (1975) points out that taste heterogeneity is positively corre-lated with nonprofit provision. James (1987a and b) also emphasizes the role of taste heterogeneity in the provision of nonprofit education.

Social cohesion depends positively on the degree of shared economic, religious, cultural, ethnic and educational background, and negatively on the degree of geographic dispersion among stakeholders for a given market size. Related stakeholders have more opportunity to meet each other and identify common demand, can more easily exercise social pressure to prevent free ridership in the revelation of demand and payment for services, and can control an organization more cheaply. Stakeholders that belong to a common organization (e.g., a church, community center, or social club) may also find it cheaper to employ that organization to form or manage another nonprofit organization. Often, the goals of the "parent" organization are unrelated to those of the nonprofit organization (see also Olson, 1971). Examples of such situations are numerous: day care centers operated by churches[27], homeless shelters established by community centers, theaters supported by large local companies, neighborhood-association sponsored food stores (cooperatives), ski clubs sponsored by workplaces, and banking institutions operated by trade unions.

In sum, the supply of nonprofit organizations is likely to be greater in communities where diverse but internally cohesive groups exist[28]. This supply-side effect is strengthened by the demand-side finding that demand heterogeneity, which is greater in communities where diverse groups exist, also stimulates nonprofit provision.

6.3 Product Attributes

We established earlier that the demand for nonprofit provision is restricted to trust and collective goods, which are characterized by various degrees of nonexcludability, nonrivalry and asymmetric information. The greater these degrees, the greater is the probability that a good will be provided by a nonprofit organization. For example, among health services, facility-intensive care has stronger collective attributes than care that can be administered in the office of a family practitioner. Thus while demand for nonprofit provision may exist for both types of care, the demand is likely to be stronger for facility-intensive care. Similarly, all things equal, day care for children, which has both trust and collective attributes, is a more likely candidate for nonprofit provision than elementary or higher education,

---

27   But not all church-operated day care centers fall within this category, as some may be directed, for example, at spreading religion.
28   See Galaskiewicz (1985) and James (1987a and b) for discussions of the relationship between community networks and nonprofit provision.

which have weak trust aspects[29]

Demand for the nonprofit form depends not only on the strength of a good's trust or collective attributes, but also on the total utility that the good provides to stakeholders. For a given cost of participating in the formation and control of a nonprofit organization, high utility goods are more likely to be candidates for nonprofit provision than other goods. Utility may be measured in terms of expense relative to total budget, which indicates potential utility gain, or in terms of the size of the loss if provision is unsatisfactory.

7   Conclusions

The theory presented in this paper synthesizes and expands on extant theories, especially those of Weisbrod (1975) and Hansmann (1980). In terms of Figure 1, Hansmann's theory can be summarized by arrows from 'Demand' to 'Unsatisfied Demand' (via market failure), and from there directly to 'Nonprofit Provision'. The Weisbrod theory can be summarized by arrows from 'Demand' to 'Unsatisfied Demand' (via market failure), from there directly to 'Government Provision', back to 'Unsatisfied Demand' (via government failure), and then to 'Nonprofit Provision'. While these analyses provide important insights into the role of the nonprofit sector, neither provides a complete motivation for the formation of nonprofit organizations, and both ignore the steps between unsatisfied demand and nonprofit provision. However, these steps are crucial, as no organization comes into existence just because of the existence of demand. Moreover, the conditions of the supply of the nonprofit form of organization differ from those of both for-profit and government organizations. A nonprofit organization will be formed only if a group of interested stakeholders (individuals or organizations) has the ability to exercise control over the organization. Stakeholder control is a *sine qua non* for the existence of nonprofit organizations, because it avails the trust required for patronizing the organization, revealing demand to it, and making donations to it. These are key elements in the demand for nonprofit organizations, and must be satisfied for these organizations to exist. Nonprofit organizations are thus a case in which demanders must generate their own supply.

---

29   For further discussion of differences in the degree of trust and collective attributes of goods in different industries, see Ben-Ner and Van Hoomissen (1990).

However, only those stakeholders who anticipate that the benefits of control outweigh its costs will participate in the formation and control of a nonprofit organization. This net benefit must also be greater than the net benefit achieved by purchasing elsewhere. Noncontrolling stakeholders will also purchase from the nonprofit organization, trusting it because of the nonrivalry of its services (which suggests that they cannot be exploited by controlling stakeholders who partake in the consumption of the same units), or simply preferring its price-quantity-quality package over that of other organizations.

Direct control by stakeholders is never complete, and the residual agency problem may deter stakeholders from patronizing it. In order to enhance stakeholder control, founders of nonprofit organizations impose an organizational structure aimed at guarding their present and future group interests. Three prominent features of this structure include (a) the absence of ownership shares, (b) the nondistribution-of-profits constraint, and (c) the open books policy. Respectively, these (a) prevent concentration of control in the hands of a few stakeholders-owners, (b) enhance control over hired managers, serve as a distribution of economic surplus rule, and signal the reinvestment of the surplus in the organization, and (c) ensure free access to information required for the exercise of control. In addition, the statutes of nonprofit organizations vest formal control in boards of directors representing stakeholders.

Clearly, not all stakeholders will have equal demand for nonprofit organizations, nor will they all have similar abilities to control them. Factors such as stakeholders' education, income, social cohesion, and demand heterogeneity affect both the degree to which they suffer from market and government failures and therefore their demand for nonprofit provision, as well as their ability to provide the requisite conditions for nonprofit supply, primarily the ability to exercise control. Thus the geographical prevalence of nonprofit organizations will depend on characteristics of stakeholders in different communities[30].

The industrial incidence of nonprofit organizations depends on attributes of different goods and services. The primary attributes that are relevant to nonprofit provision are the degrees of excludability, rivalry and informational asymmetries that are associated with dif-

---

30   We explore these issues empirically in Ben-Ner and Van Hoomissen (1991a), providing support for the main hypotheses presented in this paper.

ferent goods. On this basis we concluded that services rather than consumer goods are the most likely candidates for nonprofit provision. Table 1, which presents the industrial distribution in New York State, confirms this hypothesis. Furthermore, among services, industries with stronger rivalry, nonexcludability, and asymmetric information attributes, such as health and social services, are heavily populated by nonprofit organizations, whereas services with strong private good attributes (essentially nonrival and excludable), such as personal and financial services, are provided mainly by the for-profit sector. These hypotheses are broadly confirmed by the industrial distribution figures presented Table 1.

Table 1: For-Profit, Nonprofit and Government Employment Shares in New York State, by Industry Group 1987, in percent

	For-profit	Nonprofit	Government
ALL SERVICES	51	21	28
Financial Services	95	1	3
Personal and Business Services	99	1	0
Amusement & Recreation	79	8	12
Health Services	31	47	22
Legal Services	97	3	0
Education & Libraries	3	32	65
Social Services	9	87	4
Museums, Bot. & Zoo. Gardens	1	92	6
Membership Organizations	39	61	0
Other Services (prof'l, etc.)	98	0	1
Government	0	0	100
ALL NON-SERVICES	92	1	7
Agriculture	99	1	0
Mining	100	0	0
Construction	100	0	0
Manufacturing	100	0	0
Transportation	78	0	22
US Postal Service	0	0	100
Communications	99	1	0
ALL OTHER INDUSTRIES	98	0	2
Commerce	99	1	0
Printing & Publishing	76	0	24
Electricity, Gas & Sanitation	99	0	1
ALL INDUSTRIES	73	11	17

(1)Reproduced from Ben-Ner and Van Hoomissen (1990), where sources for the data are given.
(2)Totals may not add up to 100 due to rounding.
(3)The nonprofit sector here comprises organizations covered by section SOl(c)(3) of the United States Internal Revenue Code. Other nonprofits (mostly in membership organizations) are included as for-profit organizations. The 501(c)(3) segment employs about 92% of the nonprofit sector workforce (Rudney, 1987).

REFERENCES

BEN-NER A., 1986, "Nonprofit Organizations: Why Do They Exist in Market Economies?" in *The Economics of Nonprofit Institutions: Studies in Structure and Policy,* ed. Susan Rose-Ackerman, 94-113, Oxford, Oxford University Press.

——, 1987, "Birth, Change and Bureaucratization in Nonprofit Organizations: An Economic Analysis", in *Politics, Public Policy and the Voluntary Sector,* ed. Robert Herman, 119-137, Proceedings of the Fifteenth Annual Meeting of the Association of Voluntary Action Scholars.

——, 1991, "Cooperation. Conflict, and Control in Organizations", Forthcoming in Samuel Bowles, Herbert Gintis and Bo Gustafsson (eds.), *Democracy and Markets: Participation, Accountability and Efficiency,* Cambridge, Cambridge University.

BEN-NER A. and VAN HOOMISSEN T., 1989, *A Study of the Nonprofit Sector in New York State; Its Size, Nature, and Economic Impact,* Albany, NY, The Nelson A. Rockefeller Institute of Government.

——, 1990, "The Nonprofit Sector's Growth in the 1980s : Facts and Causes", in *Nonprofit Management and Leadership* 1(2): 99-116.

——, 1991a, "An Empirical Investigation of the Joint Determination of the Size of the For-Profit, Nonprofit and Government Sectors", University of Minnesota, Mimeo.

——, 1991b, "The Provision of Mixed Goods: Markets, Contracts, and Consumer Control", University of Minnesota, Mimeo.

BERGSTROM T. and GOODMAN R., 1973, "Private Demand for Public Goods", in *American Economic Review* 63: 280-96.

DUBIN J. and NAVARRO P., 1988, "How Markets for Impure Public Goods Organize: The Case of Household Refuse Collection", in *Journal of Law, Economics, and Organization* 4(2): 217-41.

EASLEY D. and O'HARA M., 1983, 'The Economic Role of Nonprofit Firms", in *Bell Journal of Economics* 14:531-38.

ELLMAN I., 1982, "Another Theory of Nonprofit Corporations", in *Michigan Law Review* 80: 999-1050.

FAMA E. and JENSEN M., 1983, "Separation of Ownership and Control", in *Journal of Law and Economics* 26: 301-25.

FRIEDMAN L., 1984, *Microeconomic Policy Analysis*, Mc Graw-Hill.

GALASKIEWICZ J., 1985, *Social Organization of an Urban Grants Economy: A Study of Business Philanthropy and Nonprofit Organizations*, Orlando, Academic Press.

GROSSMAN S., and HART O., 1986, "The Costs and Benefits of Ownership: A Theory of Vertical and Lateral Integration", in *Journal of Political Economy* , 94 (August): 691-719

GUI B., 1987, "Productive Private Nonprofit Organizations: A Conceptual Framework", in *Annals of Public and Cooperative Economics* 58(4): 415-35.

———, 1990, "The 'Non-Distribution Constraint' in Economic Organizations", in *Ricerche Economiche*, XLIV(1): 115-30.

HALL, DOBKIN P., 1987, "A Historical Overview of the Private Nonprofit Sector", in *The Nonprofit Sector: A Research Handbook*, ed. Walter W. Powell, 3-26, New Haven, Yale University Press.

HANSMANN H., 1980, "The Role of Nonprofit Enterprise", in *Yale Law Journal*, 89: 835-98.

———, 1987, "Economic Theories of Nonprofit Organization", in *The Nonprofit Sector: A Research handbook*, ed. Walter W. Powell, 27-42, New Haven, Yale University Press.

———, 1988, "The Ownership of the Firm", in *Journal of Law, Economics, and Organization* 4:267-304.

HART O. and MOORE J., 1990, "Property Rights and the Nature of the Firm", in *Journal of Politicial Economy*, 98 (December), 1119-58.

HEFLEBOWER R.B., 1980, *Cooperatives and Mutuals in the Market System*, Madison, WI, University of Wisconsin Press.

HOLTMANN A., 1988, "Theories of Nonprofit Organizations", in *Journal of Economic Surveys*, 2.

JAMES E., 1987a, "The Political Economy of Private Education in Developed and Developing Countries", in *World Bank Discussion Paper* EDT 81.1987.

———, 1987b, "The Public/Private Division of Responsibility for Education: An International Comparison" in *Economics of Education Reciew*.

JAMES E. and ROSE-ACKERMAN S., 1986, "The Nonprofit Enterprise in Market Economies", in *Fundamentals of Pure and Applied Economics,* eds. Jacques Lesourne and Hugo Sonnenschein, New York, Harwood Academic Publishers.

MOE T. M, 1990, «The Politics of Structural Choice: Toward a Theory of Public Bureaucracy", in *Organization Theory: From Chester Barnard to the Present and Beyond,* ed. Oliver E. Williamson, Oxford, Oxford University Press.

NELSON R.R. and KRASHINSKY M., 1973, "Two Major Issues of Public Policy : Public Subsidy and the Organization of Supply", in *Public Subsidy for Day Care of Young Children,* eds. Richard Nelson and Dennis Young, Lexington, MA, D.C. Heath.

OLSON M., 1971, *The Logic of Collective Action,* Cambridge, MA: Harvard University Press.

PRESTON A., 1988, "The Nonprofit Firm: A Potential Solution to Inherent Market Failures", in *Economic Inquiry* 26: 493-506.

ROSE-ACKERMAN S., 1986, "Altruistic Nonprofit Firms in Competitive Markets: The Case of Day-Care Centers in the United States", *Journal of Consumer Policy,* 9: 291-310.

RUDNEY G., 1987, "The Scope and Dimensions of Nonprofit Activity», in *The Nonprofit Sector: A Research Handbook,* ed. Walter W. Powell, 55-64, New Haven, Yale University Press.

SIMON J. G., 1987, "The Tax Treatment of Nonprofit Organizations: A Review of Federal and State Policies", in *The Nonprofit Sector: A Research Handbook,* ed. Walter W. Powell, 67-98, New Haven, Yale University Press.

VAN HOOMISSEN T., 1988, "Price Dispersion and Inflation: Evidence from Israel", in *Journal of Political Economy,* 96 (December): 1303-14.

——, 1991, "On the Choice of Organizational Form", University of Minnesota, Mimeo.

WEISBROD, B. A., 1975, "Toward a Theory of the Voluntary Nonprofit Sector in a Three-Sector Economy", in *Altruism, Morality and Economic Theory,* ed. Edmund Phelps, 171-95, New York: Russell Sage Foundation.

——, 1988, *The Nonprofit Economy,* Cambridge, MA, Harvard University Press.

WILLIAMSON O., 1985, *The Economic Institutions of Capitalism: Firms, Markets, Relational Contracting,* New York and London, The Free Press and Collier Macmillan Publishers.

YOUNG D. R., 1986, "Entrepreneurship and the Behavior of Nonprofit Organizations: Elements of a Theory", in *The Economics of Nonprofit Institutions: Studies in Structure and Policy,* ed. Susan Rose-Ackerman, 161-184, Oxford and New York, Oxford University Press.

THE ECONOMIC RATIONALE FOR THE "THIRD SECTOR"
Nonprofit and other Noncapitalist Organizations

by

Benedetto GUI*

Department of Economic Sciences

University of Venezia

Introduction

If the third sector is defined as comprising economic microorganizations "...located between the private, for-profit, and the public sector..." (Anheier and Seibel, 1990, p. 7), we notice that economic theory has mostly dealt separately with its subsets: nonprofit organizations (henceforth NPOs), clubs, insurance and financial mutuals, worker cooperatives, other types of cooperatives[1]. This paper is intended to suggest a unitary approach to the third sector, which is

* Thanks are due to Avner Ben-Ner, Ottorino Chillemi, Henry Hansmann, Steven Martin, and Milica Uvalic for reading and commenting on previous drafts. Valuable comments have also been made by Domenico Mario Nuti, Serge Christophe Kolm, and other participants in a seminar held at the European University Institute in Florence in April 1989. Anonymous referees have further helped reduce the number of errors and weaknesses, whose responsibility of course is only mine.

1 Surveys of the economic literature on NPOs can be found in Gui (1987), Hansmann (1987), Holtmann (1988); on clubs see among others Sandler and Tschirhart (1980); on worker cooperatives and labour-managed firms see Bartlett and Uvalic (1986), and Bonin and Putterman (1987); on mutuals and cooperatives in general see Heflebower (1980). Among the contributions that use a more general framework see: Hansmann (1988); Fama and Jensen (1983); Ben-Ner and Neuberger (1981); Weisbrod (1988).

regarded here as composed of organizations where a category of agents other than investors is awarded the role of explicit, intended beneficiaries of the organizational economic activity.

After providing some definitions, notably that of the "potential surplus" of an organization (Section 1), a classification of economic micro-organizations is presented that permits neatly separating the third sector from the "capitalist" sector, and to distinguish "public benefit" from "mutual benefit" organizations within the third sector (Section 2). As a second step, in Section 3 I survey the various reasons why a category of agents might prefer to deal with an organization statutorily intended to benefit them, rather than transact with for-profit organizations. Then, in Section 4 I briefly tackle the issue of control over third sector-organization, whether and why it should be in the hands of beneficiaries themselves – the mutual benefit option – or in those of donors and trustees – thus giving rise to a public benefit organization. Last, having discussed it at length elsewhere (Gui, 1989, 1990), in Section 5 I only hint at the role of the "nondistribution constraint" by which nonprofit organizations are characterized within the third sector. A short concluding Section completes the paper[2].

1   The distribution of an organization's surplus

Herein the term organization refers to an entity that is distinct from all agents that are involved in its activity, and does not include any of them. The considerations that follow are more relevant in the case of large, formal organizations, where many people are involved and the functions played by each of them are more clearly stated.

---

2   Inevitably, several important themes do not find an adequate treatment in the following pages. I mention among others: the role of the third sector, as an alternative not to the for-profit sector, but to government; the behaviour of third sector organizations, as distinguished from their role; the motivations of those who supply resources to the third sector, and in particular of entrepreneurs. On all three see for example the literature review in James and Rose-Ackerman (1986), and their quotations. As to the last theme, I only notice that the puzzle that nonprofit entrepreneurship poses to economists is not much greater than with other third sector organizations such as cooperatives. In fact, the great dispersion of economic benefit among their members renders here too the acquisitive motivation of promoters implausible. An interesting effort to broaden the perspective on the forces driving entrepreneurship in NPOs is found in Young (1983, 1986). See also Ben-Ner and Van Hoomissen (this issue).

Any economic organization – NPOs included – pursues a distributive goal, i.e. it aims at devoting in some form or other its surplus to the advantage of a "beneficiary category", such as buyers, consumers of nonexcludable goods, aid recipients, workers, sellers, and investors. Two categories have been purposedly excluded from the above list: donors, who may certainly receive "psychic income", but this will be seen as a side effect of their donations benefitting (in the usual sense of the term) another category; directors, who are, for simplicity, considered the executors of the organization's will and not bearers of legitimate interests themselves (at least, qua directors).

Notice that beneficiaries can have various, conflicting interests (for instance, in consumer cooperatives, healthfulness versus cheapness), and the trade-offs between them can differ widely among agents. In order to limit disputes, usually the statutes specify a "privileged" interest, and thus try to shift the balance toward it (e.g. in natural food cooperatives it is healthfulness that is privileged).

Statutes also specify the "dominant" category, which is awarded the ultimate decision making power in the organization. In addition to the categories listed above with reference to the beneficiary role, the dominant role may also be assigned to donors and trustees (i.e., directors not immediately accountable to any of the other categories). Both the beneficiary and the dominant roles may be assigned to only part of a certain category[3].

The distribution of an organization's surplus does not necessarily occur in explicit forms (such as dividends or bonuses). Implicit forms also exist, either overt or covert (think respectively of favourable prices for members and unduly generous nonmonetary benefits to managers). Implicit distribution occurs before the determination of the "accounting" surplus, which is the object of explicit distributive decisions. Thus, in order to discuss distributive decisions in a global sense, it is convenient to refer to the "potential" surplus of an organization, defined as the net revenue that would result if any implicit distribution were avoided – e.g., in a consumer cooperative, if member-customers were charged market prices (see Ben-Ner and

---

3   Examples are voting and nonvoting shares in joint stock companies, with the latter only awarded the beneficiary role; member (i.e., dominant) and nonmember donors in charitable organizations; member or nonmember customers in consumer cooperatives, with the latter excluded from both roles; subsidized (i.e. beneficiary, typically the students) and unsubsidized customers in university cafeterias.

Table 1 A classification of economic micro-organizations

BENEFICIARY CATEGORY \ DOMINANT CATEGORY	BUYERS	AID RECIPIENTS	CONSUMERS OF NON-EXCLUDABLE GOODS	WORKERS	SELLERS	INVESTORS	DONORS OR TRUSTEES
BUYERS	CONSUMER COOPERATIVES SOCIAL AND SPORTING CLUBS						NONPROFIT HOSPITALS AND NURSING CARE
AID RECIPIENTS		SELF-ADMINISTERED AID					ORGANIZATIONS CARING FOR THE POOR
CONSUMERS OF NON-EXCLUDABLE GOODS			COMPULSORY IRRIGATION UNIONS CONDOMINIUM HOUSING				ENVIRONMENTS ORGANIZATIONS, EDUCATIONAL RADIO AND TV
WORKERS				WORKER COOPERATIVES			JOB CREATION ENTERPRISES, ESOP
SELLERS					DAIRY OR WINE COOPERATIVES		"THIRD WORLD SHOPS"
INVESTORS						JOINT STOCK COMPANIES	INVESTMENT FUNDS AND TRUSTS

Neuberger, 1981). It is the potential surplus that the organization is statutorily bound to devote to the beneficiary category, by either distributing it explicitly (if permitted) or surrendering it in the form of implicit distribution[4].

Notice that the potential surplus is not independent of the assignment of the beneficiary and dominant roles, which determines the information flows and the distribution pattern of the organization. In fact, these may influence the willingness of transactors to deal with the organization – or, equivalently, transaction costs – and therefore affect the size of the potential surplus (see section 3 and in particular, situation 3; for a simple modelling of this effect see Gui, 1988).

Last, implicit distribution is not a zero sum transfer. By modifying either the price or the quality of transactions with the beneficiaries, it affects their quantity decisions. This allocative effect can lead to either an increase or a decrease in the joint surplus of the organization and the category's members[5].

2   A classification of economic micro-organizations

Private organizations can be classified according to which the dominant and, respectively, beneficiary categories are[6]. This is done

---

4   Distribution to beneficiaries must not necessarily occur immediately, say, in the current period. Accumulation of wealth by the organization can also serve their interests, e.g. by financing quality-improving investment, or simply by smoothing the provision of services over time (for an intertemporal model of a grant-receiving NPO, see Austen-Smith and Jenkins, 1985).

5   A case where implicit distribution may lead to Pareto-superior allocations occurs in the performing arts. Here, fixed costs are overwhelming, while marginal costs are low. NPOs reduce prices below average costs, and therefore toward marginal costs, thanks to donations (see Hansmann, 1981b; a similar configuration of costs is assumed also by Holtmann, 1985, to present a theory of NPOs based on uncertain demand). The opposite tends to occur when surplus distribution (even explicit) is apportioned according to the volume of some type of transaction with members, and nonmembers are excluded from that type of transaction. This is the long-debated "Ward-Vanek effect" in the economics literature on worker-managed firms (see: Bartlett and Uvalic, 1986; Bonin and Putterman, 1987).

6   The classification presented in Table 1 differs in several respects from that proposed by Hansmann (1980). Apart from restricting his analysis to

in Table 1, where the relevant cells are filled with examples. For simplicity, only "pure" cases are considered, in which each role is only assigned to one category (e.g., profit-sharing firms are a mixed case, since both shareholders and employees are beneficiaries).

The cases on the main diagonal can be designated as "mutual benefit", since the beneficiary and the dominant categories coincide: those having decision-making power can manage the organization to their own benefit. For instance, workers constitute both the beneficiary and the dominant category in worker-cooperatives. The privileged interest is not specified in the table. In the example of workers, this could be either high wages or security of employment.

The remaining cells can be labelled "public benefit". They are characterized by noncoincidence between the dominant and the beneficiary category. As the table shows, the only relevant "public benefit" cells belong to the last column, in which the dominant role is assigned either to trustees or to donors. Typical examples are nonprofit hospitals and organizations caring for the poor. However, Table 1 indicates that categories other than consumers can be the beneficiaries of public benefit organizations, not only of non-capitalist mutual benefit organizations. This is worth stressing since the attention of researchers in the economics of NPOs has been confined to organizations intended to benefit either consumers or aid recipients (see also section 4 below).

The last row in Table 1 refers to organizations whose beneficiaries are investors. Here, as a rule, the privileged interest is a high return on the wealth permanently committed to the organization[7]. Since the title to share in the surplus derives from a once and for all contribution, no further transaction between the member and the organization is required. Each share is then an unconditional claim to the flow of future residual income and therefore lends itself to "capitalization": membership rights become regular financial assets. In this sense both joint stock companies and investment funds can be

---

organizations serving consumers or aid recipients, he focuses on the single transaction that commits money to the organization (whether a purchase or a donation) rather than on the destination of the surplus resulting from all the organization's transactions; in the case of donations this leads him to discuss the protection of donors' will (1980, p. 845) rather than the other side of the coin, i.e., the promotion of beneficiaries' interest.

7   Atypical situations exist where limited companies are formed to pursue public benefit aims, with both private and public money.

called "capitalist", while the former can be identified as "for-profit" proper.

Let us now look at the remaining types. Regarding public benefit organizations, capitalization of future income is excluded by definition; thus their non-capitalist nature is absolutely patent. As to the remaining mutual benefit typologies, notice that in order to enjoy a fraction of the organization's surplus, members have to repeatedly interact with the organization; e.g., sell or buy from it, perform a certain job in its office, or use its facilities (in the case of a club). This on the one hand, leads to the imposition of constraints on the saleability of membership rights (colleague members are not indifferent as to whom they have to deal with), and on the other, conditions the appropriation of the future surplus by the individual member, albeit to various extents. Since capitalization is not given priority, these organizations too can be called "non-capitalist"[8], and therefore be included in the third sector, together with public benefit private organizations[9].

3   Advantages and disadvantages of being the beneficiaries

The first question that is suggested by the classification of Section 2 is why should the members of a category other than investors prefer, when dealing with an organization, to be established as its

8   Unfortunately, the boundaries are always somewhat blurred (for instance the statutes of some cooperatives, especially in the US, make them quite close to capitalist organizations). My use of the term capitalist refers to internal principles of organization, and therefore differs from Williamson's (1985), who includes also third sector organizations among capitalist institutions, in that they are part of (predominantly) capitalist systems. Alchian and Woodward are particularly explicit in adopting this view (they go as far as to include even the family among "capitalist institutions"; 1988, p.76).

9   Unfortunately, the use of the term "third sector" is not univocal. Some authors – among which Douglas (1983) – use it to refer to NPOs alone. The recent book by Anheier and Seibel (1990) is rather confusing in this regard: in the introduction they define the third sector as including cooperatives, while the rest of the volume deals almost exclusively with NPOs. Even more discordant uses of the term "third sector" can be found (for example Clayre, 1979, refers to participatory enterprises). The view adopted in this paper that NPOs represent only part of the third sector, together with cooperative, mutuals, clubs, etc. corresponds to the use of the French expression "economie sociale", which is also adopted by the EEC (see Archambault's paper in Anheier and Seibel).

explicit beneficiaries, rather than rely on normal contractual arrangements (and, say, let investors perform both the dominant and beneficiary roles).

Several reasons have been suggested in the literature to answer this question. They correspond to the situations that are listed below. (In reality mixtures of these situations can be found).

1) a) The organization would exert ordinary market power to the detriment of the category. An obvious example are traditional consumer cooperatives, that were born as a response to oligopolistic retail markets[10]. Similarly, b), where transacting entails a significant accumulation of specific assets on the part of the category's members, dealing with an organization with conflicting interests would expose them to *ex-post* monopoly, in the form of opportunistic attempts to appropriate a disproportionate share of the quasi-rent of these assets (post-contractual market power). In fact, plants for the joint treatment of industrial waste water – connection to which is a significant nonrecoverable investment – are sometimes managed in cooperative form by their users[11].

2) The market is not cleared, with some members of the category prevented from finding a partner in the transaction (or "rationed"). These members would benefit from the organization aiming at providing transaction opportunities to the category. The best example is mass unemployment during economic crises.

3) There is asymmetric information, as at least one important characteristic of the transaction (let us call it "quality"), with the category's members being the less informed party. The nursing care of

---

10   See also Ben-Ner's (1987) discussion of the advantage of forming worker cooperatives in face of an oligopsonistic local labour market. In fact, by forming an organization to their own benefit, the members of the category may also take advantage of any market power the organization is in a position to exert toward other categories (an attack, not a defense strategy).

11   Avoiding *ex-post* monopoly is the rationale for vertical integration suggested by Klein, Crawford and Alchian (1978), who see mutual ownership of country clubs as a protection of a specific quasi-rent. The three authors also refer to specific human capital as an asset that needs particular protection; this argument is developed by Alchian and Woodward (1988), who suggest that in some cases this is a good reason for the firm being managed to the benefit of workers (and controlled by them). Avoiding post-contractual exploitation on the part of the organization is indeed an important reason for investors to control an organization (see also Hansmann, 1988).

elderly people is a good example in this regard. The members of the category are exposed to both moral hazard (the organization opportunistically supplies lower quality than agreed), and adverse selection (low quality organizations might drive high quality competitors out of the market). Their damage is twofold. First, they may engage in transactions that they would refuse if better informed (i.e., whose quality is below the member's reservation level for the agreed price). Second, they may refuse mutually advantageous transactions because they do not trust the organization. In the latter case the organization is also damaged by asymmetric information. This is the typical situation to which Hansmann applies his concept of "contract failure"[12].

4) There is asymmetric information, with the members of the category more informed than the organization, not only about their own characteristics and behaviour, but also about those of their colleagues. The beneficiary position gives the category's members the incentive to counter: a) moral hazard, by modifying their own behaviour and monitoring colleagues (e.g., so as to avoid shirking, not only as to labour supply, but also as to loss preventing activities in the case of damage insurance); b) adverse selection, by disclosing information regarding co-members (e.g., as to the reliability of applicant borrowers). This seems to be the case of property and liability insurance mutuals and of credit cooperatives, with risk and reliability being the relevant quality characteristics [13].

---

12   "Contract failure" is said to occur when, due in particular to asymmetric information, "patrons" – i.e. buyers or donors – are unable "...to police producers by ordinary contractual devices" (Hansmann, 1980, p. 845). Among other examples Hansmann (1990) suggests that mutual savings banks, that are run by trustees to the benefit of depositors, have been formed for precisely this reason, i.e. to protect uninformed depositors from bankers engaging in exceedingly risky ventures (here deposit security is the relevant "quality"). Hansmann suggests that similar arguments hold with life insurance mutuals. For a recent modelling of the "contract failure" theory of NPOs see Chillemi and Gui (1991). Notice that also the contract failure argument applies to investors as well.

13   Hansmann observes that the best response to this type of market failure would be, if conceivable, that the organization "owned" the insured or the borrowers, rather than the other way round, which has to be seen as a second best option (1985a, 1988). A different view of the role of insurance mutuals is presented by Smith and Stutzer (1990), who argue that participating insurance policies (that are typically offered by mutuals) act as a sorting device for low-risk demanders of insurance.

5) The relevant characteristics of the transaction – the same for all customers – are numerous. Adequate satisfaction of the category's members cannot be assured through normal market relationships, due to one or more of the following reasons: the number of different "bundles of characteristics" offered on the market is smaller than the number of characteristics, which prevents a market price for each characteristic from being implicitly determined (Drèze, 1976, uses this result in search for a rationale for worker-managed firms); the true characteristics of transactions and their conformity with one's own preferences are known only through direct experience, while both writing complete contingent contracts and interrupting an ongoing contractual relationship entail high costs; new occurrences call for frequent readjustments of characteristics. Provided its members are sufficiently homogeneous, elimination of the conflict of interest between the organization and the category eases the maintenance of a stricter conformity of characteristics to preferences and of prices to normal costs (conflict prevents the "voice" of beneficiaries having a more direct influence over the organization's choices; see Krashinsky, 1986, p. 123). Day centers for children and schools are probably the best examples[14].

6) The transaction concerns a nonexcludable public good, so that recourse to individual self-regarding action would lead to underprovision or even no provision at all. The free rider problem is the first obstacle to efficient collective action. However, provided some members of the category are ready to voluntarily contribute to production costs, the further problem of "marginal impact monitoring" arises: the payer is unable to ascertain whether his contribution is actually used to improve the quantity or the quality of supply, rather than being simply pocketed by somebody (see Ellman, 1982, p. 1009). A response to the latter problem is making consumers the beneficiaries of the organization that provides the public good. A typical example is donor-supported educational broadcasting.

7) The transaction concerns an excludable public good, such as a theater performance. The problem is similar to the previous case,

---

14   This is the situation of consumers searching for a "special quality", as stressed by Ellman (1982, p. 1035). Hansmann, instead, never considers situations in which quality is inherently a multidimensional magnitude (in situations 3 and 4 quality could be simply considered as a scalar), notwithstanding that they fit into his definition of contract failure. Ben-Ner (1987, pp. 440-441) applies this argument to workplace characteristics, as a reason for the formation of worker cooperatives.

although less severe. Allocative efficiency can be improved by better knowledge of the category's members' willingness to pay, which is the magnitude according to which price discrimination should be shaped. Elimination of interest conflicts between the category and the organization reduces the reluctance of individuals to reveal their demands, while horizontal monitoring by colleague beneficiaries can reinforce the effect. Price discrimination can even take the form of voluntary contributions above a base fee[15].

8) The category is constituted of intended recipients of aid and therefore is the beneficiary by definition.

While in situation 8 the only reason for assigning the beneficiary role is to redistribute surplus – which can be seen as positively affecting social welfare, not allocative efficiency – in the remaining situations the reassignment of the beneficiary role may improve allocative efficiency: the initial situation is one of "market failure", and the reassignment of the beneficiary role represents an adequate, albeit not necessarily complete, cure. In fact, after the reassignment, the joint surplus of the category and the organization is increased (*ceteris paribus*). This should remain true also when extending our focus to the whole market, since competition, if any, will tend to align the behaviour of competitors with that of the organization under consideration, and therefore move it in the right direction[16].

Furthermore, as a result of the reassignment of the beneficiary role, redistribution can also occur to the advantage of the category (for example, in the case of monopolistic retailing, by becoming the beneficiaries, consumers would get both the surplus previously accruing to the monopolist, and the additional surplus ensuing from prices moving down toward marginal cost). As already observed, in all situations, part of the gain can be lost when implicit distribution takes place. Notice that in situation 2 another redistributive effect can result: the advantage enjoyed by the organization's beneficiaries, who escape rationing, could, at least partly, occur at the expense of other market participants, who, in turn, consequently become rationed. In

---

15   See Hansmann (1981b) and Ben-Ner (1986, case 3 in particular).

16   In situation 2 the reassignment of the beneficiary role would lead to an improvement in allocative efficiency if, for instance, unemployment were due to downward inflexible wages (classical unemployment), an obstacle that would be passed round by residual worker compensation. At worst, the effect on allocative efficiency might be nil, as in a textbook situation of Keynesian unemployment.

the example above, workers employed elsewhere could be displaced as an effect of the employment-maintaining policy adopted by a competitor organization taken over by workers.

Obviously, besides the above listed advantages of being the beneficiary, there are disadvantages that have to be taken into consideration (this is why above I have used the *ceteris paribus* clause). First, depriving investors of the beneficiary role may entail an efficiency loss (in particular, investors are likely to suffer from market failures of types 1b and 3 above; see Hansmann, 1988, p. 281-283). Second, attached to the beneficiary role is a greater risk to be borne by the category's members. In this regard note that individual beneficiaries can be sheltered from risk by using the accounting surplus as a buffer against variability in the potential surplus, up to a certain point. However, to the extent that beneficiaries are free to refuse to transact with the organization without incurring significant penalties, an unusual share of risk ends up being borne by other categories (creditors of all types); however, this does have a cost all the same, in the form of less favourable terms of transaction with such categories (see the discussion in Gui, 1985, with reference to worker cooperatives). Third, since the dominant role will also have to be reassigned (either to the beneficiaries themselves or to trustees or donors), the cost of control over the organization will be affected too, possibly in an adverse manner (see Hansmann, 1988).

Of course, the reassignment of the beneficiary role is not the only response to the market failures examined. Others exist, either within the private sector (cost-plus contracts, reputation, professionalism, etc.) or with the intervention of public authorities (see Hansmann, 1980, sect. 6; Krashinsky, 1986, pp. 116-117).

4   Public Benefit versus Mutual Benefit

A further problem arises: once a category is established as the beneficiary of the organization, who is going to play the dominant role and why? In other words, for what reasons should an organization established to serve a certain category adopt the public benefit or the mutual benefit form?

In general it can be said that control on the part of beneficiaries can assure a stricter conformity of the organization's activity with its established goals, due to both information and incentives considerations. Exceptions to this general statement are found in situation 8;

the beneficiaries might not give priority to those interests that the donors have established as privileged. An obvious example is spending, in alcohol consumption, money donated with the aim of improving education or health care. Furthermore, control by beneficiaries can be desirable *per se*, as an opportunity for personal and social advancement. Similarly, the mutual benefit option can be preferred by founders and donors, in order to push the category to assume responsibility.

On the other hand, the mutual benefit solution can be hindered by the costs of collective action (especially in setting up the organization, but also during subsequent operation). The elements that influence such costs include among others: group homogeneity and cohesion; number of members; transaction costs connected with distance and frequency or continuity of transactions; value of transactions of individual members; lack of cultural requirements on the part of beneficiaries[17].

Of course, the previous argument does not imply that when such costs are high, the job of serving the interests of the category will be automatically turned over to a public benefit organization, since this requires the willingness on the part of someone else to devote resources to the benefit of the category. Furthermore, a public benefit governance of the organization also entails specific costs, stemming from lack of economic incentives to monitor performance (this is a central theme of the "property rights school"; see Steinberg, 1987, pp. 127-130, for an overview of empirical results regarding NPOs; see also Pauly, 1987).

---

17   Ben-Ner and Van Hoomissen (this issue) explore this subject in detail. See also: Hansmann, 1988, 1989; Krashinsky, 1987, p. 123; Ben-Ner, 1986, p. 108. A general reference is Olson, 1965, p. 43. The inability of the category's members to start a successful initiative does not necessarily preclude the mutual benefit solution. In fact, the peculiar difficulties of the early stages can be overcome by (or with the aid of) outside entities, such as public agencies, philanthropists, cooperative associations and so on. The pattern that sees outside support leaving room to self-governance is quite common in the history of noncapitalistic organizations. In a sense what is required for the viability of the mutual benefit form is the ability to successfully govern the organization once started. It can even result that, in this second phase, active member participation is not so important for continuation (this seems to be the case of the above mentioned life insurance mutuals; see Hansmann, 1985a).

Specific arguments hold in the various situations listed above. In cases 4, 5, and 7, in order to reap fully the advantage of being the beneficiaries, the members of the category must accomplish some actions. This is more likely to occur if the category's members exert direct control over the organization, i.e., also play the dominant role. The importance of having "residual rights of control" (Hart, 1988) seems to be especially great in situation 4, while in situations 5 and 7 some forms of consultation might also be effective.

In situation 6, if the category is large and membership is not made compulsory[18], control by beneficiaries necessarily involves only some of them, so that a neat mutual benefit response is nearly impossible. In some cases whether the organization has to be seen as public benefit or as mutual benefit is not at all obvious. One might say that it depends on whether non-members are considered as intended or unintended beneficiaries; see, for example, Hansmann (1985b) and Ellman (1982) on whether members' contributions to business associations have to be viewed as donations or as purchases. An example in which the public benefit nature is evident are NPOs engaged in environmental activities.

In the case of aid recipients (situation 8), the arguments related to insufficient cultural requirements, lack of group cohesion, and possible differences between donors and beneficiaries in establishing the privileged interest, seem to reinforce each other so that nearly all charitable organizations are controlled either by donors or by trustees. Some exceptions are found, especially in development aid, where one can find more or less informal organizations of recipients set up to allocate among themselves goods or money received from developed countries. Such an arrangement can be explained partly by the "responsibility" argument and partly by the costs of administering the allocation of aid among recipients on the part of a funding organization that is located thousands of kilometers away and has insufficient knowledge of local language, habits and so on.

As to situations in which market power or rationing is the crucial issue (situation 1 or 2), none of the arguments just presented is decisive in favour of either solution; the same can be said of situation

---

18   There exist examples of private non-voluntary mutual benefit organizations, such as those caring for the maintenance of agricultural infrastructures (e.g. Italian compulsory agricultural Unions named "consorzi obbligatori"). A similar situation occurs in condominium housing as to some (local) public goods.

3, where contract failure is the issue (a different opinion is expressed in this regard by Hansmann, 1981a, p. 597). Possible reasons which might explain the dominance of the mutual benefit form in the first two situations and of the public benefit form in the third are to be found elsewhere. For instance, in the fact that for market power to significantly hurt an individual, the volume of his transactions in that market must be large – and therefore the costs of control relatively small – while with contract failure this is not necessarily so. Or in the more explicitly charitable nature of organizations operating in the health care industry (where contract failure plays a certain role), rather than, for example, in consumer wholesale (where market power might be a problem), and therefore in a greater role of philanthropy in the formation and financing of the former.

A related question is why only very few examples can be found in which the interests of beneficiary categories that are different from consumers and aid recipients are promoted in the public benefit mode. One reason is that transactions qua sellers or workers are usually much more specialized and more often repeated than transactions qua consumers; so the cost-of-control argument once more applies. A second reason is that in most cases these functions define the professional status of a person, which on the one hand provides a further stimulus to playing an active role, and on the other, exposes a non-participatory response to the charge of paternalism.

The second reason suggested above helps to explain why organizations aimed at benefitting workers often adopt, at least formally, a participatory statute even in cases in which the beneficiaries play no role in starting them and only a minor one in controlling them. This is the case, for example, of worker cooperatives formed in the US during the Great Depression to engage unemployed labourers in public works. The same can be said of worker cooperatives that exclude any remuneration of capital shares and limit wages to prevailing levels, in order to devote their potential surplus to providing a job for handicapped worker-members. A notable exception is represented by those US companies in which Employee Stock Ownership Plans (ESOPs) own the majority of shares (even 100% in some cases), but the control is in the hands of trustees[19]. Another exception is provided by some

19   Hansmann (1989) explains this seemingly paradoxical situation, in which workers bear the risk without having control, on the one hand, by the high cost of collective decision-making on the part of large nonhomogeneous constituencies, and, on the other, by the fact that in such a way control is still not in the hands of a potentially adversarial category.

voluntary organizations aimed at benefitting sellers located in particularly disadvantaged communities. A noticeable example are the so called "third world shops" that market handicraft or agricultural products directly shipped from selected poor areas.

5   Third Sector organizations and constraints on distribution

An important characteristic of third sector organizations is that constraints on distribution are often imposed. The extreme case is that of NPOs, where the so called "nondistribution constraint" forbids any explicit form of surplus distribution to the dominant or other non-beneficiary categories[20]. The role of this constraint – to the extent that it is actually enforced (see Hansmann, 1981a) – is to help force distribution toward the beneficiary category (most often in an implicit form). It is only in public benefit organizations that the nondistribution constraint plays an important role. Only there, in fact, do nondominant beneficiaries need protection from other categories turning explicit distribution to their own benefit (see Gui, 1989, 1990). Of course, the nondistribution constraint has to be supplemented by rules that also hinder an unduly pattern of implicit distribution, e.g. excessive salaries to managers, or opportunistic self-dealing on the part of trustees (see, for example Hansmann, 1981a).

Unless they control the organization directly, the nondistribution constraint is particularly valuable to donors – a category that is typical of public benefit organizations (see Preston, 1988) – who face contract failure not differently from the purchasers of goods of nonverifiable quality (see situation 3 in Section 3 similarities also exist with situation 6). In fact, it is only the assurance that their contributions will be channeled to beneficiaries that makes them willing to donate (for a formal modelling of the relationship between uninformed donors and service producing organizations see Easley and O'Hara, 1983, 1988).

In mutual benefit organizations, instead, the role of the nondistribution constraint is a minor one, since the beneficiary cat-

---

20   See for example the definitions of NPO in Hansmann (1987) or James and Rose-Ackerman (1986). Notice that in some cases in public benefit organizations explicit monetary distribution is admitted – to the beneficiary category, of course (think of money subsidies to the poor).

egory also controls the organization and is therefore in a position to block any overt distribution to other categories. All the constraint does, is to force implicit rather than explicit distribution. In many cases this is almost irrelevant (e.g., in a club reducing next year's membership fees following a large profit, is nearly equivalent to an immediate distribution of profit among members). However, in other cases the constraint can somewhat help pursue the statutorily privileged interest, protecting it against directors or even some members giving priority to another interest of beneficiaries'. For example, in consumer cooperatives, blocking profit distribution according to patronage, can help maintain an orientation toward high quality and healthfulness (see Hansmann, 1980, pp. 889-890).

The constraint also blocks profit distribution according to share capital. This is certainly effective in privileging distribution according to patronage, and therefore the interest of members qua transactors, rather than qua investors. However, the nondistribution constraint is too restrictive for this purpose, since it unnecessarily discourages capital contribution by members, while a simple ceiling to the remuneration of shares seems more reasonable. This is the usual regime in cooperatives (they account for a significant share of mutual benefit typologies). Here membership – and therefore decision-making power – is formally attached to the ownership of capital shares, while the statutorily privileged interest is, say, a high remuneration of member-supplied milk to be processed. The remuneration of capital shares is usually limited just to protect some members against their colleagues using the organization to serve first of all their interest as investors[21].

6   Summary and conclusions

Focusing on the choice of the categories of agents to be awarded the beneficiary and/or the dominant roles, as I do in this paper, leads to a useful classification of micro-economic organizations. The third

---

21   In for-profit organizations, instead, for what has been said above no implicit channel of distribution should exist; thus the imposition of constraints to distribution would conflict with the mutual benefit nature of these organizations. In fact, possible constraints (such as in limited dividend companies) are not imposed by the beneficiaries themselves in order to protect the aims of the organization, but by the government, in order to protect other categories (in particular customers at risk of monopolistic exploitation).

sector is characterized by having a category of agents other than investors as the beneficiary. Another distinguishing characteristic is a greater or lesser lack of appropriability of the organization's income stream in comparison to "capitalist" organizations. Third sector organizations are presented as a response to various market failures, in particular market power, asymmetric information, and public goods.

The crucial distinction within the third sector is between "public benefit" and "mutual benefit" organizations, the former identified by the fact that their beneficiaries – who are not necessarily consumers or aid recipients, but may also be workers or sellers – do not control the organization. I contend that imposing the nondistribution constraint, i.e., adopting the nonprofit form, is only important in public benefit organizations, while in mutual benefit organizations it may even be an unnecessary hindrance. In fact, no substantial distinction in the economic functions played by mutual benefit organizations incorporated as NPOs rather than as cooperatives can be found.

If, rather than focusing on the distribution of accounting profits, the purposive distribution of benefits in any forms is considered; or, similarly, if "non-profit" is meant to denote "non-self-benefit" – as I think it should –, it follows that the true nonprofit organizations are the public benefit ones.

REFERENCES

AKERLOF G., 1970, The Market for "Lemons": Quality Uncertainty and the Market Mechanism, in *Quarterly Journal of Economics* 84, pp. 487-500.

ALCHIAN A. A. and WOODWARD S., 1988, The Firm is Dead; Long Live the Firm: A Review of Oliver E. Williamson's «The Economic Institutions of Capitalism», in *Journal of Economic Literature* 26, March, pp. 65-79.

ANHEIER H.K. and SEIBEL W. (eds.), 1990, *The Third Sector: Comparative Studies of Nonprofit Organizations,* Berlin, de Gruyter.

ARCHAMBAULT Edith, 1990, "Public Authorities and the Nonprofit Sector in France" in: Anheier and Seibel (eds.), pp. 293-302.

AUSTEN-SMITH D. and JENKINS S., 1985, "A Multiperiod Model of Nonprofit Enterprises", in *Scottish Journal of Economics* 32 (2), June, pp. 119-134.

BADELT Christoph, 1990, "Institutional Choice and the Nonprofit Sector", in H.K. Anheier and W. Seibel (eds.), pp. 53-63.

BARTLETT W. and UVALIC M., 1986, "Labour-Managed Firms, Employee Participation and Profit Sharing: Theoretical Perspectives and European Experience", in *Management Bibliographies & Reviews* 12 (4), pp. 3-66.

BEN-NER A., 1986, "Non-Profit Organizations: Why Do They Exist in Market Economies", in: S. Rose-Ackerman (ed.), *The Economics of Nonprofit Institutions*, Oxford, O.U.P.

BEN-NER A., 1987, "Producer Cooperatives: Why Do They Exist in Capitalist Economies", in: W. W. Powell, *The Nonprofit Sector*, New Haven (Conn.), Yale U.P.

BEN-NER A. and NEUBERGER E., 1981, *Aspects of Income Distribution in the Self-Managed and Nonprofit Variants of the Universal Form Organization*, State University of New York at Stony Brook, mimeo.

BEN-NER A. and VAN HOOMISSEN T., 1991, "Nonprofit Organizations in the Mixed Economy: A Demand and Supply Analysis", in *Annals of Public and Cooperative Economics* 62 (4), this issue.

BONIN J. P. and PUTTERMAN L., 1987, "The economics of Cooperation and the Labor-Managed Economy", in *Fundamental of Pure and Applied Economics*, vol. 14, London, Harwood Academic Press.

CHILLEMI O. and GUI B., 1990, "Uninformed Customers and Nonprofit Organizations: Modelling 'Contract Failure' Theory", in *Economics Letters* 35 (1), pp. 5-8.

CLAYRE A. (ed.), 1979, *The Political Economy of Cooperation and Participation: A Third Sector*, Oxford.

DREZE J., 1976, "Some Theory of Labor-Management and Participation", in *Econometrica* 44, pp. 1125-1139.

EASLEY D. and O'HARA M., 1983, "The Economic Role of the Nonprofit Firm", in *Bell Journal of Economics*, Autumn.

EASLEY D. and O'HARA M., 1988, "Contracts and Asymmetric Information in the Theory of the Firm", in *Journal of Economic Behavior and Organization* 9, pp. 229-246.

ELLMAN I. M., 1982, "Another Theory of Nonprofit Corporations", in *Michigan Law Review*.

FAMA E. F. and JENSEN M. C., 1983, "Separation of Ownership and Control", in *Journal of Law and Economics* 26 (2), pp. 301-325.

GUI B., 1985, "Limits to External Financing: A Model and An Application to Labor-Managed Firms", in: D. K. Jones and J. Svejnar (eds.), *Advances in the Economic Analysis of Participatory and Labor-Managed Firms*, vol. 1, pp. 107-120.

GUI B., 1987, "Productive Private Nonprofit Organizations: A Conceptual Framework", in *Annals of Public and Cooperative Economy*, 58 (4), pp. 415-434.

GUI B., 1988, *Nonprofit Organizations and Surplus Distribution*, University of Trieste, Department of Economics and Statistics, W. P. n. 12.

GUI B., 1989, *Beneficiary and Dominant Roles in Organizations: The Case of Nonprofits*, Firenze, European University Institute W. P. n. 383, June.

GUI B., 1990, "The 'Nondistribution Constraint' in Economic Organizations", in *Ricerche Economiche* 44 (1), pp. 115-130.

HANSMANN H., 1980, "The Role of Non-Profit Enterprise", in *Yale Law Journal* 89 (5), pp. 835-901.

HANSMANN H., 1981a, "Reforming Nonprofit Corporation Law", in *University of Pennsylvania Law Review*, 129 (3), pp. 497-623.

HANSMANN H., 1981b, "Nonprofit Enterprise in the Performing Arts", in *Bell Journal of Economics* 12(2), Autumn.

HANSMANN H., 1985a, "The Organization of Insurance Companies: Mutual versus Stock", in *Journal of Law, Economics and Organization*, Spring.

HANSMANN H., 1985b, *What is the Appropriate Structure for Nonprofit Corporation Law?*, PONPO Working Paper n. 100, Yale University.

HANSMANN H., 1987a, "Economic Theories of Nonprofit Organizations", in Walter W. Powell (ed.), *The Nonprofit Sector*, Yale U.P., New Haven (Conn.).

HANSMANN H., 1988, "Ownership of the Firm", in *Journal of Law, Economics and Organization*, 4, pp. 267-304.

HANSMANN H., 1989, *Politics and Markets in the Organization of the Firm, inaugural lecture for the Sam Harris Professorship,* Yale University, January.

HANSMANN H., 1990, "The Economic Role of Commercial Nonprofits: The Evolution of the U.S. Savings Bank Industry", in H.K. Anheier and W. Seibel (eds.), pp. 65-76.

HART O.D., 1988, "Incomplete Contracts and the Theory of the Firm", in *Journal of Law, Economics and Organization* 4 (1), 119-139.

HEFLEBOWER R. B., 1980, *Cooperatives and Mutuals in the Market Systems,* Madison (Wis.), The University or Wisconsin Press.

HOLTMANN A. G., 1985, "A Theory of Nonprofit Firms", in *Economica* 50, pp. 439-449.

HOLTMANN A. G., 1988, "Theories of Nonprofit Institutions", in *Journal of Economic Surveys* 2(1).

JAMES E. and ROSE-ACKERMAN S., 1986, *The Nonprofit Enterprise in Market Economies,* Fundamentals of Pure and Applied Economics, n. 9, Chur (Switzerland), Harwood Academic Publishers.

KLEIN B., CROWFORD R. and ALCHIAN A. A., 1978, "Vertical Integration, Appropriable Rents and the Competitive Contracting Process", in *Journal of Law and Economics* 21, pp. 297-326.

KRASHINSKY M., 1986, "Transaction Costs and a Theory of Nonprofit Organizations", in S. Rose-Ackerman (ed.), in *The Economics of Nonprofit Institutions,* Oxford, O.U.P.

OLSON M., 1965, *The Logic of Collective Action,* Cambridge (Mass.), Harvard University Press.

PAULY M. V., 1987, "Nonprofit Firms in Medical Markets", in *American Economic Review* 77 (2), pp. 257-262.

PRESTON A. E., 1988, "The Nonprofit Firm: A Potential Solution to Inherent Market Failures", in *Economic Inquiry* 26 (3), pp. 493-506.

SANDLER T. and TSCHIRHART J.T., 1980, "The Economic Theory of Clubs: An Evaluative Survey", in *Journal of Economic Literature* 18 (4), December, pp. 1481-1521.

SMITH B.D. and STUTZER M.J., 1990, "Adverse Selection, Aggregate Uncertainty, and the Role for Mutual Insurance Contracts", in *Journal of Business* 63 (4), pp. 493-510.

STEINBERG R., 1987, "Nonprofit Organizations and the Market", in W.W. Powell, *The Nonprofit Sector*, New Haven (Conn.), Yale U.P.

YOUNG D., 1983, *If Not for Profit, for What?*, Lexington (Mass.), Heath.

WEISBROD B.A., 1988, *The Nonprofit Economy*, Cambridge (Mass.), Harvard Univerity Press.

WILLIAMSON O.E., 1985, *The Economic Institutions of Capitalism*, New York, The Free Press.

SELF-SERVING PHILANTHROPY
AND PARETO OPTIMALITY

by

Dennis A. KAUFMAN[*]

Department of Economics

University of Wisconsin-Parkside

Introduction

The motives for charitable giving are numerous and complex, ranging from such diverse factors as caring about the consumption and welfare of others, conforming to social expectations and norms, and living up to one's own code of ethics or religious beliefs, to receiving social acclaim and enhancing one's own reputation[1]. In economic theory, these various motives can be represented formally by some form of interdependency among the donors and recipients of a charitable good. By modelling individual interdependencies, a more robust explanation of voluntary charitable giving is possible. The most common approach found in the theoretical literature on charitable giving has been to assume that a donor's preferences depend on one or more of the following: own private consumption; the total quantity of a charitable good provided; and, the donor's actual contribution to the charitable good.[2] This literature has primarily analyzed the efficiency of government subsidy/tax schemes, lump-sum income transfers, and direct public grants to charities using models where

---

*   Special thanks are due to an anonymous referee.
1   See for example Batson and Toi (1982), Becker (1974), Collard (1978), Ireland and Johnson (1970), Kennett (1980), Margolis (1982), and Olson (1965).
2   See Andreoni (1988, 1989, 1990), Cornes and Sandler (1984a), Posnett and Sandler (1986), Roberts (1984), and Steinberg (1987).

donor/recipient interdependencies are respresented by either pure, impure/mixed, or transfer public goods[3].

Although recent research has produced several models of giving, which explain a wide spectrum of philanthropic activity and provide insights into the optimal tax treatment of charitable giving, these models fail to capture some of the salient characteristics of certain types of giving to nonprofit organizations. If a donor directly benefits from the consumption a public good provided by a charity, then that donor has a incentive to make a positive contribution to its provision, even though the actual contribution is likely to be less than the donor's relative marginal benefit. On the other hand, if a donor does not derive utility from the charitable good, then the donor has less of an incentive to donate and so the nonprofit organization's fundraising ability is reduced. If this reduced incentive to contribute is combined with the absence of direct grants from public tax revenues, then a nonprofit may encourage "self-serving" or "competitive" giving in order to generate adequate funds. Charitable giving is competitive or self-serving if (i) a donor perceives that own giving and the giving of others are *not* substitutes for each other, and, (ii) the value that a donor places on his or her own contribution depends negatively upon the contributions of others. In self-serving philanthropy, an increase in a donor i's giving increases i's utility, but an increase in the contributions of others decreases i's utility. Casual observation reveals many possible instances of self-serving philanthropy. For example, self-serving philanthropy occurs when the public recognition and adulation produced by a donor's beneficence is relative to and hence diminished by the contributions of others, which dilute the relative magnitude of that social acclaim.

Although it is widely believed that an individual's voluntary giving is influenced by the contributions of others and fundraising appeals, the relatively few empirical economic studies investigating this "stylized fact" have produced conflicting results[4]. Feldstein and Clotfelter (1976) acknowledge the possibility of a "demonstration

---

3   Other related papers include Bagnoli and Lipman (1989), Bernheim (1986), Cordes, Goldfarb, and Watson (1986), Kaufman (1987, 1990), Kingma (1989), Kranich (1988), Lemche (1986), Steinberg (1987), Sugden (1982, 1984).
4   In the empirical literature, see Clotfelter (1985), Feldstein and Clotfelter (1976), Schiff (1990), and Schwartz (1970). See also Guttman (1986, 1987).

effect" associated with "leadership gifts" but argue that their empirical findings do not support the existence of such an effect. On the other hand, Andreoni and Scholz (1990) present empirical results that indicate a donor's giving increases in response to an increase in the contributions of those in the donor's "social reference space", which includes such factors as income, education, age, and occupation. Neither of these studies deals explicitly with self-serving behavior. The relationship between donor contributions and fundraising efforts and techniques has also been examined in the social psychology literature. For example, Mark and Shotland (1982) and Reingen (1978) study the effectiveness of the timing and content of various solicitation appeals and procedures that are designed to influence a potential donor's preferences and elicit the largest possible contribution. These studies have shown that solicitation appeals such as "even a penny will help", "please make a generous family contribution", and "the average contribution of your neighbors has been approximately..." result in higher contributions as compared to when no appeals are made.

Interdependencies or "externalities" among donors generally imply two economic consequences. First, because of the "free riding" behavior of individuals, private voluntary contributions underprovide the charitable public good and so the resulting equilibrium is not Pareto optimal. Second, government subsidy, tax, or income redistribution policies are required to achieve the efficient level of the charitable good and Pareto optimality[5]. This paper extends the theory of charitable giving to the case of self-serving philanthropy and, by analyzing several special specifications of donor preferences, offers additional insights into the private provision of charitable goods when donors engage in self-serving behavior and are not in the population served by those goods. In particular, this paper identifies conditions that ensure the Pareto optimality of an equilibrium in an economy with a charitable good, without resorting to government subsidies or income redistribution. As a corollary, it is shown that if a donor's welfare depends upon the deviation of his or her own giving from a designated "fair share" contribution (such as the average contribution of others), then the contributions equilibrium is Pareto optimal. One implication of this corollary is that a nonprofit

---

5   See, for example, Andreoni (1990), Archibald and Donaldson (1976), Bergstrom (1970), Bergstrom *et al* (1986), Goldman (1978), Greenberg (1980), Hochman and Rodgers (1969), Lemche (1986), Rader (1980), Roberts (1987, 1990), Warr (1982), and Winter (1969).

organization can manipulate the level of giving by influencing how donors perceive the relative value of their contribution. In addition, it is shown that if government income redistribution efforts are absent or impossible, then a contributions equilibrium is again Pareto optimal. Finally, an example demonstrates that under self-serving behavior, the equilibrium level of contributions may actually exceed a desired target level, even though the equilibrium level is optimal. The paper concludes with a brief discussion of the implications of self-serving philanthropy for nonprofit organizations and possible directions for future research.

1   The Model

Consider an economy with a single, private consumption good x, a nonprofit organization that provides a charitable public good y, and two types of individuals: donors and beneficiaries. Donors (beneficiaries) are denoted by the nonempty set D (R) and indexed by $i = 1, ..., n$ $(r = n + 1, ..., N)$. Each donor i is endowed with w_i of the private good; x_i is i's consumption of the private good, g_i is i's contribution to the provision of y, and G_i denotes the contributions from all other donors, $G_i = \Sigma_{j\neq i}g_j$. For each donor, the consumption good x and own giving g are assumed to be normal goods. Each beneficiary $r \in R$ consumes his or her entire endowment w_r of the private good x. Donors and beneficiaries are assumed to interact only through the charity; no direct private good transfers among individuals are possible, either between donors and recipients or among donors themselves. The charitable good y is provided solely by donors $i \in D$ but is consumed exclusively by beneficiaries $r \in R$. There is no public (government) provision of y. The charitable good is produced by means of a strictly increasing production function F that utilizes donor contributions as inputs, that is, $y = F(\Sigma_{i \in D}g_i)$. For simplicity, it is assumed that $y = \Sigma_{i \in D}g_i$. An allocation $((x'_i, g'_i)_{i \in D}, y')$ is defined as a consumption-contribution bundle, (x'_i, g'_i), for each $i \in D$ and a level of the charitable good y'.

The "altruistic" preferences of donor i are represented by a concave, twice continuously differentiable utility function $v_i = v_i(x_i, g_i, G_i)$ where v_i has the partial derivatives $\delta v_i / \delta x_i = v_{ix} > 0$, $\delta v_i / \delta g_i = v_{ig} > 0$, and $\delta v_i / \delta G_i = v_{iG}$, which may be positive, negative, or zero. The assumption $v_{ig} > 0$ implies that for whatever reason, be it moral or philosophical principles or religious beliefs, a donor derives utility from the act of voluntarily contributing g_i to the provision of the charitable good y. Even though each donor $i \in D$ contributes to y's provision, i does not directly consumer or derive utility from y. A donor i is *self-serving* at an allocation $((x'_i, g'_i)_{i \in D}, y')$ if i's marginal rate of substitution between the contributions of others G_i and own giving g_i is negative at $((x'_i, g'_i)_{i \in D}, y')$, that is, $MRS^i_{Gg}(x'_i, g'_i, G'_i) = v_{iG}(x'_i, g'_i, G'_i) / v_{ig}(x'_i, g'_i, G'_i) < 0$. The possibility of self-serving philanthropy distinguishes the model presented here from other impure or transfer public goods models. These public goods models assume that the giving of others is a substitute for own giving, which then consequently elicits free-riding behavior, and that a donor i obtains utility from either (i) i's own consumption of the charitable good y, as in Andreoni (1988, 1990), Cornes and Sandler (1984) and Steinberg (1987), or, (ii) the beneficiaries' consumption of the charitable good y when i does not directly consume y, as in Roberts (1984, 1990). Under either assumption (i) or (ii), a donor i's utility depends positively upon y and hence G_i, which implies that $v_{iG} > 0$ at all allocations. Obviously, models that assume $v_{iG} > 0$ do not allow for self-serving philanthropy. Finally, since each beneficiary $r \in R$ consumes the charitable good y and w_r, r's preferences are represented by a strictly increasing utility function $u_r(y)$.

Each donor $i \in N$ assumes that G_i is exogenous; that is, donor i assumes that i's contribution does not affect the contributions of others and so $\delta G_i / \delta g_i = 0$ [6]. Thus, donor i chooses the most preferred bundle (x_i, g_i) within i's budget set $B_i(p_x, \omega_i) = \{(x_i, g_i) \in R^2_+ : p_x x_i + g_i \leq p_x \omega_i\}$ where the price of x is p_x and the price of g is one. That is, i's utility maximization problem given G_i is

$$\underset{\{x_i, g_i\}}{\text{maximize}} \ v_i(x_i, g_i, G_i) \text{ subject to } (x_i, g_i) \in B_i(p_x, \omega_i).$$

The solution to this problem gives i's contribution function, $g_i = f_i(G_i, \omega_i, p_x)$, and private good demand function, $x_i = d_i(G_i, \omega_i, p_x)$. An allocation $((x'_i, g'_i)_{i \in D}, y')$ is *individually* feasible if for each donor $i \in D$, $(x'_i, g'_i) \in B_i(p_x, \omega_i)$ and $y' = \Sigma_{i \in D} g'_i$.

An allocation $((x^*_i, g^*_i)_{i \in D}, y^*)$ is a *Nash equilibrium* if $y^* = \Sigma_{i \in D} g^*_i$, and, for each $i \in D$, $(x^*_i, g^*_i) \in B_i(p_x, \omega_i)$ and $v_i(x^*_i, g^*_i, G^*_i) \geq v_i(x_i, g_i, G^*_i)$ for all $(x_i, g_i) \in B_i(p_x, \omega_i)$ [7]. To ensure an interior Nash

---

6   Alternatives to the assumption that each donor i takes G_i exogenously have appeared in Cornes and Sandler (1984b), Guttman (1986, 1987), Scafuri (1988), and Sugden (1985).

7   Given the assumptions of the model, a Nash equilibrium exists as a result of Berge's Maximum Theorem and Kakutani's Fixed Point Theorem.

equilibrium ($0 < g^*_i < \omega_i$ and $0 \leq x^*_i < \omega_i$ for all $i \in D$), it is assumed that for each i, $MRS^i_{xg}(\omega_i, 0, G_i) < p_x$ for all $G_i > 0$. Since the beneficiaries $r \in R$ are "passive" non-contributing recipients of the charitable good y, they do not factor in the determination of a Nash equilibrium. An allocation $((x^*_i, g^*_i)_{i \in D}, y^*)$ is *Pareto optimal* if there does not exist a feasible allocation $((x_i, g_i)_{i \in D}, y)$ such that (i) for all $i \in D$, $v_i(x_i, g_i, G_i) \geq v_i(x^*_i, g^*_i, G^*_i)$, and, (ii) for all $r \in R$, $u_r(y) \geq u_r(y^*)$, with strict inequality holding for some individual $k \in D$ or $t \in B$. It is important to note that Pareto optimality and social welfare is defined in terms of the utility of both beneficiaries and donors. This inclusion appears very natural and appropriate, but it implies that donors are the sole source of any potential Pareto improvement. Since $u_r(y) \gtrless u_r(y')$ if and only if $y \gtrless y'$, any Pareto improvement must not decrease the level of the charitable good y. Obviously, if y decreases, then all beneficiaries are worse off.

2   Properties of the Model

If altruistic individuals and charitable public goods exist in an economy, then a Nash equilibrium generally is not Pareto optimal[8]. In a general setting of nonidentical preferences and nonidentical endowments, Proposition 1 below establishes a sufficient condition under which self-serving philanthropy produces a Nash equilibrium that is Pareto optimal. This condition requires that, at a Nash equilibrium $((x^*_i, g^*_i)_{i \in D}, y^*)$, all donors are self-serving and have identical marginal rates of substitution between others' giving and own giving. If a donor i is self-serving at a Nash equilibrium, then i perceives his or her contribution as a beneficial private good and the contributions of others as a harmful public "bad". Hence, if the "altruistic" giving of each donor becomes self-serving, then donor contributions at a Nash equilibrium produce a Pareto optimal allocation:

Proposition 1: If, at a Nash equilibrium $((x^*_i, g^*_i)_{i \in D}, y^*)$, all donors $i \in D$ are self-serving and $v_G/v_g = \alpha < 0$ for all i, then $((x^*_i, g^*_i)_{i \in D}, y^*)$ is Pareto optimal.

---

8   For further discussions of the validity of the first and second fundamental theorems of welfare economics given various interdependent preference domains, see Archibald and Donaldson (1976), Kranich (1988), Lemche (1986), Osana (1972), Rader (1980), and Winter (1969).

Although the condition that $v^*_{iG} / v^*_{ig} = \alpha$ for all $i \in D$ is a strong condition, it is satisfied in at least two cases of donor preference specification. The first case arises when nonprofits employ various fundraising techniques and solicitation strategies that are designed to alter donor preferences. For example, by publicizing the target level of contributions (the fundraising campaign goal) or recommending giving guidelines that suggest specific "fair share" donations, nonprofits are often able to change how a donor perceives the marginal benefit of his or her contribution[9]. The second case arises when donors are identical.

The first case is achieved when (i) preferences and endowments are nonidentical and (ii) the benefit derived from own giving depends upon the deviation of the donor's contribution from a designated "fair share" contribution. Although fair share contributions are frequently based on the donor's own income, for the case of self-serving philanthropy it is assumed that the fair share contribution is based upon the giving of others. Suppose a donor i's preferences are given by the utility function $v_i(x_i, g_i, G_i) = \phi_i(x_i, z_i; \lambda)$ where $z_i = (g_i - \lambda G_i)$ and λG_i denotes i's fair share contribution. The value of the fair share parameter λ is set exogenously by the charity. Donor i's utility ϕ_i is assumed to increase as the deviation of i's contribution from the fair share contribution, z_i, decreases (that is, $\delta\phi_i / \delta z_i < 0$). Given this specification of donor preferences, donors are always self-serving since for all $i \in D$, $v_{iG}/v_{ig} = -\lambda$. Thus, assuming that the fair share parameter λ is constant, Proposition 1 becomes:

Corollary 1: If each donor i's preferences are represented by $v_i(x_i, g_i, G_i) = \phi_i(x_i, z_i; \lambda)$ where $z_i = (g_i - \lambda G_i)$ and $\lambda \in R_+$ is the given "fair share" parameter, then a Nash equilibrium $((x^*_i, g^*_i)_{i \in D}, y^*)$ is Pareto optimal.

Since a donor's preferences are a function of the fair share parameter λ, a change in λ constitutes a change in the donor's preferences. As a result, a nonprofit organization can manipulate donor preferences by changing the fair share parameter λ and thereby influence the level of total giving. Specifically, introducing λ into donor utility functions implies that a donor i's contribution function is

9   "Fair share" donations are often based upon individual income levels or average giving for a particular professional, income, or age group. For example, the pledge card for the United Way of Kenosha and Racine Counties, Wisconsin, suggests a "Giving Guide" donation of one hour's pay per month.

now a function of λ, that is, $g_i = f_i(\lambda, G^*_i, \omega_i, p_x)$, and so in equilibrium, $g^*_i = f_i(\lambda, G^*_i, \omega_i, p_x) = h_i(\lambda, \omega, p_x)$ where $\omega = (\omega_1, ..., \omega_n)$. Next, let $S(\lambda)$ represent the solicitation expenditures necessary to induce donors to incorporate λ into their utility functions and assume that $S'(\lambda) > 0$ and $S''(\lambda) > 0$. In this case, a nonprofit can maximize net contributions by solving

$$\underset{\lambda \in \mathfrak{R}_+}{\text{maximize}} \; \Sigma_{i \in D} h_i(\lambda, \omega, p_x) - S(\lambda)$$

Since a change in λ represents a change in preferences, the usual Pareto criterion cannot be used to compare the equilibria associated with each set of preferences, which are now parameterized by λ. Fortunately, meaningful welfare comparisons are possible when preferences change by applying the Pareto criterion twice, evaluating the equilibrium obtained under the "λ_1-preferences" and the equilibrium obtained under the "λ_2-preferences" with respect to both λ_1- and λ_2-preferences. If the λ_1-equilibrium is preferred under *both* sets of preferences to the λ_2-equilibrium, then the former is "socially superior" to and more desirable than the later[10].

The following example illustrates that although an increase in λ may increase in each donor's equilibrium contribution, that is $\delta h_i / \delta \lambda > 0$, a Pareto inferior equilibrium from the perspective of donors may result. Suppose that $p_x = 1$ and there are two donors j and k with identical utility functions $v_i(x_i, g_i, G_i) = \phi_i(x_i, z_i; \lambda) = x^5_i(g_i - \lambda G_i)^5$ and identical endowments $\omega_i = 1$, $i = j, k$. A symmetric Nash equilibrium is obtained by solving the system of two equations given by $g_i = (1 - \lambda G_i)/2$, $i = j, k$. Suppose that the charity is choosing between two values of the fair share parameter λ, $\lambda_1 = .25$ and $\lambda_2 = .5$ and that $S(\lambda) = 0$. The symmetric Nash equilibrium associated with λ_1 is $((3/7, 4/7)_{i \in D}, 8/7)$, where $y_1 = 8/7$ and $z_i = 3/7$; the symmetric Nash equilibrium associated with λ_2 is $((1/3, 2/3)_{i \in D}, 4/3)$, where $y_2 = 4/3$ and $z_i = 1/3$. Although increasing λ clearly increases total giving ($y_2 > y_1$), both donor's are worse off at the λ_2-equilibrium than at the λ_1-equilibrium, regardless of which preference ordering is used to evaluate the two equilibria. Specifically, each donor i prefers the λ_1-equilibrium over the λ_2-equilibrium since under λ_1-preferences, $\phi_i(3/7, 3/7; \lambda_1) > \phi_i(1/3, 1/3; \lambda_1)$, and under λ_2-preferences, $\phi_i(3/7, 3/7; \lambda_2) > \phi_i(1/3, 1/3; \lambda_2)$, $i = j, k$.

---

10   For a further discussion of the use of this welfare criterion, see Weisbrod (1977) and Kaufman (1990). The latter examines the desirability of an exogenous change in preferences (from selfish to altruistic preferences) in the private provision of a impure public good.

Although maximizing total contributions maximizes the utility of beneficiaries, Corollary 1 implies that any increase in λ that increases contributions above the initial Nash equilibrium level will decrease the utility of donors and result in a Pareto inferior allocation from the perspective of donors and their original preferences, which were contingent upon the initial λ. If the charity is concerned *only* about the provision of the charitable good and the welfare of the beneficiaries, then a decrease in the welfare of the charity's supporting constituency may not be a problem. Nevertheless, based on casual observation, it appears that in the long run, many nonprofit organizations are sensitive to their funding constituency and typically avoid "biting the hands that feed them". Furthermore, it is reasonable to conjecture that the expenditures required to persuade donors to adopt preferences with higher values of the fair share parameter λ increase as λ increases. In the extreme, fundraising expenses consume total contributions and the charitable public good cannot be provided.

In the second case, donors are assumed to be identical. Benefactors of a particular charity often share common ideals and values and have similar incomes. Consequently, donors tend to be fairly homogeneous with respect to their preferences and incomes. Corollary 2 below shows that if all donors have identical preferences and endowments and if a symmetric Nash equilibrium exists, then the equilibrium is Pareto optimal. This corollary implies that given a set of donors with "fairly" similar preferences and endowments, then a Nash equilibrium will be "fairly" close to a Pareto optimum (assuming sufficient continuity).

Corollary 2: If all donors $i \in D$ are identical (that is, for all $i \in D$, $v_i(x_i, g_i, G_i) = v(x_i, g_i, G_i)$ and $\omega_i = \omega$) and are self-serving at a symmetric Nash equilibrium $((x^*_i, g^*_i)_{i \in D}, y^*)$, then $((x^*_i, g^*_i)_{i \in D}, y^*)$ is Pareto optimal.

The above results are contingent upon a particular specification of donor preferences but require no restrictions on feasible alternative allocations. Andreoni (1990) shows that, in the case of an impure public good, total giving depends upon the distribution of income and will increase when income is transferred by lump-sum taxes from less altruistic to more altruistic individuals. Since some nonprofits do not receive direct government grants, they must instead rely solely on private voluntary contributions. Usually, nonprofits are unable to unilaterally alter the distribution of donor endowments in order to increase voluntary giving. Proposition 2 considers self-serving behavior when income redistribution among donors is not possible and so Pareto improving allocations are restricted to the set of *individually* feasible allocations. Proposition 2 states that given the distribution of donor endowments, there does not exist an *individually* feasible allocation that Pareto dominates the initial Nash equilibrium.

Proposition 2: If all donors $i \in D$ are self-serving at a Nash equilibrium $((x^*_i, g^*_i)_{i \in D}, y^*)$, then $((x^*_i, g^*_i)_{i \in D}, y^*)$ is Pareto optimal for the given distribution of endowments.

However, even in the case of self-serving philanthropy, it is possible to construct a Pareto superior allocation but such an allocation would generally require a redistribution of donor endowments among donors, which could be accomplished either by a voluntary (and enforceable) agreement among donors or by government lump-sum taxes and excise subsidies (or taxes), as shown by Roberts (1990)[11]. The following example substantiates this claim and shows that it is possible to find a redistribution of donor endowments and an alternative allocation that strictly Pareto dominates the original Nash equilibrium.

Suppose there m beneficiaries and two donors, 1 and 2, with identical endowments $\omega_1 = \omega_2 = 1$, and utility functions $v_1(x_1, g_1, G_1) = 4x^5 g^5 - 2G_1$ and $v_2(x_2, g_2, G_2) = 4x^5 g^5 - .125 G_2$, respectively. Assuming that $p_x = 1$, a Nash equilibrium is given by the allocation $((x'_i, g'_i)_{i \in D}, y') = ((.5, .5)_{i \in D}, 1)$; at this equilibrium $MRS^1_{G_g} = -1$ and $MRS^2_{G_g} = -.0625$. Since donor 2's relative marginal disutility of others' giving is smaller than donor 1's, an endowment transfer from 1 to 2 and an increase (decrease) in 1's (2's) contribution produces a Pareto improvement. Specifically, the allocation $((x'_1, g'_1), (x'_2, g'_2)), y') = ((.35, .61), (.63, .41)), 1.02)$ is feasible and strictly Pareto superior to the Nash equilibrium since $v_1(.5, .5, .5) < v_1(.35, .61, .41)$ and $v_2(.5, .5, .5) < v_2(.63, .41, .61)$, for the donors, and $y^* = 1 < 1.02 = y'$ for the beneficiaries. Note that $x'_1 + g'_1 = .96 < \omega_1$ and $x'_2 + g'_2 = 1.04 > \omega_2$. The immediate policy implication of Proposition 2 and this example is that although the Nash equilibrium is Pareto optimal *without* government redistribution programs, *with* income redistribution through lump-sum taxes and a supporting subsidy scheme, a strictly Pareto superior allocation is possible even though all donors are self-serving and some donors experience an actual decrease in their endowment income.

---

11   See also Andreoni (1988, 1990), Bernheim (1986), Hochman (1977), Hochman and Rodgers (1969), Kingma (1989) and Warr (1982).

3   A Final Example

As mentioned above, charities frequently publicize the goal of a fundraising campaign in order to induce greater giving. The following example illustrates that if each donor's utility depends upon the difference between a designated target level of total contributions and the actual level of the contributions of others, then, at self-serving Nash equilibrium, donors will contribute more than the targeted level.

Suppose the preferences of each donor are represented by the utility function $v_i(x_i, g_i, G_i) = ln\ (x_i) - (G_i - \mu)^2/g_i$ where μ denotes the target level of contributions. Donor i's marginal utility of g_i, $v_{ig} = (G_i - \mu)^2/g^2_i$, is non-negative for all non-negative G_i and g_i. This implies that as the contributions of others approach the desired target $(G_i \rightarrow \mu)$, donor i derives less marginal utility from a given contribution g_i. Similarly, donor i's marginal utility of G_i, $v_{iG} = -2\ (G_i - \mu)/g_i$, is negative (non-negative) for $G_i > \mu\ (G_i \leq \mu)$. Thus, the marginal utilities of g_i and G_i suggest that the parameter μ is a reasonable proxy for what donor i thinks *should* be given to the charity.

For computational purposes, it is assumed that there are twenty-seven donors $(n = 27)$, $p_x = 1$, $\omega_i = 1$ for all $i \in D$, and $\mu = 8.91 = 27\ (.33)$, which means that the target level of contributions is almost one-third of the total donor endowment. If donors were to divide the cost of y equally, then a donor's "fair share" contribution would be $\mu/27 = .33$. The level of the charitable activity is given by $y = \Sigma_{i \in D} g_i$. From the first order conditions of i's utility maximization problem, i's contribution function g_i is defined implicitly by

$$g^2_i - (G_i - \mu)^2(\omega_i - g_i) = 0.$$

Solving the above system of equations produces a symmetric Nash equilibrium $((x^*_i, g^*_i)_{i \in D}, y^*) = ((.64, .36)_{i \in D}, 9.72)$, which by Corollary 2 is Pareto optimal. At this equilibrium, each donor i gives more than i's "fair share" $(g^*_i = .36 > .33 = \mu/27)$ and total contributions exceed the target level $(y^* = 9.72 > 8.91 = \mu)$. Since each donor is self-serving at the Nash equilibrium, donor i would prefer an allocation in which others' contributions are smaller and i's own contribution is larger. Consequently, each donor attempts to compensate for the negative effects of others' giving by increasing own giving. Finally, since equilibrium contributions exceed the target level $(y^* > \mu)$, the nonprofit "over-produces" the charitable good.

4   Conclusions and Future Research

First, one underlying implication of the above analysis is that nonprofit organizations should acquire some knowledge of the nature of donor preferences. The specification of donor preferences is crucial and provides the basis for the results on Pareto optimality. This does not suggest that a charity should spend its finite resources on mechanisms that reveal donor contribution functions, an extremely difficult endeavor, but instead it indicates that the charity may benefit from the determination of the functional relationships among the arguments of donor preferences. Knowing that a donor's utility and hence contributions depends upon the deviation of his or her contribution from some fair share contribution permits the nonprofit to devise and utilize more efficient (cost minimizing) solicitation procedures. In addition, if a charity is engaged in changing donor preferences, then it is necessary to arrive at an explicit definition, interpretation, and functional representation of the costs incurred by the charity as it induces donors to adopt alternative preferences.

Second, a somewhat paradoxical conclusion of this model of charitable giving is that if the "altruistic" behavior of a donor becomes self-serving, then private voluntary giving produces a Pareto optimal equilibrium. Intuitively, this result can be explained as follows. First, at a self-serving Nash equilibrium, any increase in a donor $i's$ contribution would make some other donor j worse off, holding all other contributions constant. Second, although all donors could benefit from a small reduction in each donor's contribution, such a reduction would lower the quantity of the charitable good provided and thereby would make the beneficiaries worse off. Thus, it is not possible to make donors better off without harming beneficiaries and conversely. In addition, if the initial equilibrium contributions are not Pareto optimal, then a change in donor preferences that elicits self-serving philanthropy can increase total giving and generate a Pareto optimal equilibrium with respect to the *modified* preferences.

Third, the self-serving model also reveals one important implication for nonprofit organizations that are involved in encouraging greater giving from its supporting constituencies. If donors are induced to adopt certain alternative altruistic preferences, then the persuading charity must proceed very cautiously because an induced change in donor preferences may increase total giving, but it may not necessarily produce a socially superior equilibrium (that is, a Pareto superior allocation with respect to both the original and "new" preferences).

Finally, future research based on the self-serving philanthropy model could proceed in at least two worthwhile directions. First, the model could be placed in a game theoretic framework and extended to the case where multiple nonprofit organizations compete among themselves for a finite pool of private contributions. Suppose, for example, that there are two charities A and B and each charity chooses a "fair share" parameter λ_A and λ_B, respectively. One reasonable conjecture is that although a small increase in λ_A may induce a donor i to increase his or her contributions to charity A, a large increase in λ_A may result in a decrease in i's contribution to A and an increase in i's contribution to B. The second direction is to extend the results of the existing literature on the efficiency and desirability of subsidy and lump-sum taxation schemes to the case of self-serving philanthropy. One would expect that the policy implications for self-serving philanthropy are qualitatively different than those that have been established for the pure, impure, and transfer public goods models.

APPENDIX

Proof of Proposition 1: By way of contradiction, assume that there exists a feasible allocation $((x'_i, g'_i)_{i \in D}, y')$ that is Pareto superior to the Nash equilibrium $((x^*_i, g^*_i)_{i \in D}, y^*)$. Then, the following holds: (i) for all $i \in D$, $v'_i \equiv v_i(x'_i, g'_i, G'_i) \geq v_i(x^*_i, g^*_i, G^*_i) \equiv v^*_i$; and, (ii) for all $r \in B$, $u_r(y') \geq u_r(y^*)$, with strict inequality holding in (i) or (ii) for some $j \in D$ or some $t \in B$.

The concavity of v_i implies that for all donors $i \in D$,

$$v'_i - v^*_i \leq v^*_{ix}(x'_i - x^*_i) + v^*_{ig}(g'_i - g^*_i) + v^*_{iG}(G'_i - G^*_i) \tag{1}$$

where $v^*_{ix}, v^*_{ig},$ and v^*_{iG} are the partial derivatives of v_i evaluated at the Nash equilibrium. The first order necessary conditions of donor i's utility maximization problem imply that $0 < v^*_{ix}/v^*_{ig} \leq p_x$ at the Nash equilibrium. Dividing through by v^*_{ig} and substituting, inequality (1) becomes

$$(v'_i - v^*_i)/v^*_{ig} \leq (v^*_{ix}/v^*_{ig})(x'_i - x^*_i) + (g'_i - g^*_i) + (v^*_{iG}/v^*_{ig})(G'_i - G^*_i)$$

$$\leq p_x(x'_i - x^*_i) + (g'_i - g^*_i) + (v^*_{iG}/v^*_{ig})(G'_i - G^*_i) \tag{2}$$

By assumption, all donors are self-serving and $v^*_{iG}/v^*_{ig} = \alpha < 0$ for all $i \in D$. Furthermore, since $((x'_i, g'_i)_{i \in D}, y')$ is feasible, summing (2) over all $i \in D$ yields

$$\Sigma_{i \in D}(v'_i - v^*_i) \, / \, v^*_{ig} \leq a \, \Sigma_{i \in D}(G'_i - G^*_i)$$

$$= \alpha \, (n - 1) \, (y' - y^*) \tag{3}$$

Next, suppose that for all $i \in D$, $v'_i \geq v^*_i$, and for some $t \in R$, $u_t(y') > u_t(y^*)$. Since u_t is strictly increasing in y, it follows that $y' > y^*$, and so (3) implies $\Sigma_{i \in D}(v'_i - v^*_i) \, / \, v^*_{ig} < 0$. Hence, there exists a donor $k \in D$ such that $v'_k < v^*_k$, which contradicts hypothesis that $v'_i \geq v^*_i$ for all i. Alternatively, suppose that for all $r \in R$, $u_r(y') \geq u_r(y^*)$, for all $i \in D$, $v'_i \geq v^*_i$, and, for some donor $j \in D$, $v'_j > v^*_j$. Then, from (3), $0 < \Sigma_{i \in D}(v'_i - v^*_i) \, / \, v^*_{ig}$ and so it follows that $y' < y^*$. But, this implies that $u_r(y') < u_r(y^*)$ for all $r \in R$, which contradicts hypothesis that $u_r(y') \geq u_r(y')$. Consequently, the Nash equilibrium $((x^*_i, g^*_i)_{i \in D}, y^*)$ is Pareto optimal.

Proof of Corollary 1: For each donor $i \in D$, let ϕ^*_{iz} denote the partial derivative of i's utility function ϕ_i with respect to the deviation $z_i = (g_i - \lambda G_i)$ evaluated at the Nash equilibrium $((x^*_i, g^*_i)_{i \in D}, y^*)$. Since for all $i \in D$, $v^*_{iG}/v^*_{ig} = \phi^*_{iz}(-\lambda) \, / \, \phi^*_{iz} = -\lambda$, Proposition 1 applies and $((x^*_i, g^*_i)_{i \in D}, y^*)$ is Pareto optimal.

Proof of Corollary 2: Since all donors $i \in D$ have identical utility functions and the Nash equilibrium is symmetric, it follows that $v^*_{iG} / v^*_{ig} = V^*_G / v^*_g = \alpha$ for all i. By Proposition 1, the Nash equilibrium $((x^*_i, g^*_i)_{i \in D}, y^*)$ is Pareto optimal.

Proof of Proposition 2: By way of contradiction, assume that there exists an *individually* feasible allocation $((x'_i, g'_i)_{i \in D}, y')$ that is Pareto superior to the Nash equilibrium $((x^*_i, g^*_i)_{i \in D}, y^*)$. Then, (i) for all $i \in D$, $v'_i \equiv v_i(x'_i, g'_i, G') \geq v_i(x^*_i, g^*_i, G^*) \equiv v^*_i$, and (ii) for all $r \in B$, $u_r(y') \geq u_r(y^*)$, with strict inequality holding in (i) or (ii) for some $j \in D$ or some $t \in B$. Since $((x'_i, g'_i)_{i \in D}, y')$ is individually feasible, inequality (2) now becomes

$$(v'_i - v^*_i) \, / \, v^*_{ig} \leq (v^*_{iG} / v^*_{ig}) \, (G'_i - G^*_i) \tag{4}$$

for all $i \in D$. Since each i is self-serving, $v^*_{iG} / v^*_{ig} < 0$.

As before, suppose that for all $i \in D$, $v'_i \geq v^*_i$, and for some $t \in R$, $u_t(y') > u_t(y^*)$. Since it follows that $y' > y^*$, there must exist a donor k such that $G'_k > G^*_k$. This implies that the right hand side of (4) is negative for donor k and so $0 \leq (v'_k - v^*_k) \, / \, v^*_{kg} < 0$, a contradiction.

Alternatively, suppose that for all $r \in R$, $u_r(y') \geq u_r(y^*)$, and for all $i \in D$, $v'_i \geq v^*_i$, with $v'_j > v^*_j$ for some donor j. Inequality (4) implies that $G'_i \leq G^*_i$ for all donors i, and, in particular, $G'_j < G^*_j$ for donor j. Summing over all donors yields

$$\Sigma_{i \in D} G'_i = (n-1) y' < (n-1) y^* = \Sigma_{i \in D} G^*,$$

and so $y' < y^*$. But, this implies that $u_r(y') < u_r(y^*)$ for all $r \in R$, again a contradiction. Consequently, the Nash equilibrium $((x^*_i, g^*_i)_{i \in D}, y^*)$ is Pareto optimal for the given distribution of endowments.

REFERENCES

ANDREONI J., 1988, "Privately Provided Public Goods in a Large Economy: The Limits of Altruism", in *Journal of Public Economics*, 35, 57-73.

ANDREONI J., 1989, "Giving with Impure Altruism: Applications to Charity and Ricardian Equivalence", in *Journal of Political Economy*, 97, 1447-1458.

ANDREONI J., 1990, "Impure Altruism and Donations to Public Goods: A Theory of Warm-Glow Giving", in *Economic Journal*, 100, 464-477.

ANDREONI J. and SCHOLZ J., 1990, *An Econometric Analysis of Charitable Giving with Interdependent Preferences*, Social Systems Research Institute, # 9023, University of Wisconsin-Madison.

ARCHIBALD G.C. and DONALDSON D., 1976, "Non-paternalism and the Basic Theorems of Welfare Economics", in *Canadian Journal of Economics*, 9, 492-507.

BAGNOLI M. and LIPMAN B.L., 1989, "Provision of Public Goods: Fully Implementing the Core through Private Contributions", in *Review of Economic Studies*, 56, 583-601.

BATSON C.D. and TOI M., 1982, "More Evidence that Empathy is a Source of Altruistic Motivation", in *Personality and Social Psychology*, 43, 281-292.

BECKER G., 1974, "A Theory of Social Interactions", in *Journal of Political Economy*, 82, 1063-1093.

BERNHEIM B.D., 1986, "On the Voluntary and Involuntary Provision of Public Goods", in *American Economic Review*, 76, 789-793.

BERGSTROM T.C., 1970, "A "Scandinavian Consensus" Solution for Efficient Income Distribution among Nonmalevolent Consumers", in *Journal of Economic Theory*, 2, 383-398.

BERGSTROM T.C., BLUME L. and VARIAN H., 1986, "On the Private Provision of Public Goods", in *Journal of Public Economics*, 29, 25-49.

CLOTFELTER C.T., 1985, *Federal Tax Policy and Charitable Giving*, Chicago, The University of Chicago Press.

COLLARD D.A., 1978, *Altruism and Economy: A Study in Nonselfish Economics*, New York, Oxford University Press.

CORDES J.S., GOLDFARB R.S. and WATSON H.S., 1986, "The Relative Efficiency of Private and Public Transfers", in *Public Choice*, 49, 29-45.

CORNES R. and SANDLER T., 1984a, "Easy Riders, Joint Production, and Public Goods", in *Economic Journal*, 94, 580-98.

CORNES R. and SANDLER T., 1984b, "The Theory of Public Goods: Non-Nash Behavior", in *Journal of Public Economics*, 23, 367-379.

FELDSTEIN M. and CLOTFELTER C., 1976, "Tax Incentives and Charitable Contributions in the United States", in *Journal of Public Economics*, 5, 1-26.

GOLDMAN S.M., 1978, "Gift Equilibria and Pareto Optimality", in *Journal of Economic Theory*, 18, 368-370.

GREENBERG J., 1980, "Beneficial Altruism", in *Journal of Economic Theory*, 22, 12-22.

GUTTMAN J., 1986, "Matching Behavior and Collective Action", in *Journal of Economic Behavior and Organization*, 7, 171-198.

GUTTMAN J., 1987, "A Non-Cournot Model of Voluntary Collective Action", in *Economica*, 54, 1-19.

HOCHMAN H.M., 1977, "The Optimal Treatment of Charitable Contributions", in *National Tax Journal*, 30, 1-18.

HOCHMAN H.M. and RODGERS J.D., 1969, "Pareto Optimal Redistribution", in *American Economic Review*, 59, 542-557.

IRELAND T. and JOHNSON D., 1970, *The Economics of Charity*, Blacksburg, Virginia: Center for the Study of Public Choice.

KENNETT, D.A., 1980, "Altruism and Economic Behavior", in *Economics and Sociology*, 39, 183-198.

KAUFMAN D.A., 1987, *Altruism and Welfare*, Ph.D. Thesis, University of Kansas.

KAUFMAN D.A., 1990, *Altruism and Welfare in a Public Goods Economy*, University of Wisconsin-Parkside.

KINGMA B.R., 1989, "An Accurate Measurement of the Crowd-out Effect, Income Effect, and Price Effect for Charitable Contributions", in *Journal of Political Economy* 97, 1197-1207.

KRANICH L.J., 1988, "Altruism and Efficiency: A Welfare Analysis of the Walrasian Mechanism with Transfers", in *Journal of Public Economics*, 36, 369-386.

LEMCHE S.Q., 1986, "Benevolent Preferences and Pure Public Goods", in *Journal of Public Economics*, 30, 129-134.

MARGOLIS H., 1982, *Selfishness, Altruism, and Rationality*, New York, Cambridge University Press.

MARK M. and SHOTLAND T., 1983, "Increasing Charitable Contributions: An Experimental Evaluation of the American Cancer Society's Recommended Solicitations Procedures", in *Journal of Voluntary Action Research*, 12, 8-21.

OLSON M., 1965, *The Logic of Collective Action*, Boston, Harvard University Press.

OSANA H., 1972, "Externalities and the Basic Theorems of Welfare Economics", in *Journal of Economic Theory*, 4, 401-414.

POSNETT J. and SANDLER T., 1986, "Joint Supply and the Finance of Charitable Activity", in *Public Finance Quarterly*, 14, 209-222.

RADER T., 1980, "The Second Theorem of Welfare Economics when Utilities are Interdependent", in *Journal of Economic Theory*, 23, 420-424.

REINGEN P.H., 1978, "Inducing Compliance with a Donation Request", in *Journal of Social Psychology*, 106, 281-281.

ROBERTS R.D., 1984, "A Positive Model of Private Charity and Public Transfers", in *Journal of Political Economy*, 92, 136-148.

ROBERTS R.D., 1987, "Financing Public Goods", in *Journal of Political Economy*, 95, 420-437.

ROBERTS R.D., 1990, *Government Subsidies to Private Spending on Public Goods*, Washington University in St. Louis.

SCAFURI A., 1988, "On Consistency of Conjectures in the Private Provision of Public Goods", in *Journal of Public Economics*, 37, 395-398.

SCHIFF J., 1990, *Charitable Giving and Government Policy*, Westport, Connecticut, Greenwood Press.

SCHWARTZ R., 1970, "Personal Philanthropic Contributions", in *Journal of Political Economy*, 78, 1264-1291.

STEINBERG R., 1987, "Voluntary Donations and Public Expenditures in a Federalist System", in *American Economic Review*, 77, 24-36.

SUGDEN R., 1982, "On the Economics of Philanthropy", in *Economic Journal*, 92, 341-350.

SUGDEN R., 1984, "Reciprocity: The Supply of Public Goods through Voluntary Contributions", in *Economic Journal*, 94, 772-787.

SUGDEN R., 1985, "Consistent Conjectures and Voluntary Contributions to Public Goods: Why the Conventional Theory Does Not Work", in *Journal of Public Economics*, 27, 117-124.

WARR P., 1982, "Pareto Optimal Redistribution and Private Charity", in *Journal of Public Economics*, 19, 131-138.

WEISBROD, B., 1977, "Comparing Utility Functions in Efficiency Terms, or, What Kind of Utility Functions Do We Want?", in *American Economic Review*, 67, 991-995.

WINTER S.G., 1969, "A Simple Remark on the Second Optimality Theorem of Welfare Economics", in *Journal of Economic Theory*, 1, 99-103.

DOES GOVERNMENT SPENDING CROWD OUT DONATIONS ?
Interpreting the Evidence

by

Richard STEINBERG

Department of Economics

Virginia Polytechnic Institute and State University

Introduction

Models of the motivation for voluntary donations developed by Warr (1982) and Roberts (1984) imply the following startling conclusion: government expenditures crowd out donations to related services on a one-for-one basis. Thus, government spending on social services is essentially useless. Every increase in government spending is matched by a corresponding decrease in donations, so total spending remains constant. Governmental expenditures are only useful past the point where donations are driven to zero. Since government expenditures require coerced taxation, whereas donations are purely voluntary, the proper role of government is quite narrow in their idealized world.

While their conclusion is derived under restrictive assumptions, the assumptions are not outrageously unrealistic. Regardless, their work has highlighted the importance of crowdout considerations when formulating the appropriate role for government. When crowdout is near total, governmental expenditures are a relatively inefficient vehicle for obtaining service expenditures. In contrast, when crowdout is negative (that is, government expenditures are to some extent, matched by private donations), government spending is especially productive.

Crowdout is also important in the design of tax code provisions concerning charitable donations. Feldstein (1980) argued that tax breaks (deductions or credits) for giving are efficient whenever the price elasticity of donations is greater than one (in absolute value). The reason is that donations provide services which otherwise would have to be financed through taxation. When giving is price elastic, the increment to giving fostered by the tax break exceeds the treasury's revenue loss, so a given level of social-service expenditure can be obtained with lower total tax collections.

Roberts (1987) extended Feldstein's model to incorporate crowdout effects. He showed that when crowdout is zero, Feldstein is exactly right, but when crowdout is total, tax breaks for donations are superior to direct governmental provision regardless of the price elasticity of giving. In between, tax breaks are superior when price elasticity exceeds a critical value (between zero and one in absolute value) which is inversely proportional to the extent of crowdout.

Warr and Roberts derived their conclusion under two admittedly restrictive assumptions. First, they assumed that the set of donors is exogenously determined. Bergstrom, Blume, and Varian (1986) showed that partial crowdout may result when this assumption is relaxed, but Bernheim (1986) noted that total crowdout will still result if the sets of donors to competing causes overlap. Second, they assumed that donations are made solely to increment expenditures on a pure public good. In effect, they assume that donations of others and government expenditures are regarded as a perfect (Hicksian) substitute for one's own donation in each donor's utility function. This restriction has been relaxed by many authors, including Cornes and Sandler (1984), Schiff (1985), Posnett and Sandler (1986), Steinberg (1987), and Andreoni (1989). In these models, crowdout predictions are ambiguous in both magnitude and direction. Government spending can be more than 100% effective in a raising total spending (negative crowdout, or crowdin) or less than 0% effective (super crowdout), as well as total or partial. This ambiguity is inherent, and diverse results can occur even when government spending is regarded as an imperfect substitute for one's own giving and all goods are normal.

Other authors have investigated the form taken by governmental expenditures and the behavioral response of non-profit organizations, the recipients of both government grants and charitable donations. Rose-Ackerman (1981) detailed some of these factors: matching requirements accompanying grants (which reduce the effective price of giving and may lead to crowdin), strings attached to grants (which may induce non-profits to select an output mix more, or perhaps less in tune with the wishes of donors), and information revealed to donors by grant receipt (donors may regard grant recipients as especially meritorious or efficient because the recipients have received an implicit government seal of approval). In a later paper, Rose-Ackerman (1987) argued that even non-matching grants with no strings attached can have effects, for they free the manager of the non-profit from compromising his or her ideology to satisfy major donors.

One further distinction becomes relevant in federal (or other multilevel) systems of government. If, for some reason, social service grants from the central government to some locality were to change, both the local government and local donations would react. This reaction would be composed of a direct response to the grant and an indirect feedback caused by this response, as donors and local governments react to induced changes in each other. I denote the total reaction as "joint crowdout". Joint crowdout of donations signifies the ultimate effect of a central government expenditure change on donations, allowing local government expenditures to simultaneously adjust. Similarly, joint government crowdout denotes the ultimate effect on local government spending, allowing donations to simultaneously adjust. In distinction, "simple crowdout" signifies the direct effect only-say, the effect of the grant on donations when local government expenditures are held constant.

Whereas crowdout measures are important when deciding the overall role of government, joint crowdout measures are important for questions of federalism. If joint crowdout is total, the central government should avoid social-service provision. If there is joint crowdin, central government expenditures are especially efficient.

Joint crowdout results from simple donative crowdout, simple government crowdout, and interactions between the two. Simple government crowdout has been much studied (see, i.e., Craig and Inman, 1986, and the references contained therein), both analytically and empirically. Briefly, the form of the grant is critical.

Consider first a general grant (like revenue sharing). One would expect that states would use the grants (in part) to provide tax relief to residents, so that total state spending would rise, but by less than the size of the grant. Standard models make a further prediction – that grants should have the same effect on state expenditures as that of an increase in community income. Further, except for corner solutions, there should be no difference between grants targeted to specific programs and general grants. Grant makers cannot assure that incremental spending on the targeted service will equal the size of the grant, for they cannot observe how much the state was willing to spend in the absence of the grant.

These predictions have not been borne out in most empirical studies, which find that general grants have bigger impacts than community income, and targeted grants have bigger impacts than general grants. This phenomenon has become known as "the flypaper effect," for money seems to stick where it hits. The existence of the flypaper effect has been challenged on econometric grounds (i.e., Moffit, 1984, ascribed it to nonlinearities in the median voter's budget set which were not taken account of in the statistical specification). Alternatively, the basic economic model has been replaced by more elaborate ones which made predictions consistent with observed estimates (i. e., Hamilton, 1983, who considered scale economies in public-good production or Craig and Inman, 1986, who modelled the political decisionmaking process in a representative government).

Open-ended matching grants should have greater impact on state spending than non-matching grants, for matching reduces the effective price of state spending. This prediction is generally borne out in the literature. However, most matching grants have binding caps (they match only up to a maximum amount, and the limit is nearly always reached). In this case, matching serves to increase the community's income, but does not affect the relevant marginal price of state government spending.

In Section 1 of this paper, I briefly summarize existing estimates of simple and joint crowdout, including tentative estimates from work in progress. In Section 2, I discuss some general problems with available data. I conclude with some recommendations and a brief summary. Appendices deal with the merits of specific data sets and with difficulties in constructing control variables.

1   A Survey of Crowdout Estimates

The typical empirical study regresses some measure of donations on some measure of government spending and a vector of control variables. As much of this work predates my 1987 paper, it is not surprising that reported results do not distinguish between simple and joint crowdout. Thus, for example, Jones (1983) explained family donations in the U.K. using the sum of central plus local government spending on social services and housing. Schiff (1985; 1990) explained

U.S. donations using several government expenditure variables in the same equation (representing distinct levels of government). Abrams and Schmitz (1978) explained U.S. donations claimed for tax purposes using only federal government expenditures on health education and welfare.

To make the econometric implications clear, suppose that only two levels of government make expenditures, denoted F (for federal) and S (for state). Donations in a state are denoted D, and the true model is one of joint crowdout. Further, donors regard F and S as perfect substitutes, and state voters regard D and F as perfect substitutes. Thus, the structural model (omitting control variables) is:

$$D = \alpha_1 + \beta_1 (S + F) + \varepsilon_1$$
$$S = \alpha_2 + \beta_2 (D + F) + \varepsilon_2$$

The reduced form of this model is:

$$D = a_1 + b_1 F + \eta_1$$
$$S = a_2 + b_2 F + \eta_2$$

The econometric implications are:

(1)   OLS estimates explaining donations by the sum of federal plus state spending can be interpreted as biased estimates of simple crowdout. This bias results from endogeneity of one component of the government spending measure. Reece (1979), Pacqué (1982), Amos (1982), Jones (1983), Abrams and Schmitz[1] (1984), and Steinberg (1985) all suffer this defect. Schiff (1985; 1990) entered F and S as separate control variables, but the endogeneity bias infecting the coefficient on S will, in general, spill over and infect the coefficient on F.

(2)   OLS estimates utilizing federal, but not state government expenditures are a proper reduced form. However, information from the other reduced form equation is not utilized, so estimates may not be efficient. Further, the coefficient on F estimates joint crowdout. Simple crowdout cannot be inferred from such an equation. Abrams and Schmitz (1978) utilized this approach.

---

1   Abrams and Schmitz (1984) omit the federal level entirely but incorporate the lagged sum of state plus local government spending. A more elaborate set of assumptions is necessary to properly interpret and complete this specification, but estimates of simple crowdout are plausibly produced.

(3)   An unbiased estimate of the structural equation for donations can be obtained by instrumental variables. This approach was taken by Kingma (1989). His coefficient should be interpreted as an estimate of simple crowdout.[2]

(4)   The reduced form can be estimated as a system using the seemingly-unrelated regression technique. Coefficients of this system are efficient estimates of joint crowdout of both donations and of state spending. Further, the structural   coefficients estimating simple crowdout are a simple (if nonlinear) function of the reduced-form coefficients.[3] This approach is taken by Steinberg (1983, 1984), Lindsey and Steinberg (1990), and Schiff and Steinberg (in progress).

(5)   Alternatively, one may believe that information lags affect behavior. In this case, direct estimates of the structural model would not suffer from bias, for the endogenous right-hand variables would be predetermined. Estimated coefficients reveal simple crowdout; joint crowdout can be inferred by taking the present value of the simulated stream of reactions to a federal change. This approach (and several variants) was taken by Steinberg (1983).

(6)   Those studies (not summarized here) which estimate a single equation, explaining state spending by federal grants (but omitting charitable contributions) are proper reduced-form estimates of *joint* government crowdout. Simple government crowdout cannot be inferred from these estimates.

Most studies view non-profits as passive conduits of funds, mechanically implementing donor desires for replacement of government services. In contrast, Schiff and Weisbrod (in progress) postulated endogenous behavioral responses by non-profits which affect our interpretation of crowdout estimates.

To direct simple crowdout of donations, they add four other relevant effects. First, some government grants and purchase contracts go directly to non-profit organizations. If these are cut back, there is a direct revenue effect. Second, government money may insulate non-

---

2   Kingma also incorporated instruments for gifts by other donors, which makes his estimates more "pure" (in a structural sense) then even simple crowdout. For the distinction between crowdout holding the gifts of others constant (ceteris-paribus simple crowdout) and crowdout allowing others to adjust to a new Nash equilibrium (mutatis-mutandus simple crowdout), see my 1986 paper.

3   In particular, the implied simple donative crowdout parameter is $b_1/(b_2 + 1)$.

profits from the need to engage in commercial activity (both related and unrelated to the charity's purpose). Cutbacks may force them to increase sales of less-preferred private output, the revenue-source substitution effect. Third, cutbacks may affect the nonprofit's choice of solicitation expenditure level, the fundraising effect. Finally, grants may affect the equilibrium number of nonprofit organizations, the entry/exit effect. Each of these effects is separately estimated in their work through the use of organization-level data.

What one would like is the change in the charity's net receipts (those available for the provision of substitute services) after allowing all mitigating behavioral responses by charities. Therefore, one would not like to hold, say, fundraising expenditures constant when estimating crowdout. Donor-level data can be employed to properly estimate the mutatis mutandus *gross* crowdout effect. However, such estimates need to be supplemented with estimates produced from organization-level data in order to calculate the corresponding *net* crowdout effect of interest.

In Table 1, I report estimates of simple crowdout, in Table 2, estimates of joint donative crowdout. Where the authors of these papers were not clear, the classification is my own, following the guidelines above. Tables 3-6 report more detail on joint crowdout, providing estimates of joint crowdout of state spending to infer the total of the relevant crowdouts.

Simple donative crowdout estimates span the gamut from partial crowdout (a negative coefficient between zero and negative one) to crowdin (a positive coefficient). Point estimates always exceeded negative one, and in most cases, we can reject the hypothesis of total crowdout. Thus, if any of these estimates are persuasive, they speak against the pure public goods models of Warr (1982) and Roberts (1984). In most studies, we can reject the hypothesis that crowdout is zero for at least some specifications, and estimated crowdout ranges from 1/2% to 35% per unit of government spending.

Cases of crowdin are rarer. Pacqué (1982) found significant crowdin caused by cultural affairs spending in the Federal Republic of Germany; Schiff (1985) found significant crowdin caused by state government spending, noncash transfers by the state and local social welfare spending in the U.S.A. Similarly, Schiff (1990) found significant crowdin caused by state and local government welfare spending, but federal welfare expenditures caused significant crowdout. Schiff and Weisbrod (in progress) found significant crowdin caused by cash assistance to the poor, payments to private organizations for services

Table 1 : Estimates of Simple Crowdout

Study	Crowdout parameter[a]	Measure of Government Spending	Measure of Donations
(1) Reece (1979)	− 0.011[e]	AFDC + old age assistance + aid for disabled per recipient for all regressions	charity
	− 0.100[e]		charity + gifts + religious + educational + political
	− 0.100[e]		
	− 0.032[e]		charity + religious + educational + political
			(all above from U.S. Consumer Expenditure Survey, (1972-73), cross-section)
(2) Pacqué (1982)	− 0.06 to − 0.35[c,d]	Social Service Expenditures	Deductions on German (FRG) federal income tax returns for all regressions (aggregate panel)
	0.118[c]	Health + Recreation	
	0.11 to 0.31[c,d]	Cultural Affairs	
		(all above were combined federal + state + local)	
(3) Amos (1982)	− 0.002 to − 0.462[d,f]	Total transfers; AFDC; public welfare payments	Deductions on U.S. federal income tax returns. (cross-section)
(4) Steinberg (1983)	− 0.001 to − 0.003	Intergovernment grants for Recreation	Local United Way (U.S.) allocations to specified service for all regressions. (aggregate panel)
	0.004 to 0.009[d]	Intergovernment grants for hospitals	
(5) Jones (1983)	− 0.015 to − 0.016[b,d]	Central + local Government spending on social services and housing	Family donations from family Expenditure Survey (U.K.) (time series)
(6) Abrams and Schmitz (1984)	− 0.30[d]	State and local social welfare payments per $1000 personal income	Deductions on U.S. Federal income tax returns. (cross-section)
(7) Schiff (1985)	+ 0.344[d]	State government spending	Total Donations
	− 0.662[d]	Local Govt. Spending	Total Donations

Study	Crowdout parameter[a]	Measure of Government Spending	Measure of Donations
	− 0.058[d]	Cash transfers by state	Donations to Social Welfare
	+ 0.046[d]	Noncash transfers by state	Donations to Social Welfare
	+ 0.030[d]	Social Welfare by Local	(all from U.S. National Survey of Philanthropy), (cross-section)
(8) Steinberg (1985)	− 0.005[d]	Central + Local Government Spending on Social Services and Housing	Family Donations from Family Expenditure, Survey (U.K.) (time series)
(9) Kingma (1989)	− 0.135[d]	Total Support from all sources other than station members	Donations to Public Radio Stations in U.S. (cross-section)
(10) Lindsey & Steinberg (1990)	− 0.0139	Federal Grants for Social Services	Deductions on U.S. Federal income tax
	− 0.060[d]	Other Federal Grants	returns for all regressions. (aggregate panel)
(11) Schiff (1990)	− 0.397[d]	Federal Welfare Spending	Total Donations
	+ 0.125[d]	State and Local Local Welfare Spending	Total Donations (all from U.S. time series aggregate estimates, 1930-1986)
(12) Schiff and Steinberg (in progress)	− 0.0179	Federal Grants for Public Assistance	Social welfare
	+ 0.2932	Federal Grants for Health	Health
	+ 0.1818	Federal Grants for Education	Higher Education
	− 0.2859	Federal Grants for Education	Lower Education
	− 0.0157[d]	Total Federal Grants	Social Welfare
	− 0.0515	Total Federal Grants	Health
	− 0.2496	Total Federal Grants	Higher Education

Table 1 continued

Study	Crowdout parameter[a]	Measure of Government Spending	Measure of Donations
	− 0.0303	Total Federal Grants	Lower Education
			(All from U.S. National Survey of Philanthropy, cross-section)
(13) Schiff & Weisbrod (in progress)	+ 0.02[d]	Cash assistance to Poor	Net receipts of Nonprofit Organization (cross-section) from U.S. tax forms of exempt organizations
	+ 0.03[d]	Payments to Private Organizations for Services to Needy	
	− 0.12[d]	Other State Public Welfare Expenditures	
	+ 0.02[d]	Social welfare Spending by Local Governments	

[a] Change in donations caused by a $1 increase in government spending.
[b] My calculation from reported elasticities and available data.
[c] Elasticity; conversion to crowdout parameter not possible from available data.
[d] Reported coefficients different from zero at .05 significance level or better. Where parameter is a function of estimated coefficients, the significance test is for the estimated coefficients, not the parameter.
[e] This is the effect of an increase in government spending *per recipient* on giving *per donor*. Conversion to a crowdout parameter is not possible from available data.
[f] Although donations are *per itemizer*, the article does not report the units for government spending, so interpretation as a crowdout parameter is questionable.

Table 2: Estimates of Joint Donative Crowdout

Study	Crowdout parameter[a]	Measure of Government Spending	Measure of Donations
(1) Abrams & Schmitz (1978)	− 0.236[b,c]	Federal expenditure on health, education, and welfare	Deductions on U.S. Federal income tax returns (time series)
(2) Steinberg (1983)	+ 0.0003 to + 0.0006[c]	Total Intergovernmental Transfers	United Way Allocations to Hospitals
	+ 0.002 to + 0.009[c]	Intergovernmental Transfers for Health	United Way Allocations to Hospitals

Study	Crowdout parameter[a]	Measure of Government Spending	Measure of Donations
	− 0.0006 to + 0.0013	Total Intergovernment Transfers	United Way Allocations to Recreation
	− 0.0188 to + 0.0253[c]	Intergovernmental Transfers for Recreation	United Way Allocations to Recreation (all aggregate panel of U.S. data)
(3) Steinberg (1984)	− 0.0014[c]	Intergovernmental Transfers for Health	United Way Allocations to Hospitals
	+ 0.03[c]	Intergovernmental Transfers for Recreation	United Way Allocations to Recreation (all aggregate panel of U.S. data)
(4) Lindsey & Steinberg (1990)	− 0.0456	Federal Grants for Social Services	Deductions on U.S. federal income tax returns for all
	− 0.0209[c]	Other Federal Grants	regressions (aggregate panel)
(5) Schiff & Steinberg (in progress)	− 0.047	Federal Grants for Public Assistance	Social Welfare
	− 0.173	Federal Grants for Health	Health
	+ 0.18	Federal Grants for Education	Higher Education
	− 0.283	Federal Grants for Education	Lower Education
	− 0.033[c]	Total Federal Grants	Social Welfare
	− 0.05	Total Federal Grants	Health
	− 0.297	Total Federal Grants	Higher Education
	− 0.036	Total Federal Grants	Lower Education all from U.S. National Survey of Philanthropy (cross-section)

[a] Change in donations caused by a $1 increase in government spending.

[b] My calculation from reported elasticities and available data.

[c] Reported coefficients different from zero at .05 significance level of better. Where parameter is a function of estimated coefficients, the significance test is for the estimated coefficients, not the parameter.

Table 3: Joint Crowdout Estimates from Steinberg (1983)[a]

	Change in Donations to Specified Service	Change in Own-financed Local Government Expenditures on Specified Service	Change in Total Expenditures on Specified Service
(1) Effect of an increase in intergovernmental transfers for health on hospital sector	+ 0.0046[b]	+ 0.0397	+ 1.0442
(2) Effect of an increase in intergovernmental transfers for recreation on recreation sector	+ 0.0033[b]	− 0.7017[b]	+ 0.3016

[a] Predicted effect of a $1 intergovernmental transfer on the present value of induced expenditures, discounted at 10% (nominal). These numbers are the simple averages of coefficients reported in various specifications.
[b] Reported coefficients different from zero at .05 significance level or better. However, the parameter reported here is a complicated nonlinear function of those coefficient estimates.

Table 4: Joint Crowdout Estimates from Steinberg (1984)[a]

	Change in Donations to Specified Service	Change in Own-Financed Local Government Expenditures on Specified Service	Change in government User Fees for Specified Service	Change in Total Expenditure for Specified Service
(1) Effect of an increase in intergovernmental transfers for health on Hospital Sector	− 0.014[b]	+ 0.19[b]	− 0.04[b]	+ 1.15
(2) Effect of an increase in intergovernmental transfers for recreation on recreation sector	+ 0.03[b]	+ 0.76[b]	+ 0.36[b]	+ 2.15

[a] From "reduced form" equations
[b] Significant at .01 or better

Table 5: Joint Crowdout Estimates from Lindsey and Steinberg (1990)

	Change in Donations ($s)	Change in Own-Financed State Government Expenditures on Social Services ($s)	Change in Total Expenditures on Social Services ($s)
(1) Effect of Social Services Grants	− 0.0456[a]	+ 1.2766[b]	+ 2.2310[b]
(2) Effect of Non-Social Services Grants	− 0.0209	1.4621[b]	+ 1.4412[b]

[a] significant at .10
[b] significant at .01

**Table 6: Joint Crowdout Estimates
from Schiff and Steinberg (in progress)**

Effect of a $1 Increase in Per Capita Total Federal Grants on				
For Service	Money Donations[a] ($S)	Time Donations[a] (Seconds)	Own-Financed State and Local Government Expenditures[a] ($S)	Total Expenditures[a,b] ($S)
Welfare	− 0.033	+ 15.6	− 0.949	+ 0.018
Health	− 0.05	− 93.6	− 1.03	− 0.08
Higher Education	− 0.297	− 15.6	− 0.81[c]	− 0.107
Lower Education	− 0.036	− 56.4	− 0.81[c]	+ 0.154
Effect of a $1 Increase in Per Capita Federal Grants to Specified Service				
Welfare	− 0.047	+ 180	+ 0.62	+ 1.57
Health	− 0.173	+ 984	− 2.59	− 1.76
Higher Education	+ 0.18	− 43.2	− 1.01[c]	+ 0.17
Lower Education	− 0.283	− 204	− 1.01[c]	− 0.293

[a] Per Capita
[b] Does not include an imputation for volunteer time.
[c] Government spending data used here did not report higher and lower education separately, so a combined regression was run.

to the needy, and social welfare spending by local governments. However these studies suffer, to an unknown extent, from the endogeneity bias discussed earlier. I found significant crowdin caused by grants to U.S. hospitals in some estimates contained in my 1983 study, but the magnitude of this crowdin was small.

There is no reason to suppose that crowdout is the same for every country and for every good, and indeed, estimates vary. However, there are too few independent estimates of crowdout for the same partition of goods and services to detect a clear pattern.

Joint crowdout of donations has been much less studied. In most cases, there was partial joint crowdout of less than 30¢ per dollar, though numerically small but statistically significant estimates of crowdin did occur.

The total picture is revealed by those studies which explained state or local spending as well as donations. In my 1983 paper, I found that intergovernmental grants to localities for health increased total expenditures by a bit more than the grant itself. Rather than using intergovernmental aid to replace some portion of locally tax-financed government expenditures, local governments seemed to partially match the grant[4]. In sum, donations rose by about 1/2¢ and local government spending by about 4¢, so a $1 grant led to just over $1.04 in spending.

Preliminary results from Lindsey and Steinberg (1990) show a similar pattern, albeit between higher levels of government. A $1 increase in federal grants targeted to social services appeared to cause a fall of about 4.6¢ in donations, while causing state tax-financed social service expenditures to rise by about $1.28[5]. Social service grants appeared to be especially productive despite simple and joint crowdout of donations, with total expenditures rising by more than $2 for each grant dollar provided.

Grants not targeted for social services had a smaller effect on state spending, but own-financed expenditures still went up. Donors, responding to a smaller rise in government spending, only cut donations by about 2¢. Overall, these grants appeared to cause a $1.44 increase in total expenditures per dollar.

---

4   I should note that I had no data on the structure of state grants to localities. The obtained result would not be surprising if state grants were of the open-ended matching variety.

5   This result is not due to matching requirements. Open-ended matching grants were removed from the measure of social service grants, and matching rates were incorporated into a price of government services variable.

2   General Problems with Data

What is the proper measure of donations? It is easiest to measure and incorporate monetary donations, but even this component is problematic when a quid pro quo is provided. Part of the cost of a fundraising banquet is a payment for food and entertainment, yet all is typically reported as a donation[6]. One would also want measures of donations of assets and in-kind donations. Finally, one would want to measure donations of time as well as money. The difficulty here is in imputing a value to volunteer labor. Traditional measures value an hour of volunteer labor at the foregone wage rate. This measure appropriately measures the donor sacrifice, but not the value of time to the recipient charity. The volunteer labor market may not enjoy efficient job matching, so these two measures may differ (Steinberg, 1990). Finally, if workers at nonprofit firms accept lower wage rates as a form of implicit donation (Preston, 1988; 1989), this can be viewed as a difficult-to-measure form of "partial volunteering" (Weisbrod, Wolff, and Bird, in progress).

While donations by living persons are important, they are not the only source of donations. Corporations, foundations, and bequests also contribute to the donative total, and I know of no crowdout study which included any of these. Fortunately, the bulk of donations are made by living persons (at least in the U.S.), though the percentage is much lower if we exclude religious giving (Hodgkinson and Weitzman, 1986).

For-profit service providers (in industries such as health care, day care, or nursing homes) should, perhaps, also be incorporated. In some cases, for-profit provision is an entirely commercial activity, suggesting that no social issues are involved. In other cases, for-profits are involved principally because of third-party payments by governments, and are thus relevant components of the crowdout picture.

Having measured the various components of giving, one must decide whether to aggregate them as one dependent variable, or incorporate a separate equation explaining each form of donation. Although no crowdout study has addressed the issue, one study (O'Neal, Steinberg, and Thompson, 1990) found that asset gifts respond distinctly to tax incentives.

---

6   At least on U.S. tax returns, this practice is discouraged. Donors are not supposed to deduct the fair market value of goods and services provided to them in (implicit or explicit) exchange for their donation. However, IRS interest in enforcing this provision is very recent, and it is quite difficult to enforce.

Schiff (1984) and Schiff and Steinberg (in progress) explained both time and money contributions using separate equations. There are many more reasons to suspect that volunteering and monetary contributions are imperfect substitutes, so there is no reason to try to aggregate these two. Unlike money, time donations provide the donor with training, skill certification, social opportunities, control over nonprofit output, and information about the quality and efficiency of the recipient charity. In any case, without a solution to the imputation problem, it is not possible to aggregate here.

Any data on donations must be matched with data on government spending, and this matching is difficult for six reasons. First, many surveys do not reveal the location of the donor, out of respect for maintaining anonymity[7]. Second, those surveys which reveal donor location typically question only a few donors in each location, too few to reliably estimate average giving in each jurisdiction. Third, consistent definitions of goods provided by government and goods provided through donations are rarely (if ever) available. Thus, for example, Schiff (1985) matched cash transfers by states, noncash transfers by states, and social welfare spending by localities (as defined by one survey) with donations to social welfare organizations (as defined by another). Even when the definitions of goods seem consistent, there may be quality differences or different sectors may fund different aspects of the good. Apparently identical classifications may indicate complementarities, not perfect substitutability. Thus, federal spending for museum and symphony orchestras may principally fund the construction of facilities, while donations are used for acquisition of paintings and musicians.

The total crowdout prediction of the "pure public good" models are not properly tested unless the match is perfect. In contrast, the impure public good models assert that even if the physical match between goods is perfect, donors will not regard giving and government spending as perfect substitutes. The *act* of giving is important, for it provides a "warm glow", assuages guilt, and reduces social pressures. In Kingma (1989), both donors to public radio stations and the stations themselves were surveyed about all sources of support (including government and

---

7   In the U.S. Consumer Expenditure Surveys, donor location is available internally but is omitted from the Public Use tapes. Reece (1979) was only able to use this data because he was employed by the agency responsible for collecting the data. Average expenditures for between 16 and 25 major metropolitan areas were published, but presents to families and friends were combined with donations in these reports.

corporate sponsors). Even with this seemingly perfect match, crowdout was partial, which supports the impure public goods models. Imperfect matching is thus a bit of a red herring, for it appears to be inherent in the donative decision.

Fifth, donations cross jurisdictional boundaries. This problem becomes more acute at the local government level, but is present at every level of government. When borderline residents in, say, the state of Maryland make contributions to an organization in the neighboring state of Virginia, and this organization helps the homeless in Virginia regions of concern to Maryland residents, organization-level data is superior. Here, Virginia government expenditures crowd out donations by Maryland donors to Virginia organizations. Donor-level data would neglect the effect of Virginia spending on Maryland donors. On the other hand, if Maryland donors contribute to a non-Maryland national philanthropy which serves Maryland's needs, then the location of the recipient organization is inappropriate for crowdout estimation. Donor-level data would enable one to estimate the effect of Maryland government spending on donations by Marylanders.

Finally, the structure of local governments is complicated. Different services (education, aid to the poor, etc.) are provided by different but partially overlapping local jurisdictions. It is perhaps for this reason that no one has attempted to estimate a three-level of government (federal/state/local) model of joint crowdout.

Estimates produced from cross-sections should differ from those produced in time series for inherent reasons. It makes sense to regard federal non-matching grants to a community as exogenous to that community. If one includes variables to control for differences in tastes across communities, then cross-section regressions explaining state expenditures and donations by federal grants would properly estimate joint crowdout. On the other hand, one would not want to take changes in aggregate federal grants as exogenous when explaining changes in aggregate state spending and donations in a time series. The election of Reagan and the concommitant reduction in federal social-service expenditures in the early years of his presidency was accompanied by only a modest rise in donations, but this does not imply that crowdout was small. The same "taste change" that led to Reagan's election may have been accompanied by a taste change that led to lower donative generosity, producing an underestimate of true crowdout (holding tastes constant).

3   Conclusions

It is important to estimate the extent of crowdout of donations and lower-level government spending by central   government expenditures. Crowdout estimates tell us how effective government spending is in raising total expenditures. It is also difficult to estimate the extent of crowdout. The importance of the subject justifies much empirical analysis even if no individual study is likely to prove persuasive.

Many problems remain with existing crowdout estimates. In my view, the top research priorities are:

(1)   To obtain better data sets in which the nature of the good supported by donations can be better matched with the nature of the government-provided good.

(2)   To better incorporate behavioral responses of nonprofit organizations in the calculation of *net* revenue responses (along lines begun by Schiff and Weisbrod, in progress).

(3)   To estimate crowdout with data from a variety of countries.

(4)   To better exploit the panel nature of some data sets, imposing the theoretical structure of my 1987 paper on the estimating procedure.

(5)   To further explore the dynamic structure of crowdout – the time path of the various dependent variables.

(6)   To obtain more complete measures of giving, including volunteer time, wage sacrifices, in-kind gifts and gifts of assets, all in a form suitable for estimation.

(7)   To estimate the relative efficiency with which expenditures by the differing sectors translate into service provision.

Although one would like to see all these shortcomings remedied within a single study, most are remedied in some existing studies. Crowdout has been estimated from time series and cross-sectional data. Donative measures include data from tax returns, donor surveys, and surveys of recipient nonprofit organizations. Crowdout has been estimated for narrowly defined goods (public radio stations) and for broad aggregates (social welfare spending). Each of these different sources has unique advantages and disadvantages. Collectively, they begin to provide a persuasive picture.

Thus despite the faults of individual studies, three conclusions seem apparent. First, crowdout of donations does occur. Second, crowdout is relatively small (usually between 1/2¢ and 35¢ per dollar of government spending). Finally, state government reactions match federal changes, the so-called flypaper effect. Whereas donative crowdout reduces the effectiveness of federal grants, state government reactions more than make up for this, so that overall, targeted federal grants are quite effective instruments for raising total expenditures on a specified good or service.

REFERENCES

ABRAMS B. and SCHMITZ M., 1978, "The 'Crowding-Out' Effect of Governmental Transfers on Private Charitable Contributions", in *Public Choice* 33, pp. 29-37.

————, 1984, "The Crowding-Out Effect of Governmental Transfers on Private Charitable Contributions: Cross-Section Evidence", in *National Tax Journal* 37, Dec., pp. 563-568.

AMOS O. M., Jr., 1982, "Empirical Analysis of Motives Underlying Individual Contributions to Charity", in *Atlantic Economic Journal* X # 4, December, pp. 45-52.

ANDREONI J., 1989, "Giving with Impure Altruism: Applications to Charity and Ricardian Equivalence", in *Journal of Political Economy* 97, Dec.

BERGSTROM T., BLUME L. and VARIAN H., 1986, "On the Private Provision of Public Goods", in *Journal of Public Economics* 29 # 1, June, pp. 25-49.

BERNHEIM B. DOUGLAS, 1986, "On the Voluntary and Involuntary Provision of Public Goods", *The American Economic Review* 76, Sept., pp. 789-93.

CLOTFELTER C., 1985, *Federal Tax Policy and Charitable Giving*, Chicago: University of Chicago Press.

CORNES R. and SANDLER T., 1984, "Easy Riders, Joint Production and Public Goods", in *The Economic Journal* 94: 580-598, Sept.

CRAIG S. G. and INMAN R.P., 1986, "Education, Welfare and the "New" Federalism: State Budgeting in a Federalist Public Economy", in Harvey Rosen, ed., *Studies in State and Local Public Finance*, Chicago: University of Chicago Press, pp. 187-228.

FEENBERG D., 1988, "Are Tax Price Models Really Identified: The Case of Charitable Giving", in *National Tax Journal* 41, pp. 629-633.

FELDSTEIN M., 1975, "The Income Tax and Charitable Contributions: Part I – Aggregate and Distributional Effects, in *National Tax journal* 28 # 1, pp. 81-100.

FELDSTEIN M., 1980, "A Contribution to the Theory of Tax Expenditures: The Case of Charitable Giving", in Henry J. Aaron and Michael Boskin, eds., *The Economics of Taxation*, Washington, D.C.: Brookings Institution, pp. 99-122.

HAMILTON B., 1983, "The Flypaper Effect and Other Anomalies", in *Journal of Public Economics* 22, December, pp. 347-362.

HODGKINSON V. A. and WEITZMAN M., 1986, *Dimensions of the Independent Sector: A Statistical Profile*, Washington, D.C.: Independent Sector, 2nd ed.

JENCKS C., 1987, "Who Gives to What?" in Walter W. Powell, ed., *The Nonprofit Sector: A Research Handbook*, New Haven: Yale University Press, pp. 321-339.

JONES P.R., 1983, "Aid to Charities", in *International Journal of Social Economics*, 10# 2.

KINGMA B., 1989, "An Accurate Measurement of the Crowd-Out Effect, Income Effect and Price Effect for Charitable Contributions", in *Journal of Political Economy*, 97.

LINDSEY L., 1987, "Federal Deductibility of State and Local Taxes: A Test of Public Choice by Representative Government", in Harvey Rosen, ed., *Fiscal Federalism*, Chicago: University of Chicago Press.

————— and STEINBERG R., 1990, "Joint Crowdout: An Empirical Study of the Impact of Federal Grants on State Government Expenditures and Charitable Donations", Working Paper #3226, National Bureau of Economic Research.

MOFFITT R., 1984, "The Effects of Grants-in-Aid on State and Local Expenditures: The Case of AFDC", in *Journal of Public Economics* 23, April, pp. 279-306.

MORGAN J.N., DYE R.F. and HYBELS J.H., 1977, "Results from Two national Surveys of Philanthropic Activity" in Commission on Private Philanthropy and Public Needs, in *Research Papers* vol. I, Treasury Dept., pp. 157-323.

O'NEIL C., STEINBERG R. and THOMPSON G. R., 1990, "Cash vs. Property Contributions", Working Paper, V.P.I. & S.U., July.

PAQUÉ K.-H., 1982, "Do Public Transfers 'Crowd Out' Private Charitable Giving? Some econometric evidence for the Federal Republic of Germany, Kiel Working Paper No. 152, August.

POSNETT J. and SANDLER T., 1986, "Joint Supply and the Finance of Charitable Activity", in *Public Finance Quarterly 14*, pp. 209-222, April.

PRESTON A., "The Effects of Property Rights on Labor Costs of Nonprofit Firms: An application to the Day Care Industry", in *The Journal of Industrial Economics 36*, # 3, March 1988, pp. 337-349.

———, 1989, "The Non Profit Worker in a For-Profit World", in *Journal of Labor Economics*, 7, October, pp. 438-463.

REECE W.S., 1979, "Charitable Contributions: New evidence on Household Behavior", in *American Economic Review* 69, pp. 142-151.

——— and ZIESCHANG K., 1985, "Consistent Estimation of the Impact of Tax Deductibility on the Level of Charitable Contributions", in *Econometrica* 53, March, pp. 271-293.

ROBERTS R. D., 1984, "A Positive Model of Private Charity and Public Transfers", in *Journal of Political Economy* 92, n° 1.

———, 1987, "Financing Public Goods", in *Journal of Political Economy* 95, pp. 420-437.

ROSE-ACKERMAN S., 1980, "United Charities: An Economic Analysis", in *Public Policy* 28, Summer, pp. 323-350.

———, 1981, "Do Government Grants to Charity Reduce Private Donations", in Michelle White Ed., *Nonprofit Firms in a 3 Sector Economy*.

———, 1987, "Ideals vs. Dollars: Donors, Charity Managers, and Government Grants", in *Journal of Political Economy* 95, pp. 810-823.

SCHIFF J., 1984, "Charitable Contributions of Money and Time: the Role of Government Policies", unpublished Ph. D. dissertation in economics, University of Wisconsin, Madison.

———, 1985, "Does Government Spending Crowd Out Charitable Contributions", in *National Tax Journal*, 38 # 4, December, pp. 535-546.

——, 1990, *"Charitable Giving and Government Policy: An Economic Analysis,* Westport, Conn: Greenwood Press.

——, and STEINBERG R., 1988, "The Effect of Federal Government Expenditure Cutbacks on Service Provision by States and Nonprofit Organizations", draft, (revision in progress).

——, and WEISBROD B., 1986, "Government Social Welfare Spending and the Private Nonprofit Sector: Crowding out and More" (draft).

SLEMROD J., 1989, "Are Estimated Tax Elasticities Really Just Tax Evasion Elasticities? The Case of Charitable Contributions", in *Review of Economics and Statistics* 71, August, pp. 517-522.

STEINBERG R., 1983, "Two Essays on the Nonprofit Sector", unpublished Ph. D. dissertation in economics, University of Pennsylvania.

——, 1984, "Empirical Relations between Government Spending and Charitable Donations", Working Paper, V.P.I & S.U., Blacksburg, Va..

——, 1985, "Empirical Relations Between Government Spending and Charitable Donations", in *Journal of Voluntary Action Research* 14, Spring-Summer, pp. 54-64.

——, 1986, "Charitable Giving as a Mixed Public/private Good: Implications for Tax Policy", in *Public Finance Quarterly* 14 # 4, Oct., pp. 415-431.

——, 1987, "Voluntary Donations and Public Expenditures in a Federalist System", in *American Economic Review 76,* March, pp. 24-36.

——, 1990, "Labor Economics and the Nonprofit Sector: A Literature Review", in *Nonprofit and Voluntary Sector Quarterly* 19, Summer, 151-170.

WARR P.G., 1982, "Pareto Optimal Redistribution and Private Charity", in *Journal of Public Economics* 19, October, 131-138.

WEISBROD B., WOLFF N. and BIRD E., 1989, "The Market for Volunteer Labor", draft, (revision in progress).

APPENDIX I: SPECIFIC DATA SETS

Many of the studies employed data obtained from personal income tax returns. These data sets have unique advantages and disadvantages. Taxpayers report each year, so it is possible to obtain panel data sets, which offer richer opportunities for control of (observed and unobserved) confounding influences. Taxpayers face the threat of prosecution if they exaggerate their donations. Finally, there are many taxpayers in each state, so that average giving in each state can be reliably estimated.

Tax data have many disadvantages. First, they report only broad aggregates – total donations of money and total donations of appreciated property. Second, demographic and socioeconomic variables which proxy the tastes for giving and for social services are absent from tax returns. Third, not all donations can be reported on tax returns. For example, a large share of U.S. taxpayers (the nonitemizers) cannot report their donations, and even itemizers cannot report donations to a category of advocacy organizations. Nonreporting is typically not random. U.S. tax data excludes locational variables for the wealthy (those earning over $200,000 in the sample employed by Lindsey and Steinberg) in order to preserve anonymity. While excluded rich people constituted only 0.2 percent of the taxpayer population, this group made about 11% of all donations. Thus, tax data may lead to underestimates of crowdout. Finally, itemization status (and hence sample inclusion) is an endogenous choice. Thus, tax data may produce sample-selection bias.

The reliability of tax data is also subject to question. The fear of prosecution may induce taxpayers to underreport legitimate giving when it is inadequately documented. On the other hand, if prosecution is unlikely and penalties are small (realistic assumptions for modest exaggeration), taxpayers have a financial incentive to exaggerate their donations. The issue is an empirical one; using a specially audited sample to determine U.S. taxpayer compliance, Slemrod (1989) found that despite exaggeration, price and income elasticity estimates remain unbiased.

The National Survey of Philanthropy (NSP) (Morgan, Dye, and Hybels, 1975) is an incredibly rich source of data with several unfortunate defects. NSP respondents report giving by type of recipient (religious organization, combined appeal, higher education, social welfare, etc.) for gifts of cash, assets, and time. They also report a panoply of demographic, socioeconomic, and attitudinal variables. Unfortunately, NSP data are available from only one year, ruling out panel-data estimation techniques. The usable sample is small (506 respondents), yielding poor estimates of average giving in some states. Finally, NSP donors appear atypical when compared with other surveys (Jencks, 1987).

Steinberg (1983, 1984) employed data on allocations to specified services by local branches of United Way of America on the theory that this would be a good proxy for average donations in each community. United fundraising organizations such as United Way act as intermediaries between donors and recipient charities, so allocations must roughly accord with the wishes of donors or else donations would dry up (Rose-Ackerman, 1980). Unfortunately, one cannot confidently assert that this proxy has the same mean as the variable it approximates. If expected United Way allocations are a constant fraction of total donations, so:

Total donations = k United Way allocations + ε; k > 1
then the coefficient on donations in the government spending equation will be too large by a factor of *k*, while all coefficients in the donative equation will be too small by the same factor. If, instead:

Total Donations = k + United Way allocations + ε; k ≥ 0
then no such bias would occur, although the usual "bias toward zero" caused by noise would still occur. The true proxy structure is unknown, so the validity of estimates produced from this data set cannot assessed.

A radically different approach was taken by Schiff and Weisbrod (in progress), who used data from the tax form filed by recipient nonprofit organizations (form 990). Clearly, this type of data allows a richer understanding of crowdout. Unfortunately, analysis is complicated by three types of problems. First, available data are not categorized properly. Form 990 combines gifts, grants and contributions in one category, and the measure of sales does not distinguish sales of private goods to the public from contracting-out type sales of public goods to the government. Surveys of governments allow some correction for the latter factor, but these surveys combine contracting-out payments to for-profit firms with those to non-profits, a limitation which is serious for some programs (such as medicaid).

Second, this 990 data is very "dirty". Tax authorities did not carefully audit reports or even insure that the forms were filled out completely. When data were transferred to tape, missing data was coded as if it took a value of zero. Both these problems have been reduced in more recent 990 tapes, which await exploitation by researchers.

APPENDIX II: CONSTRUCTION OF PRICE VARIABLES

Donations and government spending depend upon prices as well as each other. In the reduced-form models of joint crowdout, every price belongs in every equation. Typically, data are somewhat collinear (because many different prices all depend upon the voter/donor's marginal tax rate). In any case, it is difficult to construct appropriate measures of price.

For U.S. itemizers, the price of giving money is unity minus the taxpayer's marginal tax rate. This is because these taxpayers can subtract contributions from income before applying the tax rate. Others face a price of unity. State income taxes modify this price in a straightforward but tedious way.

Unfortunately, this price measure is endogenous – large gifts can cause the price to rise. Three solutions to this problem have been implemented in the literature on taxes and giving. The first, initially proposed by Feldstein (1975), is to use the so-called "first-dollar price" – unity minus the hypothetical marginal tax rate if donations had been zero. Most crowdout studies have used this measure. Logically, the measure must be extended in models of joint crowdout (as in Lindsey and Steinberg, 1990) for endogenous state taxes are also deductible and also affect the donor's marginal tax rate.

Reece and Zieschang (1985) took a more sophisticated approach. They explicitly modeled the kirks in the donor budget constraint due to progressivity, deductibility, and endogenous itemization status and estimated a maximum-likelihood model. Their procedure would require similar extension to properly model joint crowdout. The Reece and Zieschang procedure is quite labor-intensive, and no one has applied it to crowdout.

Feenberg (1987) pointed out an additional problem applicable to some cross-sectional studies. Sample variation in conditional prices may be due solely to unobserved taste variables. Consider two donors of equal income (before deductions) and equal non-charity deductions. If their tax rates differ, it can only be due to their differing tastes for giving, which push them into different tax brackets. If their non-charity deductions were free to vary, the same problem infects these deductions. Using other control variables to hold tastes constant can only remove sample variation in price at each income level, leading to perfect collinearity between the price and income variables.

Both problems are solved by inclusion of state taxes in an interstate sample or by a time-series sample encompassing changes in the rate structure. However, endogeneity is not entirely eliminated. Feenberg's solution was to use first-dollar price, including state tax effects, as an instrumental variable. This approach has merit, but leads to large estimated standard errors for all but the largest samples.

The price for gifts of appreciated assets also involves the donor's marginal tax rate, but it is more complicated due to interactions with capital gains taxes. Actual calculation of the price depends upon how long the asset would have been held in the absence of donation, which cannot be calculated without many behavioral assumptions. For details of the approaches tried, see Clotfelter (1985).

Gifts of time involve a sacrifice of the marginal value of that time. For employed workers who are not constrained in their choice of hours, this value is the after-tax wage rate, regardless of itemization status. If volunteers are motivated by future returns (as volunteering develops or certifies job skills for future employment), the price is more complicated.

In Schiff's work, alone and with me, these complications are, of necessity, omitted from the price variable (indeed, the wage rate is estimated from sample information, not directly measured). Other studies of crowdout neglect volunteering entirely.

The price of state government spending depends upon the political model. In my 1987 paper, I assumed that each voter votes as if he were decisive. The political process selects a decisive voter, who considers the marginal cost to himself of increasing total expenditures on the good by one dollar, i.e. the voter price. This voter price could, in theory, be constructed from information on state population, state and federal tax codes, and the simple crowdout parameter.

No existing study has included the simple crowdout effect in the voter price variable. This omission is justified if one is willing to assert that the magnitude of simple crowdout doesn't vary across states (an implicit assumption whenever a single crowdout parameter is estimated for the whole cross-section). In this case, we have omitted a component of price which doesn't vary across the sample, so that the price coefficient is biased only by a scaling factor and other coefficients are unbiased. Alternative assumptions entail a quite difficult estimation procedure, for one would have to appropriately incorporate an estimated parameter from part of the system as a control variable in another part.

To implement a voter price measure containing the remaining factors, one needs to identify the decisive voter. The tradition is to identify the median *income* voter as decisive. However, this tradition is justified only when many restrictive conditions hold. Thus, Lindsey (1987) explored several alternatives which were extended to crowdout in Lindsey and Steinberg (1990). Each taxpayer was assigned a price equal to unity minus the marginal federal tax rate for itemizers and unity for nonitemizers. A weighted average of these prices was constructed for each state and year, where weights reflected two factors: family size, and likelihood of voting. Family size is important because married couples filing jointly represent two potential voters, not one. The likelihood of voting was imputed from exit poll information on voter participation rates by age and income class. Finally, the voter price was adjusted to reflect the effect of open-ended matching grants (for AFDC and medicaid) on effective price.

As an alternative, we employed a weighted *median* voter price, rather than a weighted mean. This measure reflects the traditional models of political decision-making in a referendum, but adjusts for non-voting. In all our regressions so far (again, work is still progressing here), the weighted median measure outperformed the weighted mean measure.

COMPETITION BETWEEN FOR-PROFIT AND NONPROFIT ORGANIZATIONS IN COMMERCIAL MARKETS*

by

Jerald SCHIFF

Fiscal Affairs Department

International Monetary Fund

and

Burton WEISBROD

Center for Urban Affairs and Policy Research

Northwestern University

Introduction

Competition between nonprofit and for-profit firms, while not a new phenomenon, has become the focus of increased interest in recent years. Nonprofit organizations (NPOs), faced with declining support from government and unable to increase private giving significantly, appear to have increasingly turned to commercial activities[1] traditionally performed by for-profit firms. This growing inter-sectoral competition has, however, been subject to relatively little economic analysis. Those economists that have examined the competition be-

---

*   This paper was completed prior to the time that Schiff joined the Fund, and the opinions expressed do not necessarily reflect those of the IMF.
1   By "commercial" we mean output that is sold directly to consumers, as opposed to being financed, at least in part, by donations, and that provides no significant external benefits.

tween nonprofit and for-profit firms have focused primarily on the issue of whether the various tax and other advantages received by nonprofits[2] provide them with unfair advantages[3]. Congressional hearings (House Ways and Means Committee, June-July 1987) have also provided a forum for debate over this issue of "unfair competition".

In this paper, we examine an NPOs decision of whether or not to undertake commercial activities in competition with for-profit firms, and show how government tax and spending policies will influence this decision. We specifically consider the impact and desirability of current tax advantages offered to NPOs engaged in commercial activities, and conclude that inefficiencies introduced by the preferential treatment of nonprofits engaged in commercial activities may be more important than any inequities brought about by such treatment. These inefficiencies are of two types: (1) commercial activities which do not generate external benefits are subsidized, and (2) subsidies to the activities of NPOs that do provide external benefits are based on the ability of organizations to generate commercial profits, and so cross-subsidize their primary nonprofit activities, rather than on external benefits generated by the nonprofit activities.

The model, based on James (1983), hypothesizes that nonprofit managers receive disutility from commercial activities, but may nevertheless engage in them in order to cross-subsidize their preferred nonprofit activities. Approaching the behavior of the NPO in this way sheds light on several issues not addressed by more standard models. For instance, we predict that cutbacks in government support for a nonprofit organization would cause the NPO to pursue commercial profits more vigorously, and present evidence to support this view. On the other hand, the typical model, which does not allow for the NPOs distaste for commercial activities, would predict that nonprofits would always attempt to maximize profits from commercial activities, regardless of the level of support received from government. In addi-

---

2   Nonprofit organizations in the United States do not pay corporate income tax unless income is generated by an activity that is unrelated to the organization's tax-exempt purpose (see text for discussion). In addition, nonprofits are generally exempt from state and local property taxes as well as some sales taxes. They also receive various other advantages, such as lower postal rates.

3   For exceptions, see Hansmann (1981, 1989), Rose-Ackerman (1982) and Steinberg (1988).

tion, we provide a plausible explanation for the coexistence of NPOs and for-profit enterprises in the same industry; previous analyses have either ignored this issue, or presented explanations with a "knife-edge" quality.

We present our model of the behavior of an NPO in Section 1, and extend it to consider long-run equilibrium in a nonprofit industry. In Section 2, we present econometric evidence in support of the model. Following that, in Section 3, we examine competition between nonprofit and for-profit firms, and consider the impact and desirability of preferential tax treatment of NPOs. We close with a discussion of policy implications in Section 4.

1   A Model of The Nonprofit Firm

There is no consensus among economists regarding the objective function of NPOs. Because the nondistribution constraint[4] legally prohibits a nonprofit firm from distributing profits to its owners, the firm is generally not modelled as a profit-maximizer. Among the hypothesized maximands in the literature are disguised profits (discretionary spending), output quantity and quality and various inputs, such as staff size[5]. The objective function we employ, to be described below, allows us to focus specifically on a nonprofit organization's choice between producing the output for which it received its tax-exempt status – which we refer to as its "nonprofit" output – and a "commercial" output[6].

Assume that an NPO – which we identify with its "manager" – has a well-defined objective function defined over its various activities. In this model, the firm can produce either nonprofit or commer-

---

4   See Hansmann (1981) for a discussion of the non-distribution constraint.

5   For instance, Mique and Belanger (1974) model nonprofit bureaus as maximizers of an objective function defined over discretionary spending and output. Newhouse (1970) hypothesizes a nonprofit hospital that maximizes a combination of output quality and quantity. Williamson (1964) views nonprofits as maximizers of staff size.

6   The output referred to as "commercial" may be legally tax-exempt. We use the terminology to distinguish between the activity for which the NPO received tax-exempt status and other, perhaps related, activities. For instance, a university bookstore might be legally exempt, but for the purposes of this model, it would be considered commercial.

cial output. Commercial output is sold at an exogenous market price, p, while nonprofit output is financed by donations, and perhaps by profits from commercial activity. In addition to producing output, NPOs can spend some of their resources soliciting for donations. We assume that the nonprofit manager receives positive utility from producing the nonprofit output, but negative utility from engaging in commercial activity. This is consistent with the claim of nonprofit organizations that the output for which they receive tax-exempt status provides their *raison d'être* and that they view their commercial activities as, at best, necessary evils.

The objective function is maximized subject to the constraint that the firm break even[7]. We write the NPO's maximization problem as:

Maximize $U(z, x)$ subject to

$$D(z, x, S) + px - C(z, x) - S = 0$$

where z is the exempt output and x is a commercial good that the nonprofit may sell at exogenous market price p. We assume, as noted, that $U_z > 0$, but $U_x \leq 0$.

Donations, D, may come either from private sources – largely individuals, but also foundations and corporations – or from government, e.g. in the form of grants. Donations are assumed to potentially depend on both exempt and commercial output levels as well as solicitation expenditures, S. It is assumed that $D_z \geq 0$, $D_s \geq 0$ and $D_x \leq 0$. We might expect donations to fall as the commercial output of a nonprofit organization increases since, in a world of imperfect information, donors may view the fact that an organization engages in commercial activity as a signal that the quality of nonprofit output is low. Concern is sometimes expressed that engaging in commercial activities causes nonprofits to "lose sight of their charitable mission".

The firm's cost function, $C(z, x)$, is specified as a joint cost function in order to allow for economies of scope. For example, universities may be able to produce certain types of research more cheaply than for-profit firms because universities produce the research jointly with graduate instruction.

---

7   A surplus may be accumulated in any given period, but in the long run all revenue must be spent. Thus, in a single period model, the firm must break even.

1.1 Comparative Static Results

Previous analyses of nonprofit competition with for-profit firms have generally assumed that the nonprofits behave as profit-maximizers in the commercial activity. The implications of the model presented here are, however, quite different. First order conditions imply that, because the nonprofit manager receives positive utility from producing the nonprofit output, the firm will produce its nonprofit output beyond the profit-maximizing level, to the point at which $Dz + Uz/\lambda = Cz'$ where λ is the marginal utility of income. On the other hand, the organization will take less than full advantage of the profit-making potential of the commercial activity, both because the manager dislikes producing commercial output ($Ux \leq O$) and because donations may be adversely affected by commercial activity ($Dx \leq 0$). The NPO will produce x to the point at which $p + Dx + Ux = Cx$ using profits earned to cross-subsidize exempt activity[8]. So, for instance, if a museum views sales of postcards at its shop as a less preferred commercial activity, it will sell fewer than the profit-maximizing number of cards. However, it may sell some postcards to generate revenues for preferred artistic activities[9].

It can be shown[10] that, in the context of this model,

$\partial z/\partial D > 0$, $\partial x/\partial D \leq 0$, $\partial z/\partial p > 0$, and $\partial x/\partial p$ either > or < 0. This implies, first, that changes in government policies that affect donations to NPOs, either directly or indirectly, will influence the extent of nonprofit competition with for-profit firms. The fall in D acts, in effect, as an inward shift of the nonprofit manager's budget constraint, causing the organization to pursue less favored revenue sources. While the profits earned from increased commercial activities will be used to cross-subsidize nonprofit output, x, these profits will not fully offset the decline in D. In particular, the reductions in government support of the nonprofit sector in the 1980s would be expected to increase this competition[11].

---

8   The objective function could be expanded to include discretionary spending (i.e. disguised profits); in this case some of the commercial profits would be diverted to such spending.

9   Another example, offered by James (1979), the subsidization by universities, from profits earned from undergraduate education, of research and graduate education.

10   For a derivation of this and following results, see James (1983) or Schiff and Weisbrod (1986).

11   Salamon and Abramson (1985) report, e.g., that excluding Medicare and Medicaid, nonprofits lost $49.5 billion in federal government support between 1982 and 1985.

The Tax Reform Act of 1986, which reduced subsidies to charitable donors − by reducing marginal tax rates and the number of itemizers, and by eliminating the deduction for charitable contributions by non-itemizers − would be predicted to have had a similar effect[12].

Another implication of this model is that price or cost changes in the commercial market may lead to "perverse" responses by nonprofit firms. A rise in the price of the commercial good (or a fall in the cost of producing the commercial good) may, by allowing greater profit per unit of x, induce the nonprofit firm to partly avoid the distasteful activity by cutting back on production of x. Profits from sale of x will, however, rise, allowing output of z to rise as well.

The comparative static results also indicate that a nonprofit organization will solicit for donations to the point at which $Ds = 1$; i.e. it will solicit in order to maximize net revenue raised[13]. Exogenous changes in donations may influence solicitation expenditures, as they do commercial activities, although the direction is uncertain. If a reduction in government grants, e.g., increases the marginal productivity of soliciting, Ds,' then soliciting will increase with cuts in D. However, if Ds falls with reductions in D, solicitations would fall.

1.2   Entry and Exit by Nonprofits

Thus far, we have simply considered the behavior of a single NPO. However, just as the existence of profits in the for-profit sector will induce entry, so should changes that make the nonprofit sector relatively more attractive induce entry into that sector[14].

Ignoring, for now, the possibility of "mixed industries" containing both nonprofit and for-profit firms, we can view entrepreneurs as choosing between entering either the nonprofit or proprietary sector. Suppose that all potential nonprofit entrepreneurs are identical.

---

12   Tax payments on unrelated business income have increased from $39 million in 1985 to $127.9 million in 1990 (unpublished data, Internal Revenue Service, Statistics of Income). Note, however, that this may reflect, in part, increased compliance rather than simply increased commercial activity.
13   Steinberg (1986) finds that, for three of the five nonprofit industries examined, Ds is not significantly different from 1, as the model predicts. Weisbrod and Dominguez (1986), however, find that NPOs appear to solicit beyond the point at which $Ds=1$.
14   For a more detailed analysis of long-run equilibrium in a nonprofit industry, see Schiff (1988).

They will enter the nonprofit sector if $U(z, x)$ exceeds the reservation utility level available in the for-profit sector, U^*, which will depend on the level of profits available[15]. If there is free entry into the nonprofit sector, then, long run equilibrium will occur when $U(z, x) = U^*$. Any change that reduces the ability of nonprofits to produce their exempt output, or increases their reliance on commercial activities – such as a fall in government support or a change in the tax treatment of donations by individuals – will lead to exit from the sector.

2   Empirical evidence

2.1   Data and Methodology

We turn now to examine econometric evidence regarding the behavior of nonprofit organizations in general and, specifically, the response of NPOs to exogenous shifts in their budget constraints. Utilizing tax returns (IRS Form 990) from the over 11,000 NPOs active in the social services sector[16] for at least one year between 1973 and 1976[17], we estimate equations for two categories of revenue received by these organizations: contributions, gifts and grants (CONTR) and sales and other receipts, such as investment income (SALES). Utilizing the zip code of each organization, we matched each observation with the state in which it is located, allowing us to estimate the impact of changes in various categories of state and local government expenditures on revenues received by NPOs. In addition, a third equation was estimated, in which the observations were the 50 states and the dependent variable was the total number of nonprofit social welfare organizations (ORGS).

---

15   It is consistent with our description of the NPO objective function to assume that the potential nonprofit entrepreneur would also receive disutility from producing commercial output in the for-profit sector as well. That is, U^* should be a function of x as well. We return to this point when we consider mixed industries, below.
16   We consider the social services sector to include NPOs aiding specifically the poor, handicapped or otherwise needy. The definition does not include, e.g., ordinary hospitals and schools, but would include schools for the blind.
17   All nonprofits were required to file Forms 990 if their revenue exceeded $5,000 for the year.

The government spending variables included in each equation were: cash transfers to individuals (CASH), vendor payments to private agencies for provision of social services (VENDOR), other state welfare spending (WELFARE), and local welfare spending (LOCWELF). In addition, the following explanatory variables were included in the CONTR and SALES equations: age of the organization AGE), solicitation expenditures (SOLEX), tax-deductible status (DEDUCT), mean household income in the state (INCOME), a proxy for the mean price of a contribution in the state (PRICE), state population (POP), percent of population over 65 (POP65) and under 18 years old (POP18), percent below poverty (POOR), and the number of competing social service NPOs in the state (ORGS). In the ORGS equation, the same variables, other than the organization-specific ones, were included.

While the data covers four years, the regression analysis uses values averaged over the four year period. This approach is employed for several reasons; first, because NPOs are not required to file a tax return for a given year by a particular date, returns from two NPOs in the same calendar year can encompass different time periods. In addition, the dependent variables CONTR and SALES take on a value of zero for a significant portion of observations[18]. Thus, Tobit estimation appeared to be a reasonable methodology to employ[19]; given the truncated nature of the data, it would be difficult to utilize the panel data to estimate a fixed-effects model with consistent estimates[20]. The ORGs equation is estimated by ordinary least squares.

Of particular interest here is the impact on NPOs in the social welfare sector of an exogenous shift in their budget constraints[21]. We proxy such a shift by changes in government purchases of social services from nonprofit social welfare agencies, VENDOR. We interpret such revenues as representing payment for the preferred, nonprofit, output and view cuts in such payments as exogenous to any single NPO. We would predict, based on the analysis above, that a cut in VENDOR would reduce social services provided by the nonprofit

---

18   For the four-year averages, CONTR took on a zero value for 38 percent of the observations, SALES 29 percent.

19   Note that it was impossible to determine how many of the zero values for the dependent variables actually represented missing data. Our methodology implicitly assumes that all zeros were true zeros, rather than missing data.

20   See Heckman and .Macurdy (1980) for a discussion of this issue.

21   For discussion of other results, see Schiff and Weisbrod (1986).

sector, and increase total commercial sales by the sector. In addition, the number of NPOs providing social services should fall, as reduced ability to provide nonprofit output, and increased reliance on commercial activities would make the nonprofit sector a less attractive alternative.

2.2 Results

The regression results largely bear out our expectations (see Appendix Table 1 for complete results). We turn first to the SALES equation, to examine the effect of a change in VENDOR on commercial activities. To interpret the results, it is important to recognize that VENDOR is aggregated at the state level, while SALES is at the organization level; i.e. we are estimating the impact of a change in state spending for vendor payments on a given NPO's sales. In addition, the SALES variable includes both sales to government – vendor payments – by a given NPO *and* sales of commercial output. The regression results indicate that VENDOR has only a small, and statistically insignificant, impact on total SALES – including vendor payments and commercial sales – by a typical NPO. This suggests that NPOs compensate for lost preferred revenue by taking more complete advantage of the potential for commercial sales. The coefficient on VENDOR implies that a reduction in vendor payments to social welfare NPOs of 10 percent, or $225 million in one year[22], leads to only a small reduction of approximately $20 million in total sales by the nonprofit sector[23]. Thus, it appears that NPOs increase other sales, a proxy for commercial activity, by approximately $205 million. This result is consistent with the view that commercial activity provides disutility for NPO managers, so that they pursue commercial sales only when more preferred revenue sources dry up.

Our analysis above suggests that following the decline in VENDOR, total output of the preferred nonprofit good should decline, notwithstanding the increased commercial activity. We proxy total nonprofit output by the revenue available to finance such output –

---

22   VENDOR includes payments under the Medicaid program, most of which go to organizations not included in the definition of the social welfare sector used here. An estimated 74 percent of VENDOR went to Medicaid during the period 1973-76; our estimate of the impact of a cut in VENDOR assumes that any reduction in payments would affect Medicaid in the same proportion.
23   This takes into account the indirect effect of VENDOR on SALES through the induced change in the number of organizations, ORGS.

vendor payments and private donations received plus profits from commercial sales, which are available for cross-subsidization. The coefficient on VENDOR in the CONTR equation is positive and significant, and indicates that the 10 percent decline in VENDOR ($225 million) would cause an additional fall in contributions received by the nonprofit sector of some $14 million[24]. Separate data on profits from commercial sales are not available but if even if we assume, for illustrative purposes, that profits are a rather high 20 percent of sales, the increase in cross-subsidy would be only $40 million. Thus, the offset to the $225 million loss in vendor payments is quite small – on the order of 15 percent – even though commercial sales appear to increase quite dramatically[25].

The reduction in financing for preferred nonprofit output and the increased reliance on commercial sales appears, as predicted, to make the sector less desirable for nonprofit entrepreneurs. The coefficient on VENDOR in the ORGS equation is positive and significant, and indicates that the 10 percent cut in VENDOR would reduce the number of social welfare nonprofits by 180, or approximately 2 percent[26]. However, even after the exit takes place, the remaining NPOs appear to be worse off than before the reduction in vendor payments; the regression results indicate that commercial sales increase, while revenues for nonprofit output – vendor payments, private donations and cross-subsidies from commercial profits – fall for the typical NPO. We would have expected exit to continue until the remaining NPOs were as well off as before any exogenous cut in vendor payments.

---

24   This fall in private donations as a result of the fall in Vendor payments may be due to the fact that government support of a nonprofit is seen by donors as an assurance that the nonprofit is of high quality. For a discussion, see Rose-Ackerman (1981) and Schiff and Weisbrod (1986).

25   It is possible also that the level of solicitation expenditures could also respond to changes in the level of vendor payments; this would affect further the level of resources available for provision of nonprofit output. In separate regression results, not reported here, VENDOR is estimated to have a negative but insignificant effect on solicitation expenditures.

26   Another interpretation of this result is that in states that have large nonprofit sectors, the government is able to rely more heavily on vendor payments.

3   Competition Between For-Profit Firms and NPOs

We have hypothesized that NPOs enter commercial industries in order to earn profits to cross-subsidize their nonprofit activity. This model has a number of implications for the efficiency and equity of nonprofit competition with for-profit firms in commercial markets. We turn now to examine more closely this issue of competition across institutional forms.

In order to examine the outcome of competition between for-profit firms and NPOs in commercial markets, we must describe the objectives of the two types of organizations. We have already described the NPO as receiving disutility from producing commercial output, x. It is typically assumed, on the other hand, that proprietary firms are profit-maximizers, so that their utility is unaffected by the type of output produced. In order to motivate the assumption that NPOs and for-profit enterprises have different objectives in the commercial market, imagine that there are two types of potential entrepreneurs, in unlimited supplies, one of which gets disutility from producing commercial output, and the other of which does not[27]. We would expect, in this case, that the for-profit sector, which is the locus of most commercial activity, would be dominated in long-run equilibrium by those who receive no disutility from producing x, as they would be willing to accept a lower rate of profit than would those with a distaste for commercial activity. That is, we would simply not expect to see nonprofits in commercial markets, and there would be no issue of "unfair competition". This, in fact, is the case in the typical commercial industries.

This analysis must be modified, however, to account for two factors that help to explain the existence of NPOs in commercial markets; first, that nonprofits have various tax advantages relative to proprietary firms and, second, that there may be complementarities in production or consumption between the nonprofit output produced by an NPO and its commercial good.

3.1   The Impact of the Tax Subsidy for Nonprofits

We focus here on the nonprofit subsidy in the form of exemption from corporate income tax. This exemption is not unrestricted; any profits from activities that are "unrelated" to the organization's ex-

---

27   More generally, one could imagine a continuum of potential entrepreneurs, with differing degrees of disutility from commercial activity.

empt purpose are subject to the unrelated business income tax (UBIT), which has a structure similar to the corporate income tax. However, we assume for the purposes of this analysis that the commercial activity of nonprofits receives the same preferential tax treatment as its exempt activity.

This is a close approximation to reality, for several reasons. First, compliance with the unrelated business income tax (UBIT) is believed to be poor[28]. Second, courts have generally given a broad interpretation to the "relatedness test", allowing much commercial activity to receive tax advantages. Third, there are a number of important exceptions to the UBIT, such as activities carried out for the convenience of a nonprofit's members. Finally, even if an activity is unrelated, ambiguities regarding the allocation of costs between exempt and non-exempt activities allow substantial avoidance of tax. In 1990, only 38,861 NPOs, or approximately 4 percent of all NPOs, claimed unrelated business income[29].

What is the impact of the preferential tax treatment of nonprofits engaged in commercial activities? Ignore, for now, the possibility of for-profit firms competing with NPOs in either the nonprofit or commercial markets. Since the corporate tax is generally viewed as either a tax on capital in the corporate sector[30] or a tax on corporate profits[31] we can view the nonprofit exemption from corporate taxation as an implicit subsidy to either nonprofit capital or profits.

Although pure profits taxes (or subsidies) are usually presumed to have no effect on output and prices, this would not be the case in the nonprofit sector. An exemption from a profits tax in the commercial industry would have an effect analogous to that of an increase in the price of the commercial good, discussed above. On the one hand, making commercial activity more profitable would, ignoring its disutility to nonprofit managers, increase such activity. On the other hand, the tax exemption allows nonprofits to produce any given level of nonprofit output at a lower level of production of the distasteful commercial good. The net effect is uncertain. The output of the

---

28   See Goodspeed and Kenyon (1988).
29   Unpublished data, Internal Revenue Service, Statistics of Income. Note, however, that commercial income earned by for-profit subsidiaries of NPOs are taxable, but would not be recorded as unrelated business income.
30   See, e.g., Harberger (1962).
31   See, e.g., Stiglitz (1973).

nonprofit output, however, will unambiguously rise in response to the increased profitability of commercial activity. The tax exemption would induce entry into the nonprofit sector although, in the absence of competition from for-profit firms, profits in the commercial activity could remain positive in long-run equilibrium; since NPOs have a distaste for producing commercial output, the existence of positive profits does not ensure further entry. If, alternatively, we view the tax exemption as a subsidy to capital in the nonprofit sector, commercial output could again either rise or fall, nonprofit output would increase and entry would occur. Profits may again be positive in the long-run[32].

Now suppose that entry into the commercial industry is opened to for-profit firms, which are subject to corporate tax. Whether these proprietary firms would be able to enter the x industry and earn positive profits, and so drive out NPOs, would depend on: (1) the size of the tax advantage enjoyed by NPOs, and (2) the extent to which commercial activities are distasteful to nonprofits. If tax advantages were small relative to the disutility of commercial activities for NPOs, then the profits available to potential for-profit entrants would be large compared with the size of the subsidy to nonprofits, and the industry would come to be dominated by for-profits. If, however, tax advantages were large and nonprofits were almost indifferent to engaging in commercial activities, NPOs dominate. However, the closer to completely indifferent the nonprofit managers were to commercial activity, the closer to zero would profits be driven by nonprofit entry; NPOs will act much like proprietary firms in commercial markets. A combination of strong distaste for commercial activities combined with large tax advantages would be necessary to allow substantial commercial profits to be earned by nonprofit firms, in long-run equilibrium.

3.2 Tax Advantages and "Unfair Competition"

We have argued that for-profit firms may, in some cases, be driven out of commercial activities in which nonprofits operate, due to differential tax treatment. In addition, long run equilibrium may be characterized by nonprofit capital owners earning positive profits. Whether, however, this situation is one of "unfair competition" or not is another matter. Note, first, that if capital is mobile between the nonprofit and for-profit sectors, then the long run impact of a subsidy

---

32   Other results, e.g. on the incidence of the tax, will differ depending on whether the UBIT is viewed as a tax on capital or profits.

to capital in the nonprofit sector should be to increase the return to capital in both sectors, much as the incidence of the corporate income tax is thought to fall on all capital. By this view, capital owners in the for-profit sector are better off with the nonprofit tax exemption than without it[33].

However, while capital owners as a whole may be made better off, it is plausible that those proprietary firms may be harmed that were initially engaged in commercial activities later taken over by tax-preferred nonprofits. Imagine for-profit firms in an industry in long-run equilibrium without tax preferences for nonprofits. Now suppose nonprofits are granted tax exemptions. If the for-profit firms are driven out – by no means a certainty, as discussed above the for-profit capital owners will be forced to find other uses for their capital. If they were initially earning positive profits, these capital owners will be made worse off, but it is difficult to see this as unfair. On the other hand, if they were initially earning zero profits, they will likely be no worse off in the new long-run equilibrium.

Note that one at least theoretic possibility is that the for-profit firms will take on the nonprofit form to receive the tax exemption. In many cases, however, this would not be a realistic alternative, since the commercial activity would receive an exemption only if undertaken in conjunction with some other primary activity for which the organization received exempt status. We would not, for instance, expect for-profit bookstores to become universities in order to compete with nonprofit university bookstores.

For-profit capital owners may have legitimate complaints regarding unfair competition when one considers adjustment costs. It may be difficult to move capital, particularly human capital, from one industry to another and the costs involved may be seen as an unjust burden. However, as Rose-Ackerman (1982) points out, if the possibility of nonprofit competition was considered, upon entry, by for-profit firms in an industry, then claims of unfair competition lose much of their strength, even if exiting the industry proves costly.

3.3 Tax Advantages and "Inefficient Competition"

Perhaps more important than any harm imposed on for-profit firms are the inefficiencies introduced into commercial activities by nonprofit tax advantages, if these advantages allow nonprofits to

---

33   This point is also made by Goodspeed and Kenyon (1988).

expand into commercial industries. These inefficiencies are of two basic types, one involving the commercial activity, the other the nonprofit activity[34].

The first sort of inefficiency arises from the fact that the tax exemption, which is designed to subsidize the production of the nonprofit good – which presumably generates external benefits – has the effect of also subsidizing commercial output, which presumably does not. Thus, we might expect the tax exemption to lead to the provision of more than the socially optimal level of commercial output. If the tax exemption allows NPOs to drive for-profit firms from an industry, then the price of the commercial good must be lower as a result of the exemption, implying that the exemption has increased commercial output. Note that, while the price of the commercial good may be lower even at a lower level of nonprofit production, since the tax exemption lowers production costs for nonprofit firms, this would imply that consumers would be rationed. In this situation for-profit enterprises could sell at a higher price to those closed out of the nonprofit market. In fact, this may help to explain the co-existence of NPOs and for-profit firms in a given market.

The second inefficiency is due to the fact that the tax exemption for the commercial activity leads to a less than optimal subsidy to the exempt activities of nonprofits. Nonprofit output should, in a first best world, be subsidized such that the marginal external benefit is equated across organizations. However, since NPOs in our model engage in commercial activities in order to cross-subsidize nonprofit activities, the tax exemption provides subsidies that increase with the ability and willingness of an organization to engage in profitable commercial activities. This need not bear any relationship to external benefits provided. Bittker and Rahdert (1976) argue that the commercial activities of nonprofits should not be taxed because all profits must eventually be used to produce the nonprofit output. Our argument suggests that, even if this is the case, granting tax advantages to nonprofits may not be desirable, as there may be more efficient ways to subsidize charitable output.

---

34   For other discussions of the inefficiencies arising from tax preferences given to nonprofits, see Hansmann (1989) and Clotfelter (1988).

3.4 Complementarities in Production and Consumption[35]

Our analysis thus far assumes that NPOs and for-profit firms produce commercial goods at the same cost and for which consumers are willing to pay the same price. Both assumptions may be relaxed.

One possibility is that, due to the non-distribution constraint, NPOs have less incentive to produce efficiently, and so will exhibit higher costs than for-profits for any given type of output. In this case, any inefficiency involved in subsidizing nonprofit commercial activity would be exacerbated. However, it is quite plausible that NPOs may produce certain outputs more cheaply than do for-profits, due to complementarities in production, and it may be precisely those commercial activities in which we find nonprofits.

Complementarities in production – economies of scope – occur when it is cheaper to produce commercial good x when nonprofit good z is being produced by the same firm than to produce x alone. Universities, for instance, may find it cheaper to produce applied commercial research than do for-profit firms because the universities can use low-cost graduate student labor, or because research is a joint product with other university activities, such as faculty scholarship. In this case, it is not the nonprofit form per se, but the relationship between exempt and commercial output that is key. Commercial research firms would, in effect, need to form a university, or merge with one, to enjoy the same economies of scope. Some recent joint ventures between commercial biotechnology firms and universities are consistent with such an expectation.

Economies of scope, then, may help to explain the pattern of commercial activity by NPOs. Such activity is not distributed randomly across industries. Hospitals do not go into steel production and social welfare agencies do not form airlines. Rather, they engage in commercial activities in which they may have advantages. Rose-Ackerman (1982) has argued that repealing the UBIT would have the effect of spreading nonprofit commercial activity across industries rather than concentrating them in the "related" industries. She argues that this would lessen any unfair impact on for-profit businesses. However, if economies of scope are an important determinant of a nonprofit's choice of commercial activity, then such "spreading" is not likely to occur.

---

35   For further discussion, see Weisbrod (1988), chapter 6, Steinberg (1988) and Hansmann (1989).

Nonprofits might dominate a commercial activity, even in the absence of tax advantages, if there are, in fact, economies of scope. For-profit firms, unable to enter the nonprofit industry, would also find themselves at a cost disadvantage in the commercial industry. Economies of scope do not, however, offer a rationale for subsidizing the commercial activities of nonprofits. Such a subsidy would not be necessary, since nonprofits would out-compete for-profit firms without tax advantages, and would still be inefficient, unless the activity generated external benefits.

One case in which it might be efficient to offer a subsidy to commercial activities of NPOs arises if they enjoy economies of scope, but face barriers to entry in the commercial industry. In this regard, Hansmann (1981) notes that the inability of nonprofits to raise equity capital may limit the growth of nonprofits.

Complementarities in consumption occur when consumers are willing to pay more for x when it is produced or sold jointly with z than when it is produced or sold alone. This might be due, for instance, to convenience of location-university bookstores, for instance, may be able to charge higher prices than other bookstores. A nonprofit affiliation may also act as brand name advertising-e.g. Planned Parenthood condoms[36]. Again, such complementarities imply that nonprofits may dominate a commercial industry even without tax advantages, but do not provide a rationale for preferential tax treatment.

3.5 Mixed Industries

This analysis has suggested that commercial activities will tend, in the long run, to be dominated either by tax-advantaged NPOs or for-profit firms. However, NPOs engaged in commercial activities typically co-exist with for-profits.

There are several possible explanations for this co-existence. One is that these industries are not in long-run equilibrium and that, if ever reached, this equilibrium would indeed be characterized by a single institutional form in each industry. A second explanation is that long-run equilibrium is characterized by the tax-advantaged NPOs earning just enough profit to make the distasteful commercial activity worthwhile, while for-profits in the same industry, without the subsidies, earn approximately zero economic profits. There is, unfortunately, little evidence on the relative rates of profit for

---

36   See Skloot (1987) for this example.

nonprofits and for-profits in the same commercial industries. In any case, this explanation has a "knife-edge" quality to it which is not particularly appealing. Third, it is likely that in at least some of the industries, nonprofit and for-profit firms are producing differentiated goods; in some sense, then, they are not really in the same industry.

This paper provides another potential explanation of mixed industries, which relies on -the negative utility provided to NPO managers by producing commercial output. As noted above, this disutility implies that even in the case in which NPOs can out-compete for-profit firms (i.e. charge a lower price) they may be un-willing to meet the entire demand for commercial output at the market price. In this case, for-profit enterprises may meet the excess demand, albeit at a higher price.

4   Conclusions and Policy Implications

We model NPOs as maximizing an objective function defined over preferred "nonprofit" output and distasteful "commercial" good. Nonprofits compete with for-profit firms in commercial markets, in order to cross-subsidize the nonprofit activities. NPOs increase (de-crease) their commercial activities when private or government do-nations fall (rise). They may also respond to price changes in the commercial markets in a perverse manner. We argue that tax subsi-dies provided to nonprofits can cause inefficiencies in both the com-mercial and exempt industries.

The primary policy tool for dealing with nonprofit competition in commercial activities is the unrelated business income tax, or UBIT. Nonprofits are required to pay corporate tax on income from activities not "substantially related" to their exempt activity. However, as noted, most nonprofit commercial income goes untaxed, and this may lead to inefficiencies. One way of attempting to avoid this would be to strictly employ the relatedness test as it currently stands. For an activity to be "substantially related" it must, according to IRS regu-lations, "contribute importantly" to the accomplishment of the ex-empt purpose. Thus, it is not sufficient that the commercial activity contribute in some way. Courts have, however, interpreted "contrib-ute importantly" in a rather loose manner[37]. In any case, even if the relatedness test was stiffened, inefficiencies would remain. Recall that, even in the case in which there are complementarities in pro-duction or consumption, there is no obvious rationale for subsi-dization of commercial output.

Alternatively, a "commerciality" test might be substituted for the current relatedness test[38]. This has the conceptual advantage of potentially eliminating subsidization of commercial output, although defining "commercial" is not likely to be much easier than defining "related" has been.

The current policy debate over the UBIT has been conducted in isolation from other issues involving the nonprofit sector, and this is unfortunate. Taxing more of the commercial income of NPOs would lead to a reduction in nonprofit revenue and production of the output for *which* the nonprofits are presumably granted tax-exempt status. Nonprofit leaders argue that their organizations have already lost much of their government support, and that removing the commercial source of revenue would cripple them further. However, if the levels of certain nonprofit outputs are less than socially optimal, more efficient alternatives to nonprofit expansion into commercial markets should be sought. For instance, a tax on commercial profits could be combined with additional government subsidies directed to the exempt activity, or increased incentives for private donations. Each of these options likely involves some inefficiencies in practice; policy-makers need to compare the distortionary effects of various policy options to determine the second-best optimum.

REFERENCES

BITTKER Boris and RAHDERT George, 1976, "The Exemption of Nonprofit Organizations from Corporate Income Taxation", in *Yale Law Journal*, 85, 301-351.

BENNETT James and RUDNEY Gabriel, 1987, "A Commerciality Test to Resolve the Commercial Nonprofit Issue", in *Tax Notes*, September 14, 1095-1098.

CLOTFELTER Charles, 1988/89, "Tax-Induced Distortions in the Voluntary Sector", in *Case Western Reserve Law Review*, 39, 633-694.

---

37   See, e.g., St. Luke's Hospital of Kansas City v. U.S., 80-2 USTC 9533 (W.D. Mo. 1980). Performance of routine laboratory tests for nonhospital patients of doctors on the hospital staff was ruled in that case to be related.
38   Bennett and Rudney (1987) suggest this.

COPELAND and RUDNEY Gabriel, 1986, "Business Income of Nonprofits and Competitive Advantage: Part One, in *Tax Notes,* November 24, 747-756.

GOODSPEED Timothy and KENYON Daphne, 1988, "The Economic Effects of the Tax-Exemption Granted Nonprofit Firms and the UBIT", unpublished draft, Office of Tax Analysis, U.S. Treasury.

HANSMANN Henry, 1981, "The Rationale for Exempting Nonprofit Organizations from Corporate Income Taxation", in *Yale Law Journal,* 91, 54-100.

——, 1989, "Unfair Competition and the Unrelated Business Income Tax", in *Virginia Law Review* 75, pp. 605-635.

——, 1980, "The Role of Nonprofit Enterprise", in *Yale Law Journal,* 89, 835-899.

HARBERGER Arnold, 1962, "The Incidence of the Corporation Income Tax", in *Journal of Political Economy,* 70, 215-240.

HECKMAN James and MACURDY Thomas, 1980, "A Life Cycle Model of Female Labor Supply", in *Review of Economic Studies,* 47, 47-74.

JAMES Estelle, 1978, "Product Mix and Cost Aggregation: A Reinterpretation of the Economics of Higher Education", in *Journal of Human Resources,* 13, Spring, 157-186.

——, 1983, "How Nonprofits Grow", in *Journal of Policy Analysis and Management,* Spring, 350-365.

MIQUE Jean-Luc and BELANGER Gerard, 1974, "Toward a general Theory of Managerial Discretion", in *Public Choice* 17, 27-43.

NEWHOUSE Joseph, 1970, "Toward a Theory of Nonprofit Institutions", in *American Economic Review,* 60, 64-75 .

ROSE-ACKERMAN Susan, 1980, "Do Government Grants to Charity Reduce Private Donations?", in *Nonprofit Firms in a Three-Sector Economy*, Michelle White, (ed.), Washington D.C., Urban Institute Press.

——, 1982, "Unfair Competition and Corporate Income Taxation", in *Stanford Law Review,* 34, 1017-1039.

——, 1987, "Ideals versus Dollars: Donors, Charity Managers, and Government Grants", in *Journal of Political Economy* 95.

SALAMON Lester and ABRAMSON Alan, 1985, "Nonprofits and the Federal Budget: Deeper Cuts Ahead", in *Foundation News*, March-April, 48-54.

SCHIFF Jerald, 1986, "Expansion, Entry and Exit in the Nonprofit Sector: The Long and Short Run of It", Program on Non-Profit Organizations (Yale University), Working Paper Number 111.

——, and WEISBROD Burton, 1986, "Government Social Welfare Spending and the Private Nonprofit Sector: Crowding Out, and More", November, unpublished.

SKLOOT Edward, 1987, "Enterprise and Commerce in Nonprofit Organizations", in Walter Powell, editor, *The Nonprofit Sector: A Research Handbook*, New Haven, CT.: Yale University Press, 380-396.

STEINBERG Richard, 1988, "Fairness and Efficiency in the Competition Between For-Profit and Nonprofit Firms", Program on Nonprofit Organizations, Yale University, Working Paper Number 132, June.

——, 1986, "The Revealed Objective Function of Nonprofit Firms", in *Rand Journal of Economics*, 17, Winter, 508-526.

STIGLITZ Joseph, 1973, "Taxation, Corporate Financial Policy and the Cost of Capital", in *Journal of Public Economics*, 2, 1-34.

WEISBROD Burton and DOMINGUEZ Nestor, 1986, "Demand for Collective Goods in Private Nonprofit Markets: Can Fundraising Expenditures Help Overcome Free-Rider Behavior?", in *Journal of Public Economics*, 30, June, 83-96.

WEISBROD Burton, 1988, *The Nonprofit Economy*, Cambridge, MA.: Harvard University Press.

WILLIAMSON Oliver, 1964, *The Economics of Discretionary Behavior: Managerial Behavior in a Theory of the Firm*, Englewood Cliffs, N.J.: Prentice Hall.

Appendix Table 1
Regression Results*

	Tobit Equations:[1]		OLS Equation:
	CONTR[2]	SALES[3]	ORGS[4]
AGE	2.33	31.70	—
	(3.83)	(8.43)	—
SOLEX	0.002	−0.002	—
	(18.62)	(2.08)	—
AGE*SOLEX	0.0000	0.0001	—
	(0.14)	(2.48)	—
DEDUCT	567.04	921.01	—
	(8.72)	(2.22)	—
PRICE	−4.21	−15.70	1.55
	(2.22)	(1.29)	(0.77)
INCOME	11.30	206.00	−6.13
	(0.81)	(2.27)	(0.58)
POP	12.00	30.50	45.77
	(1.60)	(0.64)	(7.58)
URBAN	0.29	3.05	−0.25
	(0.59)	(0.98)	(0.63)
POOR	3.23	9.77	−5.38
	(0.96)	(0.45)	(1.83)
POP18	−11.50	−5.33	1.48
	(1.62)	(0.12)	(0.25)
POP65	−1.23	38.60	7.41
	(0.21)	(1.00)	(1.61)
CASH	0.17	0.90	−0.07
	(2.88)	(2.41)	(0.78)
VENDOR	0.07	0.15	0.21
	(1.64)	(0.52)	(4.20)
LOCWELF	0.03	−0.08	−0.05
	(1.11)	(0.53)	(1.67)
WELFARE	−0.64	−4.03	−0.18
	(2.55)	(2.52)	(0.49)
ORGS	−0.27	−0.27	—
	(1.96)	(0.31)	—
CONSTANT	−325.00	−4430.12	−10.3
	(1.02)	(2.14)	(0.04)
Number of Observations	11316	11316	50
R-squared	—	—	0.96

*T-statistic in parentheses.
[1]Raw Tobit coefficients presented.
[2]Contributions, gifts and grants received by NPO (in thousands of dollars).
[3]Sales and other receipts received by NPO (in thousands of dollars).
[4]Number of social welfare NPOs in state.

TRANSACTIONS COSTS, UNCERTAINTY, AND NOT-FOR-PROFIT ORGANIZATIONS:
The Case of Nursing Homes

by

Alphonse G. HOLTMANN

and

Steven G. ULLMANN*

University of Miami

Introduction

A number of writers have recently suggested that transactions costs, particularly those costs associated with monitoring the uncertain quality of a service, account for the emergence of not-for-profit organizations as vehicles for providing education, health care, child care, nursing home care, and numerous other services (Krashinsky 1986; Weisbrod 1988,6). To see the nature of the problem, suppose that only for-profit organizations provide a service that can be either a high cost, high quality service or a low cost, low quality service. Further, suppose that sellers know the quality of the service, but consumers, who only purchase the service one time, cannot judge the quality until after they purchase the service. Finally, assume that some consumers demand each type of service and that their willingness to pay in each case exceeds the cost of providing the service. Then, the incentive of profit maximizing firms is to provide only low quality, low cost service to each customer. These

---

*   We thank our colleagues Dan Feaster, Pat Fishe, and Todd Idson for extensive comments on an earlier version of this paper. Support from the Institute for Health Administration and Research at the University of Miami is greatly appreciated.

actions drive high quality, high cost producers out of the market, causing a type of market failure predicated on lack of information. In short, these services reflect the classic characteristics associated with asymmetric information described by Ackerlof (1970).

Nonprofit organizations, which are forbidden by law from distributing profits, reduce the incentive for providers to behave in this opportunistic manner, providing a type of guarantee of high quality service to consumers and allowing the market to provide both high quality nonprofit services and lower quality for-profit services. It is worth noting that the low quality care provided by the for-profit homes serves a socially desirable function by satisfying the demand for that type of care. The point is that both types of care should be available.

While the above stereotype is relevant to the hospital industry, the child-care industry, and the education industry, it exemplifies many of the problems of the nursing home industry: the consumer rarely purchases the service, the quality of the service is difficult to determine, and the provider has more information about quality than the consumer. We believe that the dimension of service quality that nonprofit nursing-home patients are purchasing is the implicit guarantee against "disappointment" with the care purchased. Hence, patients with more access to information and patients with less need of quality guarantees will choose for-profit over not-for-profit care. Conversely, patients most vulnerable to opportunistic behavior will choose the higher cost (Bekele and Holtmann 1987; Ullmann and Holtmann 1985; Ullmann 1989) not-for-profit care.

Of course, nonprofit status is not a perfect signal, so everyone purchasing nonprofit care will not be completely satisfied with the care. In addition, proprietary firms too have an incentive to certify quality by differentiating their product (see, Williamson 1980), providing warranties, guarantees, and merchandize return assurances that reduce the consequences to the consumer of opportunistic behavior by the producer. When monitoring is expensive and service failure is extremely costly, as in the case of nursing home care, however, ex post compensation will often not be considered a sufficient remedy by the consumer. Nonprofit status of the producer, then, in some instances, may be the appropriate guarantee of service quality.

Depending on their personal characteristics, however, consumers face differing risks of exploitation from providers of nursing home services. For example, an alert patient who requires only aid in fixing meals may select a low cost for-profit nursing home, whereas, a severely disabled patient who is paying for care through a lifetime annuity may select a nonprofit nursing home. In this paper, then, we hypothesize that transactions costs associated with securing information on the quality of care not only account for the existence of not-for-profit nursing homes, but that they are important determinants of the types of consumers who "choose" a not-for-profit nursing home over a for-profit organization.

1   Theory

In order to formally analyze the last idea mentioned above, consider a consumer who is choosing between care in a not-for-profit nursing home Q_1 and care in a proprietary nursing home Q_2. For convenience, suppose that during a given period of time the individual could consume both types of care. Assume that each unit of Q_2 purchased generates an uncertain number of units of quality care, $Q^* = zQ_2$, where z is a random variable with expected value $Ez=1$. In the not-for-profit sector, then, both quality and quantity are certain and known in advance, though in the for-profit sector, quantity is known with certainty and quality is not (hence, the random variable "z"). The consumer attempts to maximize the expected utility function $EU(Q_1,Q^*)$ subject to the constraints $Q_1 \geq 0$, $Q_2 \geq 0$, and $p_1Q_1 + p_2Q_2 = B$, where B is income and the p's are prices. The utility function is assumed to be increasing and concave in Q_1, Q_2, and z. Generally, the standard assumptions about the utility function are assumed and the analysis can be generalized to the multiple good case, though the two good case is appropriate in our example. Assuming the consumer is a von Neumann-Morgenstern utility maximizer of expected utility, we can characterize the consumer's problem as maximizing the following:

(1) $L = EU(Q_1,Q^*) + \lambda (B - p_1Q_1 - pQ_2); Q_1 \geq 0$ and $Q_2 \geq 0$.

The first order conditions for a maximum are

(2) $\partial L / \partial Q_1 = E\partial U / \partial Q_1 - \lambda p_1 \leq 0$

$(\partial L / \partial Q_1)Q_1 = 0$

$\partial L / \partial Q_2 = E[(\partial U / \partial Q^*)z] - \lambda p_2 \leq 0$

$(\partial L / \partial Q_2)Q_2 = 0$

and $\partial L / \partial \lambda = B - p1Q_1 - p_2Q_2 = 0$

There are three possible solutions to this problem, shown in Diagram 1 as points *a*, *b*, and *c*. They are:

(3)

a) $Q_2 = 0$ and $Q_1 > 0$ with $E(\partial U / \partial Q_1)/p_1 > E(z\ \partial U / \partial Q^*)/p_2$,

b) $Q_1 > 0$ and $Q_2 > 0$ with $E(\partial U / \partial Q_1)/p_1 = E(z\ \partial U / \partial Q^*)/p_2$, and

c) $Q_2 > 0$ and $Q_1 = 0$ with $E(\partial U / \partial Q_1)/p_1 < E(z\ \partial U / \partial Q^*/p_2$

Diagram 1

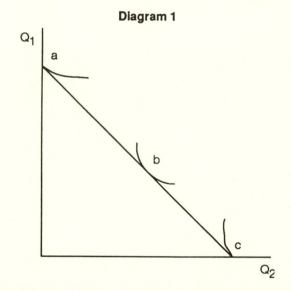

Noting that $E\ (z\ \partial U / \partial Q^*) = E(\partial U / \partial Q^*) + cov(z, \partial U / \partial Q^*)$, if the derivative of $\partial U / \partial Q^*$ with respect to z is negative (as the notion of diminishing marginal utility assumed earlier implies), $cov(z, \partial U / \partial Q^*)$ will be negative. This covariance term can be viewed as the marginal risk premium associated with consuming care in a proprietary home. As the covariance gets smaller (approaching zero), the risk associated with the proprietary homes gets smaller and $E(z\ \partial U / \partial Q^*)$ gets larger. Thus, reduced risk in proprietary care could cause an individual to shift from a point like (a) in Diagram 1 – with only nonprofit care – to a point like (c) with only proprietary care (for a detailed discussion of the covariance term see: Hey (1981, 45) and MacMinn and Holtmann (1983)).

Anyone with perfect access to information might be characterized as being able to choose the average quality of service from the for-profit sector *(Ez = 1)* with certainty, thus enhancing the marginal benefits from services in the proprietary sector. In short, those with better information or little need for information will place less value on the implicit guarantee of the nonprofit home. Hence, individuals with better information, better monitoring skills, less need for complex services, a lower potential loss from opportunistic behavior, less ability to pay, and a lower aversion to risk are more likely to be found in for-profit homes. Again, the advantage of nonprofit homes is that they reduce the risk for the poorly informed, risk averse, high income, more seriously ill patients, who are, therefore, more likely to be found in these homes.

2   Empirical Analysis

To test our hypothesis that patients who cannot monitor the quality of their care are more likely to purchase care from a nonprofit nursing home, we use the 1985 National Nursing Home Survey, which contains a sample of 5,243 current residents, 6,023 discharged patients, and 2,763 registered nurses from the 1,079 nursing homes included in the survey (National Center for Health Statistics, 1985). The sample analyzed contains 4,374 residents for whom there is complete data on the characteristics used in our econometric analysis.

In this sample, 3,043 residents are in proprietary homes and 1,331 residents are in not-for-profit homes, which includes both voluntary homes and government managed homes. Unfortunately, the current survey does not separate the government homes from other nonprofit homes. The survey does, however, provide some summary statistics that suggest that nonprofit and government managed homes may not be too different, but that they are distinct from proprietary homes. For example, nonprofit voluntary homes and government managed homes both on average hire approximately nine registered nurses per hundred beds and proprietary homes on average hire about five registered nurses per hundred beds, suggesting that combining government and nonprofit voluntary homes may not severely distort our analysis. Further, per diem rates for private pay patients are $58.67, $66.37, and 68.27 for care in proprietary homes, voluntary nonprofit homes, and government managed homes respectively, demonstrating the similarity between government and nonprofit homes.

As we have suggested, we believe there are a number of factors that influence the individual's propensity to choose a proprietary nursing home versus a not-for-profit home, and this latent propensity is reflected in the dichotomous choice reflected in the market. Hence, we estimate a logit model, which constrains the probability of choosing a proprietary home to remain between zero and one. From the coefficients of our logit model, we can derive the probability of a person with particular characteristics entering a proprietary home by the equation:

(4) $P_i = 1/(1 + e - {}^{B_j x_j})$

where P_i is the probability of being a resident in a proprietary nursing home; e is the base of the natural logarithm; B_j is the vector of coefficients of the logit function; and X_j is a vector of characteristics of the nursing home residents.

Specifically, we estimate a version of the following general function:

Probability of For-Profit Choice =

f{marital status, living children, extent of disability, payment sources, living arrangement, mental health, monthly charge}.

To reflect marital status as an independent factor, we use a set of dummy variables that characterize the resident's marital status at admission as widowed, separated, divorced, never married, and married, the base group. We predict that married residents would have someone else who might monitor the quality of their care and, thus, would be more likely to be in a for-profit home than would those who were not married. This would be reflected in a negative sign for this set of coefficients. In this same vein, we enter another dichotomous independent variable to reflect the presence of children in the family. The base category reflects the presence of children, leading us to anticipate a negative coefficient for the variable No Child.

To reflect the degree of debility of the resident, we enter seven dummy variables reflecting the need for aid in achieving basic functions of daily living. As a basis group, we use completely independent residents. This base group is compared with those needing assistance in bathing, those needing assistance in bathing and dressing, those needing assistance in bathing, dressing and using the toilet, those needing assistance in bathing, dressing, using the toilet and walking, those needing assistance in bathing, dressing, using the toilet, walking and who are incontinent, and those who have all of the above debilities and need aid in eating. We anticipate that completely independent residents are most likely to be in a for-profit home, reflecting the low need for monitoring care, and we anticipate that those with debilities are more likely to be in not-for-profit homes. However, we have no reason to suspect that the probability of being in a not-for-profit home will rise monotonically with the number of the debilities. That is, we have no clear conception of the individual's production relationship between disability and need to monitor, though this would be a fruitful area for research. We predict a negative sign for each coefficient in this category.

We enter a set of independent dummy variables reflecting the method of paying for the resident's care. The private-pay patients form the base group, accounting for approximately 48 percent of the sample. Residents who have their care paid for by Medicaid account for approximately 43 percent of the sample, and residents who have their care paid for by Medicare account for about 5 percent of the sample. Each other category accounts for one percent of the sample or less.

We believe that private-pay patients are more likely than government supported patients to be high-income individuals and to have agents, perhaps their children, with high earnings. These higher income individuals, all else equal, are able to afford the higher cost nonprofit care that offers them less risk of being disappointed with their purchase. In addition, the patient's high-earning agent will be more likely to purchase the more expensive less risky care of a nonprofit nursing home than to endure the high time cost of monitoring their principal's care in a for-profit home.

Conversely, private-pay patients are less likely to be in not-for-profit homes than patients who have their care paid for by an annuity. Patients whose care is paid for by an annuity are more likely to expect longer stays, increasing their incentive to avoid risky, low quality care. Also, it is more costly for those who have assigned their property rights from an annuity to a nursing home to recontract for care elsewhere, leading annuity supported patients to choose the less risky nonprofit homes.

Religious organizations are, of course, directly involved in operating nonprofit nursing homes, so we would expect that on average support from a religious organization would greatly increase the probability that a patient would obtain care in a not-for-profit institution.

Medicare patients are likely to have short average lengths of stay because Medicare payments are restricted to post-hospitalized patients in skilled nursing homes, not covering chronic long-term health services. Thus, these patients are likely to have a short stay in the nursing home, which reduces their risk of bearing the cost of opportunistic behavior by the home's management, or they become eligible for Medicaid support, which means that they cannot afford high cost care. In either event, they are more likely to be found in a for-profit home.

A set of dummy variables was used to reflect the resident's living arrangements before entering the nursing home, with living in an individual residence forming the base category and accounting for approximately 60 percent of the sample. Those residents located in a short-term hospital before entering the nursing home account for approximately 38 percent of the sample. The other categories include a rented room, a retirement home, a facility for the mentally retarded, a short term psychiatric unit, a veteran's hospital, a mental health center, and a group home. We anticipate that those patients entering a nursing home from some type of hospital facility are more likely than patients entering from a private residence to be in a for-profit facility. Patients entering a nursing home from a hospital are likely to have the shortest stays in a nursing home, because they are recovering from minor illnesses or because they have terminal illnesses that require a short stay. Our hypothesis is that those with the shorter length of stay in a nursing home face less risk and they are, therefore, more likely to be patients in for-profit nursing homes. We see no clear difference between entering a nursing home from any of the non-hospital types of housing and entering from an individual residence, so we predict that these non-hospital housing variables will not be significant.

A set of four dummy variables reflecting the resident's perceived mental health was entered into the estimating equation. Using excellent mental health as the base, the other categories include good, fair, and poor mental health. Those least able to evaluate services are most likely to value the reduced risk of service in a not-for-profit nursing home, suggesting that these factors should carry a negative sign in our empirical estimations.

Finally, the monthly charge for each patient was entered into the model to reflect the price variable in our theoretical model. We anticipate that higher monthly charges will be associated with those patients in nonprofit homes. We know that nonprofit homes provide more costly services (Bekele and Holtmann 1987; Ullmann and Holtmann 1985; Ullmann 1989): they are more likely to have a registered nurse on night duty and have more experienced nurses providing care, for example. The more costly services are likely to reduce the risk of disappointment, leading to a greater demand for these services by those facing the greatest risk. Of course, price of the service is likely to be related to the debility of the patient, so to some extent these two sets of variables reflect the demands of patients with greater need to reduce the risk of disappointment in service quality. The average monthly charge for the sample of patients was $1,445.

In Table 1, we report the coefficients from the logit estimating equation in column (2), the logit coefficients adjusted to make them comparable to OLS estimates in column (3), and the logit model that excludes monthly charges in column (4). Standard errors of the estimates are given below each coefficient and the significance of each coefficient is given. In column (5), the proportions of the sample in each category are given. To make our logit estimates comparable to the OLS estimates, we multiply each logit coefficient by .25 and we multiply the logit intercept by .25 and add .5, a procedure recommended by Amemiya (1981, 1488). Though the linear probability model is not appropriate for our purposes, this adjustment has the advantage that the adjusted coefficients can be interpreted as the change in the probability of being in a for-profit nursing home that is associated with that characteristic.

Using equation (4) given earlier to calculate the probability of being in a for-profit nursing home, we determine that those with the base characteristics (married, children, excellent mental health, private pay patients, no debility, and previously living in a private home) and paying the sample's average monthly charge of $1,445 have approximately a 57 percent chance of residing in a private home. It is noteworthy that using the adjusted logit intercept shown in column (3) of Table 1 and weighing the adjusted coefficient for monthly charges by the average monthly charge, we also obtain an estimated 57 percent probability of these patients entering a for-profit home.

Again using equation (4), we calculate the probability of being in a for-profit nursing home for a resident paying the average monthly charge with the base characteristics, but paying by an annuity arrangement. In this case, the resident has a 20 percent chance of being in a for-profit nursing home or an 80 percent chance of being in not-for-profit home. This result, of course, is consistent with our hypothesis that those using an initial permanent payment plan wish to avoid possible exploitation and are more likely to "choose" a not-for-profit nursing home.

Calculating the probability of being in a for-profit home for those paying the average monthly charge and with the base group characteristics but previously residing in a short-term hospital, we see that this group of residents has a 69 percent chance of residing in a for-profit home. If, as we supposed, these residents are those recovering from a short-term illness before returning home, this result is consistent with our hypothesis that those giving little value to monitoring will choose proprietary care. Of course, it may be that terminal patients leaving a short-term hospital may require a nursing home's services for the remainder of their lives. The shorter the time such a patient resides in the nursing home, the less value the patient is likely to give to monitoring the quality of care.

Considering the thirteen coefficients and the intercept in column (2) that are significantly different from zero at approximately the 95 percent probability level or above, we see that most of the results are consistent with our hypothesis. Patients who pay for their care through an annuity, for example, are much more likely to be in a not-for-profit nursing home compared to other private-pay patients. Also, married patients, who are more likely to have someone to monitor their care, are generally more apt to be in a for-profit nursing home compared to those not currently married, though only those who never married have a significantly higher probability of being in a nonprofit home.

As we predicted, the coefficient for monthly charges in column (2) is negative and highly significant. Part of the influence of this price variable is, no doubt, related to the higher cost of services provided in nonprofit nursing homes. These high costs are often associated with patients who face high risks from exploitation. To see this, notice that the coefficients for debilities are negative and more significant in the regression (column 4) in which the patient's monthly charge is deleted.

Although we believe that most of the results reported in Table 1 are consistent with the idea that patients with a greater need for protection from opportunistic behavior by the nursing home managers will choose a not-for-profit nursing home, some of the results demand other explanations. For example, the significant coefficients associated with the resident's mental health suggest that those with worse reported mental health select for-profit homes, a result apparently inconsistent with our earlier propositions. It may be that mentally ill patients are not able to choose for themselves and that their proxies choose the lower cost care of the for-profit institutions. Though this would not be an unreasonable hypothesis, the data are not detailed enough to test such a position.

As the selection of care for mentally ill patients may not reflect their choice, selection of a nursing home may not reflect the choices of other types of patients. On the assumption that private patients' desires would most likely be reflected in the selection of a nursing home that they or their proxies choose, we created a subsample of private-pay patients on which to perform our econometric analysis. This sample contained 2088 patients of whom approximately 1,364 were in for-profit homes and 724 were in nonprofit homes. The results for this sample were essentially the same as those reported in Table 1, so the results are not reported.

3   Summary and Conclusion

Generally, then, we believe that our results support the notion reported in the recent literature that risk, uncertainty, and monitoring have a role in the choices made between not-for-profit and for-profit nursing homes. Generally, individuals who have the greatest demand for less risky care – individuals without a spouse, individuals supported by annuities, individuals with greater debility, and individuals having longer stays in the home, for example – have a tendency to choose a not-for-profit nursing home. Thus, our empirical analysis supports the hypothesis that the not-for-profit constraint is a signal of reduced risk from opportunistic behavior by providers. Though further research should increase our understanding of the role of nonprofit organizations in the market place, our results are consistent with the empirical findings of other scholars (Weisbrod 1988).

Table 1
Determinants of Choice Between Nonprofit and For-Profit
Nursing Homes

Variable (1)	Logit Model (2)	Adjusted Model (3)	Logit Model (4)	%N (5)
Intercept	1.2959a (.2179)	.8240	.5787a (.2054)	
Widowed	-.0782 (.0986)	-.0196	-.0852 (.0970)	.58
Divorced	-.1573 (.1703)	-.0393	-.1336 (.1666)	.06
Separated	.2751 (.3748)	.0688	.3049 (.3701)	.01
Never Married	-.3336b (.1384)	-.0834	-.3729a (.1357)	.18
No Child	.0226 (.0896)	.0057	.0349 (.0880)	.37
MH Good	.3054c (.1575)	.0763	.3044b (.1544)	.26
MH Fair	.3091a (.1540)	.0728	.3349b (.1511)	.38
MH Poor	.4168a (.1591)	.1042	.4196a (.1560)	.30
Pay M Care	.4981a (.1779)	.1245	.1882 (.1679)	.05
Pay M Aid Sk	.2227b (.1041)	.0557	.0442 (.1005)	.15
Pay M Aid Int	.4674a (.0860)	.1169	.5866a (.0843)	.28
Pay State	.6818b (.3706)	.1720	.8809b (.3659)	.01
Pay Other Gov.	-.0901 (.2842)	-.0225	.1067 (.2807)	.01
Pay Religion	-8.021 (22)	-2.005	-8.057 (22)	.001
Pay VA	1.7607a (.6072)	.4402	1.6241a (.5991)	.01
Pay Annuity	-1.641a (.6294)	-.4104	-1.206b (.6179)	.003
Pay None	-1.748a (.6275)	-.4369	-1.462a (.5992)	.003
Pay Unknown	.6866 (.5656)	.1716	.9648c (.5568)	.005

Table 1 continued

Pay Other	-.6771	-.1693	-.3798	.001
	(.9387)		(.9342)	
Debility 1	-.2738b	-.0684	-.4132a	.16
	(.1581)		(.1567)	
Debility 2	.0574	.0143	-.2217d	.28
	(.1548)		(.1521)	
Debility 3	.0339	.0085	-.2591c	.20
	(.1628)		(.1598)	
Debility 4	-.1895	-.0474	-.4599a	.15
	(.1648)		(.1620)	
Debility 5	.0531	.0133	-.2170	.05
	(.2147)		(.2108)	
Debility 6	-.1261	-.0353	-.4414a	.10
	(.1826)		(.1786)	
Rented Rm	-.1169	-.0292	-.0830	.07
	(.1382)		(.1364)	
Retire Home	.1580	.0395	.0901	.05
	(.1548)		(.1523)	
Retarded Fac.	-.2773	-.0693	-.1075	.00
	(.4556)		(.4573)	
Short-term Hos.	.5007a	.1252	.3989a	.38
	(.0797)		(.0776)	
Psychi. Hos.	.6497c	.1624	.6192c	.01
	(.3862)		(.3833)	
Va Hos.	.3834	.0958	.3989	.02
	(.4031)		(.3971)	
Mental H.C.	-.1290	-.0325	-.1107	.01
	(.4256)		(.4182)	
Resident Fac.	-.3568	-.0892	-.3495	.01
	(.3475)		(.3436)	
Monthly Ch.	-.0007a	-.000175		
	(.00006)			
N	4,374			

Superscripts a-d denote significance levels of 1%, 5%, 10% and 15%, respectively. Standard errors are given in parentheses.

REFERENCES

AKERLOF G. A., 1970, "The Market for 'Lemons'' : Quality Uncertainty and the Market Mechanism", in *Quarterly Journal of Economics*, 488-500.

AMEMIYA T., 1981, "Qualitative Response Model: A Survey", in *Journal of Economic Literature*, 1488.

BECKER G., 1965, "A Theory of the Allocation of Time", in *The Economic Journal*, 75, September, 493-517.

BEKELE G. and HOLTMANN A.G., 1987, "A Cost Function for Nursing Homes: Toward a System of Diagnostic Reimbursement Groupings", in *The Eastern Economic Journal*, April-June, 115-122.

HEY J., 1981, *Economics in Disequilibrium*, Oxford: Martin Robertson.

HOLTMANN A.G., 1972, "Prices, Time, and Technology In the Medical Care Market", in *Journal of Human Resources*, 7:2, Spring, 179-190.

HOLTMANN A.G., 1983, "A Theory of Nonprofit Firms", in *Economica*, 50, 439-449.

KRASHINSKY M., 1986, "Transactions Costs and a Theory of Nonprofit Organizations", in S. Rose-Ackerman (ed.), *The Economics of Nonprofit Institutions*, Oxford: Oxford University Press, 113-132.

MACMINN R. and HOLTMANN A. G., 1983, "Technological Uncertainty and the Theory of the Firm", in *The Southern Economic Journal*, 50, July, 120-136.

National Center for Health Statistics, 1985, *The 1985 National Nursing Home Survey*, Hyattsville, MD: National Center.

ULLMANN S. G. and HOLTMANN A. G., 1985, "Economies of Scope, Ownership, and Nursing Home Costs", in *Quarterly Review of Economics and Business*, 25:4, Winter, 83-94.

ULLMANN S. G., 1989, "Total Charges in the Long-Term Health Care Industry", Working Paper, University of Miami.

WEISBROD B.A., 1988, *The Nonprofit Economy*, Cambridge, Mass: Harvard University Press.

WILLIAMSON O., 1980, *The Economic Institutions of Capitalism*, New York, Free Press.

FINANCIAL VULNERABILITY AND ATTRITION AS MEASURES OF NONPROFIT PERFORMANCE

by

Cyril F. CHANG*

and

Howard P. TUCKMAN*

Memphis State University

Department of Economics

A growing number of researchers have become interested in the nonprofit sector in the last decade. Theories have been advanced regarding the reasons for the creation of the sector (Ben-Ner 1986; Douglas 1987; Hansmann 1986; and Weisbrod 1986), and what makes nonprofits grow (James 1983). Scholars have examined the historic development of the sector (Hall 1987), its management (Powell and Friedkin 1987; Young 1986), its scope (Rudney 1987; Hodgkinson and Weitzman 1989), and its finances (Chabotar 1989; Clervely and Nilsen 1980; Tuckman and Chang 1990). They have also explored the impact of the marketplace on organizations within the sector (Steinberg 1987 and Milofsky 1987), and the relationship of these organizations with the government sector (Salamon 1987). This growing body of thought has substantially increased public understanding of the nonprofit economy.

---

*   The authors acknowledge the partial financial support of the Avron B. and Robert F. Fogelman Academic Excellence Fund. They also wish to thank Cecelia H. Hilgert and Susan J. Mahler from the U.S. Internal Revenue Service for providing the data used in this paper, Dwight Means, Gaylon Greer and two anonymous referees for their helpful comments, and Pichu Tang for her research assistance.

Despite these contributions, problems persist with the measurement of nonprofit performance because, in part, of the difficulties inherent in the measurement of the output of the nonprofit organizations. For example, Kanter and Summers (1987) argue that it is difficult to measure whether nonprofits succeed in goal attainment because their services are "notoriously intangible" and hard to define. Economist's attempts to define a production function for nonprofits engaged in the provision of services are hampered by the lack of suitable output measures and by competitive conditions that do not give rise to output maximizing decisions. These problems are compounded by the absence of data bases that facilitate comparison among the diverse set of nonprofits that populate the sector (Hodgkinson and Weitzman, 1989).

This article explores two dimensions of the performance of nonprofit organizations; their ability to avoid direct program cutbacks in the face of financial downturns and their ability to survive. Our analysis begins with a discussion of the conditions under which an optimal distribution of for-profit and nonprofit firms occurs. A measure of performance, financial vulnerability, is presented along with a methodology for measuring vulnerability without the use of data on program outputs. A data base comprised of the tax filings of nonprofit organizations in the 1983 and 1985 tax years is used to identify the nonprofits most likely to be financially vulnerable to financial shocks and several measures of the finances of the vulnerable nonprofits are presented. In the process, insights are offered on the extent to which severe vulnerability exists in the nonprofit sector. A second measure of performance, attrition as a measure of the inability of nonprofits to survive, is then considered. A discussion of the link between vulnerability and attrition and data are then provided to contrast attrition in the for-profit and nonprofit sectors. The analysis ends with an exploration of the question of why relatively few nonprofit organizations expire.

1   The Optimal Size of Nonprofit and For-Profit Sectors

In a world populated solely by nonprofits, the optimal number of organizations is reached when the addition of one more nonprofit produces marginal benefits to society just equal to the marginal social costs of that nonprofit's operation. When this equilibrium is reached, the addition of yet another nonprofit diminishes social welfare more than it increases it, whereas attrition results in a loss of organizations that contribute more to society than they cost. In a world where both for-profit and nonprofit organizations exist, the criteria for optimality change. An optimal allocation is achieved between the sectors when the marginal social benefits per dollar of social cost of nonprofit production just equal the marginal social benefits per dollar of social cost of for-profit production.[1] Ben-Ner (1986; 95) argues that in such a world, a nonprofit will be formed when consumers' net gain from buying from a nonprofit exceeds the benefits of buying from a for-profit firm. Nonprofit organizations with a lower ratio of marginal social benefits to costs than those of for-profits will close down. The same would be true for for-profits with a lower ratio of marginal social benefits to costs than those of nonprofits. The expectation is that social efficiency will be achieved as organizations with relatively low ratios of social benefits to costs (the less efficient) go out of business while those with relatively high ratios (the more efficient) will expand.

The same set of optimality conditions prevail when the above world is complicated by the introduction of governmental organizations. Financial problems would cause organizations that offered low benefits relative to costs to diminish the services they provide. Ultimately, this would make them less attractive as vehicles for the delivery of services and attrition of these organizations would occur. To the extent that free exit is feasible, and that these organizations' performance is based on the benefits that they provide, an efficient allocation of resources across sectors would occur. In this world, financial vulnerability and attrition would be reasonable indicators of poor performance.

In the for-profit world, competition regulates the allocation of scarce resources. While some organizational structures (e.g., monopoly) and governmental intervention (e.g., patents) can obstruct this process for periods of time, competition eventually drives out inefficient for-profit organizations. The validity of this assumption is largely supported by substantive studies of industries over time (Scherer 1970).

It is less certain whether competition will drive out less efficient organizations in the nonprofit sector. In an insightful study of the literature dealing with this question, Steinberg (1987) argues that market structure plays an important role in affecting nonprofit behavior and performance. While Steinberg believes that no "monolithic" theory of nonprofit behavior can be paramount because the forces of competi-

---

1   Government can be accomodated in this «model» by requiring that it must also produce services up to the point where the marginal social benefit of one more dollar equals that in the other two sectors.

tion and regulation temper nonprofit behavior, he advances the theory that competition does impact on nonprofit actions. The lack of a profit motive not only enables nonprofits to provide social services in a trustworthy fashion, it can also fosters inefficiency. In markets where nonprofits and for-profits compete, however, "differing internal structures perform similarly in the production, marketing, and distribution of services."

Donations represent an obstacle to the efficient operation of nonprofits because they can be used to subsidize inefficient operations. Because it is not easy for society to identify the quantitative benefits that nonprofits produce, subsidized nonprofits can continue to operate even though they offer low social benefits relative to their costs. In part, this is because donors may lack the ability to know when they are subsidizing inefficiency. They may also be led to provide funds to nonprofits based on factors that have little to do with an organization's program outputs. For example, funds may be provided because this is a "prestigious" organization to fund, because a contribution provides access to a gala event or to a desirable social circle, and/or because the organization concentrates considerable resources on soliciting funds. In each of these instances, an organization's subsidies may be driven by considerations unrelated to efficiency. In these circumstances, there is little assurance that attrition will eliminate those nonprofits least effective in the delivery of services.

Similar problems exist with respect to the delivery of social services by government organizations. Many government programs with low benefit-to-cost ratios are funded for political reasons. In addition, output measurement problems contribute to the difficulties of evaluating the relative merits of various public programs. Consequently, attrition cannot be relied upon to insure an efficient allocation of resources between this sector and the other two. While government regulatory actions and competition among the three sectors can be shown to narrow the difference in the ways that organizations operate (Steinberg, 1987; Tuckman and Chang, 1988), the task of reaching an optimal allocation of resources across the three sectors remains illusive. In this world, measures of survivability are ambiguous measures of performance from the point of view of allocative efficiency and important from the point of view of nonprofit management (Kanter and Summers, 1987; Tuckman and Chang, 1990).

2   Measurement of Nonprofit Vulnerability

Performance measures can take several forms including but not limited to the extent to which nonprofits meet their goals, use resources efficiently, adapt to the environment in which they operate, and succeed in surviving. Kanter and Summers (1987; 158) argue that survival is a useful effectiveness standard for nonprofits because it indicates an ability to persist, to satisfy clienteles, and to weather crises. However, several limitations exist with respect to this measure: it is biased against newcomer organizations, provides no guide to short-term decision making, and ignores the impacts of a nonprofit's programs.

We believe that a performance measure can be devised that does not entail the use of output data and that implicitly captures the intent of a survival measure. This is premised on the assumption that most nonprofit decision makers prefer to avoid program cutbacks when a financial shock occurs. Our measure uses a set of logical assumptions to determine whether an organization is likely to be able to avoid temporary program cutbacks. Those organizations that can avoid cutbacks are judged to be financially healthy while those that cannot are treated as financially vulnerable. A financially vulnerable organization is then defined as one that lacks the ability to avoid cutbacks in the programs and/or services that it offers when a financial shock occurs.

We have recently developed a methodology for identifying such organizations (Tuckman and Chang, 1991). Our approach is based on the assumption that a finite number of ways exist to cushion the effects of a financial shock. By identifying these, and by providing operational measures to capture a nonprofit's position relative to its peers, we can provide a quantitative indication of the nonprofits likely to experience short-term program degradation and long-term attrition. Our methodology provides a more satisfatory way of evaluating nonprofit performance than the financial-ratio approach currently found in the literature (Chabotar, 1989; Cleverly and Nilsen, 1980). This is because the measure of vulnerability does not require the use of output data and it simultaneously takes into account several dimensions of a nonprofit's financial condition.

Four criteria are used to identify nonprofits that lack the ability to offset financial shocks. These involve whether an organization has access to equity, whether its revenue sources are diversified, whether it has high administrative costs, and whether it has positive operating margins. An organization's vulnerability is measured by whether it is in the bottom quintile of the sample with respect to the four criteria. For example, an organization that is in the bottom quintile with respect to one criterion is labelled "at-risk." Organizations that fall into the bottom quintile with respect to all four criteria are most vulnerable and are labelled "severely-at-risk." It is useful to define the four criteria in greater detail.

2.1 Inadequate Equity

A nonprofit's ability to temporarily replace revenues is affected by its equity or net worth. Equity is the difference between a nonprofit's total assets and total liabilities. Such equity can be held in restricted or unrestricted and in liquid or illiquid form. While restrictions on the use of equity can limit the extent to which a nonprofit can use its equity to offset financial shocks, a nonprofit's equity position is important in at least four ways. 1) Unrestricted liquid assets can be readily converted to cash to replace lost revenues. 2) Unrestricted illiquid assets can sometimes be used as collateral to secure temporary loans. This is particularly the case if such assets are held in transferable form. 3) A nonprofit may be able to alter the mix of services it offers so that a higher proportion of its program offerings can be funded through restricted funds.[2] 4) The presence of equity may make it possible to acquire funds from capital markets.[3] Our analysis uses the ratio of equity to revenue (E/R) to measure a nonprofit's equity position. The assumption is that a nonprofit with a large net worth relative to revenues has a greater ability to replace revenue than one with a smaller net worth.

2.2 Revenue Concentration

Revenue diversification is assumed to make a nonprofit less vulnerable. For example, a temporary decline in voluntary contributions to a Girl Scout organization is more easily absorbed if the organization can increase its cookie sales or hold a gala event than if it

---

2   For example, within limits, a nonprofit nursing home can fill its empty beds with indigent patients and finance this care from a restricted fund set up for charitable purposes.
3   Capital funds obtained from bond issues cannot be used to fund current expenditures but it is possible to reduce current operating costs with a bond issue. Existing properties may be refinanced or housing costs reduced by purchase of a building.

depends solely on its donors. Likewise, an art museum may be able to avoid reducing its hours of operation if it is funded by both local and federal contributions than if it must rely entirely on the federal government. This is because access to multiple funding sources enhances an organization's chances of being able to balance a gain in one revenue source against a loss in another.

To measure revenue concentration, an index similar to the Herfindahl index is constructed (Scherer 1970). The square of the percentage share that each revenue source represents of total revenue is summed to derive a concentration index for each nonprofit in the sample. This index captures both the number of revenue sources and the extent to which a nonprofit's revenues are dispersed among several sources.[4] A nonprofit with revenues from one source has a concentration index of one whereas a firm with equal amounts of revenues from multiple sources has an index close to zero.

2.3 Administrative Costs

When a financial shock occurs, a third recourse available to nonprofits is to cut their administrative costs. Our assumption is that such cuts are easier when a nonprofit has high administrative costs relative to other operating costs than when its administrative costs are relatively low. This is because organizations that have low administrative costs are already operating at a point where additional cutbacks are likely to affect the administration of their program. A consequence is that program output will suffer.[5]

2.4 Reduced Operating Margins

A nonprofit's net operating margin (defined as its revenues less its expenditures divided by its revenues) shows the percentage that its profits represent of its revenues. The larger this percentage, the larger the net surpluses a nonprofit can draw down in the event of a financial shock. Since such a shock reduces operating margin, this is an *ex-ante* rather than an *ex-post* measure of a nonprofit's ability to withstand financial adversity. An educational institution running a profit margin

---

4   The calculation uses five revenue sources: contracts, gifts and grants, program service revenue, membership dues, sales of unrelated goods, and investment income.
5   A nonprofit with slack is less vulnerable than one without. It is not necessarily more efficient.

of 10 percent is in a better position to absorb a decline in federal funds than one running a deficit of 3 percent. Hence, operating margin is a useful indicator of ability to withstand revenue downturns without immediate cutbacks in program services.

3   Results for the 1983 and 1985 Taxable Years

3.1   The Data

Data are available from the tax returns (Form 990s) which charitable nonprofit organizations (Section 501c(3) organizations) filed with the Internal Revenue Service (IRS). The database is a random sample of organizations with gross receipts above $25,000 and assets under $10 million in the 1983 and 1985 taxable years. Also included are all nonprofits with assets above $10 million, and this biases the sample toward wealthy nonprofits (Hodgkinson and Weitzman, 1989).

The 1983 sample contains 4,370 nonprofits while the 1985 sample contains 6,168 organizations. The organizations in these samples represent a wide range of different types of nonprofits. A six-category typology is used to classify the organizations. (1) The *religious category* includes the religious institutions that report their activities to the IRS. (2) *Educational institutions* include preschool, elementary, secondary, trade school, vocational, and higher nonprofits. (3) *Health Care Institutions* include clinics, free-standing institutions, hospices, mutual benefit hospitals, nursing homes, etc. (4) *Charitable Institutions* consist of nonprofits primarily financed by public contributions. Also included are nonprofits set up by governments to dispense charitable services. (5) *Support Organizations* consist of educational and health support nonprofits such as United Way and hospital foundations set up to support the activities of their beneficiaries. (6) *Other Organizations* include government nonprofits, consumer testing nonprofits, and unidentified organizations.

3.2   The Most Vulnerable Nonprofits

Table 1 presents the number (columns 1 and 2) and percentage (columns 3 and 4) of nonprofits in each of the six categories. The percentage of organizations found to be "at-risk" is shown in columns 5 and 6. This is derived by first determining the nonprofits in each of the six categories in the bottom quintile of the entire sample with respect to at least one of the four criteria. These numbers are then divided by the total number of "at-risk" nonprofits shown at the bottom of each column. Columns 7 and 8 give the percentages of "severely-at-risk" in each category. These are the nonprofits in the bottom quintile with respect to all four criteria. The last line for columns 7 and 8 indicates the total number of most vulnerable nonprofits in the sample.

Several interesting findings emerge from Table 1. First, the number of "at-risk" nonprofits is substantially greater than the number "severely-at-risk." Over 41 percent of the nonprofits in 1983 and 40 percent in 1985 fell into the bottom quintile with respect to at least one of the four criteria. In other words, 4 out of every 10 nonprofits in the sample had at least one source of potential financial vulnerability. In contrast, only 1 nonprofit in every 1,000 was in the bottom quintile of the sample with respect to all four criteria in both 1983 and 1985.

Additional insights can be gained by exploring the question of whether the risk factors experienced by nonprofits are independent of one another. Let us first assume that the four vulnerability criteria are independent. That is, a nonprofit in the bottom quintile with respect to operating margin is no more likely to fall in the bottom quintile with respect to revenue diversification than a nonprofit with an operating margin above the bottom quintile. Similarly, one in the bottom with respect to administrative costs is no more likely to be in the bottom with respect to diversification than one with high administrative costs. The expectation is then that the percentage of "severely-at-risk" nonprofits will be 0.16 percent ($0.0016=0.2^4$). This is confirmed by the percentages observed in our data: 0.11 percent ($0.0011=5/4730$) in 1983 and 0.16 percent ($0.0016=10/6168$) in 1985. If the nonprofits had not been independent and the same nonprofits were in the bottom quintile with respect to the four criteria, the percentage would have been 20 percent (0.2). Our finding of such a low percentage of "severely-at-risk" nonprofits indicates that the four venerability criteria are independent. Most nonprofits have at least some ways to temporarily cushion their operation from a particular financial shock. Measured by the four criteria, the results presented in Table 1 suggest that the nonprofits in the sample perform well with respect to financial vulnerability.

Comparison of the "at-risk" nonprofits between the two years reveals several additional findings. For example, the health care category has a larger than expected (based on the distribution in columns 3 and 4) percentage of institutions in the "at-risk" category in both 1983 and 1985. In contrast, the percentages for educational institutions are substantially lower than expected. Charitable institutions and support nonprofits are more likely to be "at-risk" than their representation in the sample while religious and other nonprofits are not. Clearly, substantial differences exist in the financial vulnerability of different types of nonprofits.

Comparisons of the percentages of "severely-at-risk" by category with the overall percentages for the sample also suggests that differences exist in vulnerability across nonprofit types. Religious and support nonprofits tend to be overrepresented while educational institutions, charities, and other nonprofits are underrepresented. Vulnerability, as measured by the four criteria, is not equally likely within the six categories.

Table 1 suggests that most nonprofit organizations have been successful in deploying resources to provide at least some protections against temporary program cutbacks. However, a sizable percentage of nonprofits (40 percent of total) are vulnerable with respect to at least one of the four criteria.

3.3   A Financial Profile of "At-Risk" Organizations

Table 2 shows mean values and standard deviations of select financial measures for the "at-risk," and "severely-at-risk" groups in the two taxable years. These financial ratios are selected to examine the extent to which the criteria effectively identify vulnerable nonprofits. Several findings are of interest. First, the average revenue of the "severely-at-risk" group is substantially lower and the average revenue of the "at-risk" group is slightly higher than the sample average. Comparison of revenues for the two years shows that the average revenue of the "severely-at-risk" group is relatively higher in 1985 than in 1983 whereas the reverse is true for the "at-risk" group. Second, in both years the equity position of the average nonprofit improves from the beginning of the year to the end. However, the improvement in the equity position of the "at-risk" group is less than for the average nonprofit in the data base. These results suggest that vulnerable nonprofits do not have large equity and they highlight just how low the equity of "severely-at-risk" nonprofits is.

Third, the debt to asset ratio is substantially higher, on average, for the "severely-at-risk." This is consistent with the findings of financial ratio studies (Chabotar 1989). In both years, the ratio is over 3 times as large for the "severely-at-risk" than for the sample as a whole. Fourth, the current ratio data suggests that the "severely-at-risk" lack a strong cash position. In both years, the average current ratios of vulnerable organizations are substantially smaller than those of the whole sample. Fifth, note that the "severely-at-risk" group is likely to have a high percentage of its revenue from program service, reflecting a lack of diversification of revenue sources and an inability to tap other sources of funds when program service revenues begin to decline.

4   Attrition Among Nonprofits

A link exists between vulnerability and attrition. Vulnerable nonprofits continue to operate in the short run but when their deficits become excessive, and/or when they can no longer justify their existence, they cease operation and die. To date, no research has been conducted on the extent to which increases in financial vulnerability translate into increases in attrition.

Attrition is both affected by vulnerability and a separate measure of performance. Kanter and Summers (1987) argue that "in the domain of nonprofit organizations, survival can indeed be an appropriate effectiveness standard." Our investigation of the vulnerability of nonprofits raises the question of whether the attrition rate of nonprofits is high or low. If the rate is low, a presumption might be advanced that managers are successful in realizing their survival goals. If it is high then an argument can be made that managers have not attained this goal. To the extent that a nonprofit's survival is contingent on its meeting all four criteria we might expect a high attrition rate because 40 percent of our sample fails to satisfy at least one criterion. To the extent that survival is threatened only when a nonprofit satisfies none of the criteria, other things equal, attrition should be low. "High" and "low" are relative terms and thus it is useful to compare attrition in the nonprofit sector with that in the for-profit sector. If attrition is substantially lower in the former, this would suggest the need for studies to determine whether this is a sign of superior performance or a concomitant of the conditions under which nonprofits operate. If it is substantially higher, this could suggest a need to determine whether problems exist in the sector.

To answer these questions, we develop several data series that provide a basis for comparison of nonprofit and for-profit "births" and "deaths." Stock and flow data on nonprofit births and deaths are computed from the IRS Annual Reports of various years. For-profit births and deaths are obtained from the *Statistical Abstract of the United States* (1990) and the *Economic Report of the President* 1990)[6].

---

6   The difference between the change in the total number of nonprofits in each year and new additions is defined as "attrition." This methodology

Column 2 of Table 3 shows the rate of growth of new nonprofits while column 3 shows the growth in for-profits based on data presented in the *Economic Report of the President* (1990). From 1977-86, for-profits grew almost five times as fast as nonprofits. Column 4 shows the ratio of the number of new nonprofit to the number of new for-profit organizations. It indicates that the number of new nonprofits approved by the IRS was only 8 percent of the number of for-profit additions in 1977 and 6 percent in 1986. For the period as a whole, it averaged 7 percent. These data indicate that, both absolutely and relatively, the American economy gave birth to far more for-profit than nonprofit organizations in the last decade.

Column 5 shows the annual rate of nonprofit attrition and column 6 the rate of for-profit attrition. Column 7 gives the ratio of total nonprofit attritions to total for-profit attritions in each year.[7] The average nonprofit attrition rate of 3 percent (Column 5) for the period of 1977-86 is closer to the "severely-at-risk" rate of 0.16 percent than to the "at-risk" rate of 40 percent. The fact that it is higher than the "severely-at-risk" percentage suggests that factors other than finances affect nonprofit attrition and the 3 percent attrition rate can be interpreted at least two ways. On the one hand, it is sufficiently low so that it can be argued that most nonprofits succeed in realizing their goal of survival. On the other, the figures suggest that nonprofits had a higher attrition rate than for-profits. This would seem to challenge the view that nonprofits are better protected against events that threaten their survival than for-profits. Given the poor quality of the nonprofit attrition data, however, these results are better viewed as suggestive than conclusive.

5   Why Didn't More Nonprofits Die after 1981?

Salamon and Abramson (1982) document the role that government plays in financing the operations of nonprofits. Their evidence

---

introduces a problem since measurement error can occur when the IRS changes the law regarding which organizations must report, when some nonprofits file in one year and not in others, and/or when other changes occur in the population stock measured in two years. Unfortunately, we were unable to find any other way to derive an attrition series.

7   The for-profit attritions reported here are significantly lower than those customarily found in sources such as the *Economic Report of the President* (1990). This is because failures are computed as a percentage of all businesses rather than new businesses.

suggests that the severe cutbacks during the Reagan era impacted a large number of nonprofits. This raises an important question; why is it that the attrition statistics for nonprofits do not show a substantial rise after 1981? At least four explanations can be advanced. First, it can be argued that strong barriers exist to nonprofit attrition. To date, few researchers have explored the effect of barriers to exit in the nonprofit sector. Thus, the hypothesis that more nonprofits did not die because they were unable to is unconfirmed. Second, the Reagan cutbacks may have been absorbed by nonprofits by using internal resources to offset the effects of revenue cutbacks. The data presented in this paper suggest that a large number of nonprofits had the means to absorb a temporary revenue downturn. However, these are temporary means to stave off program cutbacks and more permanent measures would have been needed to replace the revenues lost from the government over time.

A third possibility is that nonprofits reacted to the cutbacks by increasing the number of unrelated business activities they engaged in. Evidence on this point and a behavioral model are presented in Weisbrod (1988). As Weisbrod suggests, a consequence of this shift toward unrelated activities may be that nonprofits provide fewer mission related services. Recent concern over unrelated business activities of nonprofits by Congress may also reflect increased nonprofit activities in this area. Substantially more research is needed before we can evaluate nonprofit performance in this regard.

A fourth possibility is that nonprofits have cut their service offerings to levels sustainable by available revenues. While this increases long term survivability, it also reduces the amount of services offered by the nonprofit sector. This may be a reasonable explanation of what happened in the 1980s but it fails to explain why the nonprofit sector's share of total employment is reported to have increased from 8.5 percent in 1977 to 9.6 percent in 1987 or why its share of national income remained the same in 1987 (5.8 percent) as it was in 1982 (Hodgkinson and Weitzman, 1989). Clearly, additional work is needed before we can fully understand the extent to which the nonprofit sector withstood the cuts that took place during this period.

Measures of nonprofit performance are necessary both to provide nonprofit decisionmakers with feedback as to how well they are doing and to allow society to evaluate the performance of the nonprofit sector. As long as the output of the nonprofit sector remains "intangible," such measures will be difficult to produce. The approach developed in this paper provides one way of evaluating nonprofit performance without the need to measure output. We believe that this approach, as well as others, can yield fruitful insights for the research community and enlighten public understanding of the performance of nonprofit organizations.

Table 1   The Distribution of Financially Vulnerable Charitable Nonprofits by Type and Year

Non profit Category	(1) (2) Number of Nonprofits in IRS Sample		(3) (4) Category percentage of the Total		(5) (6) Percentage of this Category at Risk		(7) (8) Percentage of this Category Severely at Risk	
	1983	1985	1983	1985	1983	1985	1983	1985
1. Religious	54	61	1.1%	1.0%	1.2%	1.3%	20.0%	20.0%
2. Educational	1,080	1,239	22.8%	20.1%	9.6%	7.6%	0.0%	10.0%
3. Health Care	1,926	2,143	40.7%	34.7%	50.6%	43.7%	20.0%	30.0%
4. Charity	427	663	9.0%	10.8%	11.3%	15.7%	0.0%	10.0%
5. Support	1,173	1,673	24.8%	27.1%	25.8%	30.3%	60.0%	30.0%
6. Other	70	89	1.5%	6.3%	1.4%	1.5%	0.0%	0.0%
Total	4,730	6,168	100%	100%	100% 1,951*	100% 2,475*	100% 5*	100% 10*

* = Number of organizations.

Table 2   Select Financial Characteristics of Vulnerable Nonprofits

Select Characteristics	1983		1985	
Average Revenue ($000)	*Mean*	*SD*	*Mean*	*SD*
Total	$33,642	$101,148	$33,780	$154,425
At Risk	$37,451	$138,614	$36,704	$223,942
Severely At Risk	$1,330	$707	$4,362	$10,003
Average Beginning Equity ($000)				
Total	$27,743	$82,278	$28,780	$154,425
At Risk	$17,741	$85,400	$14,795	$59,211
Severely At Risk	–$587	$1,238	$885	$2,834
Average Ending Equity ($000)				
Total	$30,173	$86,100	$31,874	$110,242
At Risk	$18,668	$83,486	$16,667	$73,690
Severely At Risk	-$ 941	$1,702	$42	$1,735
Long-Term Debt to Total Assets Ratio				
Total	0.33	0.36	0.34	0.62
At Risk	0.47	0.47	0.51	0.91
Severely At Risk	1.06	0.15	0.96	0.12
Current Ratio				
Total	27.09	79.50	30.95	88.05
At Risk	16.57	68.24	19.17	81.12
Severely At Risk	NA	NA	8.89	16.21
% of Revenue From Program Service				
Total	72%	30%	70%	31%
At Risk	81%	29%	79%	30%
Severely At Risk	NA	NA	98%	1%

The total category is a weighted average based on proportional weights for each of the six nonprofit categories. SD = standard deviation. NA = data could not be computed.

**Table 3   Estimated Number of New Additions and Attritions
For Nonprofit and For-profit Organizations 1976-1986**

Year (1)	Rate of Additions		Ratio of Nonprofit Additions to For-profit Additions (4)	Rate of Attritions		Ratio of Nonprofit Attritions to For-profit Attritions (7)
	NP (2)	FP (3)		NP (5)	FP (6)	
1977	4.6%	19.5%	0.08	NA	0.4%	NA
1978	4.3%	20.1%	0.07	2.0%	0.3%	2.42
1979	4.3%	20.5%	0.07	2.5%	0.3%	2.67
1980	4.4%	19.7%	0.07	1.7%	0.4%	1.22
1981	4.3%	20.7%	0.06	3.8%	0.6%	1.90
1982	4.6%	19.4%	0.07	5.6%	0.9%	1.88
1983	4.6%	20.0%	0.06	4.1%	1.0%	1.10
1984	5.1%	20.0%	0.07	1.4%	1.6%	0.24
1985	5.0%	20.2%	0.07	3.2%	1.7%	0.49
1986	4.6%	20.5%	0.06	0.2%	1.8%	0.04
Avg	4.6%	20.1%	0.07	3.1%	1.0%	0.74

Sources: Column 2 data from Annual Reports of Internal Revenue Service, 1977-1989. Column 3 data computed from *Economic Report of the President 1990.* Column 4 data computed from raw data that underlie columns 2 and 3. Column 5 data computed by method described in text using data from IRS Annual Reports. Column 6 dervied from data in *Economic Report of the President* and the *Statistical Abstract of the United States 1990.* Note that the failure rate is computed using all businesses rather than new businesses in the denominator. Column 7 is computed using the raw data that underlie columns 6 and 7.

REFERENCES

BEN-NER A., 1986, "Nonprofit Organizations: Why Do They Exist in Market Economies", in *The Economics of Nonprofit Institutions*, Edited by S. Rose-Ackerman, New York: Oxford University Press.

CHABOTAR K.J., 1989, "Financial Ratio Analysis Comes to Nonprofits", in *Journal of Higher Education, 60,* March/April, 188-208.

CLEVERLY W.0. and NILSEN K., 1980, "Assessing Financial Position With 29 Key Ratios", in *Hospital Financial Management, 34* (January), 30-36.

DRUCKER P., 1968, *The Age of Discontinuity,* New York, Harper and Row.

Economic Report of the President 1990, 1990, Washington, DC: U.S. Goverment Printing Office, p. 402.

HANSMANN H.B., 1986, "The Role of Nonprofit Enterprise", in *The Economics of Nonprofit Institutions,* Edited by S. Rose-Ackerman, New York: Oxford University Press.

——, 1987, "The Effect of Tax Exemption and Other Factors On The Market Share of Nonprofit Versus For-Profit Firms", in *National Tax Journal,* XL (1), March, 71-82.

HODGKINSON V.A. and WEITZMAN M.S., 1989, *Dimensions of the Independent Sector,* Third Edition, Washington, DC: Independent Sector.

Internal Revenue Service, 1987, *Annual Report 1986,* Washington, DC: U.S. Government Printing Office, p. 60.

JAMES E., 1983, "How Nonprofits Grow: A Model", in *Journal of Policy Analysis and Management, 2*: 350-65.

KANTER R. M and SUMMERS D.V., 1987, "Doing Well While Doing Good: Dilemmas of Performance Measurement in Nonprofit Organizations and the Need for a Multiple Constituency Approach", in *The Nonprofit Sector,* Edited by W.W. Powell. New Haven, Yale University Press.

KIRCHOFF B.A., 1977, "Organizational Effectiveness Measurement and Policy Research", in *Academy of Management Review, 3,* July: 347-55.

MILOFSKY C., 1987, "Neighborhood-Based Organizations: A Market Analogy, in *The Nonprofit Sector,* Edited by W.W. Powell, New Haven, Yale University Press.

O'NEIL J., 1971, *Resource Use in Higher Education: Trends in Outputs and Inputs,* New York, MacGraw Hill.

RUDNEY G., 1987, "The Scope and Dimensions of Nonprofit Activity", in *The Nonprofit Sector,* Edited by W.W. Powell, New Haven, Yale University Press.

SALAMON L.M. and ABRAMSON A.J., 1982, *The Federal Budget and the Nonprofit Sector,* Washington, DC: Urban Institute.

——, 1987, "Partners in Public Service: The Scope And Theory of Government-Nonprofit Relations", in *The Nonprofit Sector,* Edited by W.W. Powell, New Haven, Yale University Press.

SCHERER F.M., 1970, *Industrial Market Structure and Economic Performance,* Chicago: Rand McNally.

Statistical Abstract of the United States 1990, 1990, Washington, DC: U.S. Department of Commerce, pp. 521 and 523.

TUCKMAN H.P. and CHANG C.F., 1988, "Competition and Cost Convergence at Nursing Homes", in *Quarterly Review of Economics and Business, 28* (Winter), 50-65.

——, 1990, "Why Do Nonprofit managers Accumulate Surpluses And How Much Do They Accumulate?", in *Nonprofit Management and Leadership,* 1(2), 117-135.

——, 1991, "A Methodology For Measuring Charitable Nonprofit Organization Financial Vulnerability", in *Voluntary Sector Quarterly,* 20(4), Dec.

WEISBROD B.A., 1988, *The Nonprofit Economy,* Cambridge, Harvard University Press.

PART 2
Country Studies

EMPLOYMENT AND EARNINGS IN THE WEST GERMAN NONPROFIT SECTOR
Structure and Trends 1970-1987

by

Helmut K. ANHEIER

Institute for Policy Studies

The Johns Hopkins University

&

Rutgers University

Department of Sociology

Introduction[1]

This paper describes the size and scope of nonprofit sector employment in West Germany, and points to major changes that have occurred in the sector between 1970 and 1987. Comparative research on the nonprofit sector in several countries has long recognized the different cultural conceptions, legal treatment, sectoral size and embeddedness as well as the varying economic and policy importance of the nonprofit sector in other countries (James 1989; Anheier and Seibel 1990; DiMaggio and Anheier 1990). Lack of data about such

---

1   This paper reports on initial work on this size, structure and scope of the nonprofit sector in West Germany as part of the Johns Hopkins Comparative Nonprofit Sector Project directed by Lester Salamon and the present author. Assistance by the Project and the project staff, Barbara Conrad and Kusuma Cunningham in particular, is gratefully acknowledged. The paper benefitted greatly from helpful comments by Avner Ben-Ner, Gabriel Rudney, and an anonymous reviewer of this journal.

differences and similarities continues to present a great obstacle for comparative research. In this respect, the present paper hopes to contribute to a better understanding of the differences and similarities by offering a quantitative profile of the size of the West German nonprofit sector in terms of number of establishments, employment and earnings.

The nonprofit sector in West Germany plays a prominent part in social service provision, and has played a central role in the development of civil society after World War II. The nonprofit sector contributes between 2 and 3% to GDP and provides about 1.2 million jobs, representing 4.3% of total employment, and 4.2% of total wage bill in 1987. The number of nonprofit organizations is estimated to range between 200,000 and 300,000, most of which operate without paid staff. Although the main objective of this paper is to present a profile of nonprofit sector employment and earnings, it is useful to state briefly the major features of the West German nonprofit sector to put the data into a wider social context.

Several characteristics are central in describing West Germany's nonprofit sector. First, it operates in a highly decentralized political system. As political scientists remark, West Germany is a prime example of a decentralized state in a centralized society (Katzenstein 1987). The nonprofit sector contributes to centralizing social tendencies through a system of hierarchical representation by which local and regional organizations link up to form powerful peak associations. Prominent examples are the influential business and professional associations, some of which enjoy statutory and regulatory powers, or the free welfare associations which occupy central positions in social welfare delivery (Bauer and Diessenbacher 1984). As we will show, the free welfare associations have experienced higher growth than nonprofits serving businesses, which seems to indicate a relative maturation of the area of interest mediation and a continued expansion of nonprofit organizations linked to the West German version of the welfare state.

Second, large segments of the nonprofit sector are defined within a special state-church relationship which exemplifies neither separation nor union. The churches (Catholic Church and Protestant Church) enjoy far-reaching autonomy through the state's recognition that ecclesiastical law is constitutionally equivalent to administrative law in the regulation of internal church affairs. Moreover, the churches are entitled to "church tax", which is levied on income tax and collected by the state tax authorities through pay roll reductions.

As we will be shown further below, the churches are the most frequent type of organization in the West German nonprofit sector.

Third, the nonprofit sector is part of a tradition of political pragmatism in conflict management. These tendencies were reinforced by the prominent role of the churches and the principle of subsidiarity in social welfare policy in the case of the free welfare associations[2]. In a political system with corporatist tendencies, business and professional associations have historically been influential and continue to play powerful roles. Decentralized public authorities and private (nonprofit) institutions operate and negotiate in a formal, regulatory environment which, at the same time, commands and encourages cooperation as well as compromise. This policy pattern helps understand the substantial growth of the nonprofit sector during the last twenty years, even after the introduction of the German Budget Balancing Act to limit public spending.

Fourth, the country's economic system has traditionally shown a strong presence of public law corporations, cooperatives, and union-related enterprises. However, in the context of the present paper, these organizations would not be treated as part of the nonprofit sector; rather they are part of the public service economy.

1   Definitions of the Nonprofit Sector and Data Sources

The terms "nonprofit", "not-for-profit organization" and "nonprofit sector" do not exist in the German language. In German, four different terms may be used which, to varying degrees, capture some aspects of the American concept of "nonprofit organization"[3].

---

2   The principle of subsidiarity originated in Catholic thinking; in essence, it assumes that larger social and political institutions like the state should only assume direct responsibility in social, education or cultural matters; if smaller institutions like the churches, other voluntary associations, or the family cannot adequately meet demand. After World War II, the principle of subsidiarity has emerged as a central building block of social welfare policies in West Germany.

3   First, the *Vereins- und Verbandswesen*, or associational system is used in the social sciences either as shorthand for organizational forms outside the realm of government and business, or as reference to civil society, citizen's participation, and political influence networks outside the electoral system.

For purposes of this analysis, the term *Organisation ohne Erwerbscharakter* (organizations with no profit motive or commercial character) will be used. It is close to "nonprofit organizations" in the American term, but shows several substantial differences. In addition to organizations serving charitable purposes and membership associations, this term includes churches, political parties, unions, employers and business associations as well as public law economic and professional associations such as chambers of commerce, physicians, pharmacists or notaries. It excludes cooperatives, self-help groups, nonprofit housing associations, public utilities and related public corporations, and mutual organizations.

The term "organizations with no profit motive or commercial character" is widely used in official statistical accounts. This applies foremost to the two major sources of economic information on the nonprofit sector: the Census of Work Establishments (CWE) and System of National Accounts (SNA). In defining the nonprofit sector, the German SNA refers to the definition employed in the "System of Economic Activities" (SEA) of 1979:

"Nonprofit organizations are associations and institutions which either provide public goods and serve the common weal, or meet the specified interests of their members or other groups. These organizations are not primarily active for economic gains; they meet their expenses largely through membership contributions, public subsidies and, in the case of the churches, through taxes, and only to a lesser extend through production income, usually in the form of sales of services".

In contrast to most other national and international classification schemes, the SEA classifies nonprofit organizations separately from both commercial and public organizations:

In the second term, "public service/utility sector", refers to the public good character and social usefulness of the organization's purpose (Gemeinnützigkeit). The term includes charitable organizations as defined in the Fiscal Code (§55-58) and the Income Tax Law (§10b,1), but excludes political parties, most churches, cooperatives, and mutual associations.

The third term is *Gemeinwirtschaft* (public or social economy), as that part of the economy which is guided by the principle of maximizing the public good rather than private returns. It includes public enterprises and utilities, cooperatives, self-help groups, union related corporations and banks, housing societies, and charities. The term excludes political parties, business and professional associations, and organized religion.

A. COMMERCIAL SECTOR
>   Agriculture
>   Production
>> energy & mining
>> manufacturing & processing
>> construction
>   Trading
>   Communication
>   Credit, Banking & Insurance
>   Services

B. NONPROFIT INSTITUTIONS
>   Nonprofit organizations serving households
>   Nonprofit organizations serving businesses

C. PUBLIC AGENCIES & SOCIAL SECURITY

Nonprofits serving households are: a) churches, religious and political associations, welfare and youth associations, b) organizations in the fields of education, science, research and culture, sport, and health, c) unions, associations of public entities (cities), regional bodies (counties) and social security institutions, political parties, and d) other nonprofit organizations not serving businesses. Nonprofits serving businesses are business and employers associations and professional associations.

The SEA excludes from the nonprofit sector all forms of cooperatives and nonprofit building societies, both of which enter the business sector. Establishments run by nonprofit organizations (e.g. a youth center operated by one of the free welfare associations) or public law corporations (e.g. a hospital run by a Catholic diocese), are part of the nonprofit sector, whereas a forprofit business owned by a foundation, for example, is included in the corporate sector.

According to the SEA, several industries like social services, education, health and culture, consist of three different sectors (forprofit or commercial, nonprofit, and public). A special coding scheme allows for the classification of all organizations in such industries by subsectors, either as a business, nonprofit or public organization. Based on the SEA we can compare the share and relative importance of businesses, nonprofit organizations, and public institutions in all areas where nonprofit organizations typically operate.

Based on the SEA, the CWE was conducted last in 1987, which replicates similar census in 1961 and 1970. (Earlier CWEs in 1875, 1882, 1895, 1907, 1917, 1925, 1933, 1939, and 1950 used classification systems which took only rudimentary account of the nonprofit sector). In summary, the CWE presents us with a detailed picture of nonprofit sector employment; moreover, it is possible to compare, at least partially, the CWE data of 1970 with the 1987 data and gain useful insights into changes and trends in the area of nonprofit sector employment.

2   The Nonprofit Sector and the West German Economy

Table 1 presents the absolute and relative size of the nonprofit sector in relation to other sectors of the West German economy. In both the number of establishments and in terms of employment, the nonprofit sector is the seventh largest, ahead of banking/insurance, energy/mining and agriculture. In terms of total wage bill, the nonprofit sector is the eighth largest sector, with a wage bill only .3 percentage points smaller than the share of the banking and insurance sector (see Rudney, 1987, for U.S. comparisons).

The share of nonprofit establishments increased from 2.3 in 1970 to 3.1% in 1987. With a growth of almost 50%, the nonprofit sector was among the fastest-growing sectors in the economy in terms of establishments: the commercial services sector expanded at about the same rate, and only the banking/insurance sector grew faster. Between 1970 and 1987, the West German economy added a total of 295,854 (net) establishments to the economy, of which the nonprofit sector added 14,290. In other words, 4.8% or about one in twenty of all net new establishments since 1970 have been in the nonprofit sector.

In terms of employment, we find that the nonprofit sector represents the fastest growing sector of the economy between 1970 and 1987. Nonprofit sector employment almost doubled during that period, and its relative share of total employment increased from 2.4 to 4.3%. Of the 2,575,334 (net) jobs added to the West German economy between 1970 and 1987, 579,860 were in the nonprofit sector, representing 22.5% or one of every fifth job created. Only the commercial service sector shows similar growth rates.

If we compare the relative shares of branches in terms of number of establishments, employment and wage bill, we find that the nonprofit sector is the only sector of the West German economy where the employment share (4.3%) is higher than the share in the number of establishments (3.1%) and almost equal to the proportion of the total wage bill (4.2%). Some of the reasons for this characteristic of the nonprofit sector will be outlined further below. At this juncture it may suffice to mention two factors: first, the difference in the shares in the number of establishments and employment is due to the large average size of nonprofit hospitals (243 employees), which increases the average establishment size in the nonprofit sector to 15 employees, as compared to 10 for the economy as a whole. Second, kindergartens and hospitals are the most important industries in the nonprofit sector in terms of employment. They introduce two counterveiling tendencies, which together account for the equal share of employment and wage bill: Kindergartens show less than average earnings per employee (DM24,299 per year), whereas average earnings in the hospital sector are above average and amount to DM37,128, compared to DM30,841 for the nonprofit sector as a whole.

We will now examine the structure of employment in the nonprofit sector in more detail, and take a closer look at some of the reasons for its disproportionate growth.

3   The Structure of Employment

In general, as Table 1 clearly shows, employment has shifted from manufacturing and construction to services in general, either in the commercial, nonprofit or public sector. The nonprofit sector benefitted not only from a general expansion of service industries. There are three other trends which are important in this respect: the increased female participation in the labor market, the expansion of part-time employment, and public sector initiatives to reduce unemployment among youths in particular.

Table 2a examines the changes in female employment relative to other sectors of the economy. As has been shown for other countries (Hodgkinson and Weitzman 1986:38), the nonprofit sector tends to include a disproportionate share of female employment. Though in absolute terms, most women work in either manufacturing, trade or forprofit services, female employment in the nonprofit sector is relatively higher. In fact, the proportion of female employment has remained at such a high level between 1970 and 1987, so that females occupy about two out of three jobs in the nonprofit sector, in contrast to slightly more than one out of three for the entire economy. Female employment increased in the economy as a whole; in the nonprofit sector this increase came in addition to an already relatively high ratio of female employment.

While female employment increased in absolute terms, and slightly in relative terms, Table 2b shows that part-time employment increased substantially in both absolute and in relative terms in the nonprofit sector. Together, the commercial service sector and the nonprofit sector show the highest growth rates in the number of part-time jobs added to the West German economy between 1970 and 1987. However, while the nonprofit sector used to have the highest proportion of part-time jobs in 1987, it has been surpassed by the commercial service sector: in both sectors, however, three out of ten jobs are part-time, as compared to 1.5 of ten for the economy as a whole.

The period between 1970 and 1987 witnessed significant changes in the educational background and skill level of the labor force. Some of these changes are reflected in Table 2c, which shows the composition of the labor force according to major occupational categories. The table shows a general decrease of unskilled and skilled blue collar jobs in the traditional industrial sectors, though the number of skilled blue collar workers remained about the same for the whole economy. Civil servants, white collar and apprentice jobs increased their overall share in the labor force. The nonprofit sector, which increased employment by almost 100%, shows disproportionate increases in the number of white collar jobs and apprentices. In 1987, two out of three jobs in the nonprofit sector were white collar, a proportion higher only in the banking/insurance sector. Similarly, the relative share of apprentices among the total labor force was higher only in the construction industry.

The substantial growth of white collar jobs and apprentices in the nonprofit sector reflects two changes. The first can be attributed to a general professionalization of the sector: as will be shown in table 3, the largest increases occurred in the areas of social welfare, education & science and health. Those fields had been the primary beneficiaries and targets of expanded welfare and educational policies and programs in the 1970's; they had also been, during the last decade, under the greatest political pressure of accountability to deliver services efficiently and professionally.

The period between 1970 and 1987 was characterized by a shift from near full employment until the mid 1970's to relatively high unemployment throughout the 1980's. This helps explain the growth in the number of apprentices. This increase can, in part, be attributed to employment generating and job qualification initiatives launched by the Federal Employment Agencies. Throughout the 1980's the country faced the problem of high youth unemployment, which was caused when the large cohorts of "baby boomers" tried to enter the labor market at a time of economic stagnation and recession. The Federal Employment Agency designed various programs which were directed at the nonprofit sector explicitly. Increases in the number of apprentices were highest in the areas of social welfare (410.9%), science and education (3,839.3%), and employers associations (489.9%) and professional associations (420.1%) --areas which traditionally had not employed apprentices and which began to take advantage of job creation programs in the 1980s.

4   Composition of the Nonprofit Sector and Changes 1970-1987

Table 3 presents a more detailed picture of the nonprofit sector. In terms of establishments, table 3 indicates that about every third nonprofit is classified as a church or religious association. This includes the Evangelical Church of Germany and the Roman Catholic Church (including lay associations), Jewish congregations, the Islamic Community, and also non-religious associations like the Free Masons and the Anthroposophical Society. About every fifth organization in the nonprofit sector is a kindergarten, which in Germany includes day-care centers and preschools. Together, religious organizations and kindergartens account for nearly 50% of all establishment in the nonprofit sector.

In terms of employment, the result is different: though hospitals and clinics account for only 1.4% of all establishments, they represent 21.2% of employment and 25.5% of the total wage bill. The six fields, churches, hospitals, kindergartens, free welfare, homes for the handicapped and for the frail elderly account for 63.4% of all employment and 62.1% of the total wage bill in the nonprofit sector.

Some scholars suggest to exclude churches, public law professional associations, employers associations, unions and political parties from the definition of the nonprofit sector (Salamon and Anheier 1991). Following this definition makes the role of the kindergartens and hospitals even more prominent. In this case, every third (32%) nonprofit organizations are kindergartens; they employ every tenth person (10.7%; 8.4% of total wage bill) in the nonprofit sector so defined. Likewise, hospitals account for 27.3% of the total employment in the sector, and 32.6% of its total wage expenditures.

Some industries show differences in employment and wage bill shares. For example, business and professional associations represent 2.8% of the number of jobs in the nonprofit sector and 3.4% of the total wage bill. Similarly, clinics and hospitals account for 21.1% of jobs and 25.5% of the wage bill. In contrast, kindergartens include 8.3% of jobs, but 6.6% of the wage bill. Homes for the frail elderly and the handicapped show a similar pattern, whereby the share of the wage bill is lower than the relative proportion of jobs.

While a thorough analysis is complicated by the data available[4], we can nevertheless identify several factors which seem to contribute to such differences. In terms of the proportion of female and part-time employment, it is useful to compare business and professional associations and hospitals on one hand to kindergartens and homes for the frail elderly on the other. For business and professional associations, with an average annual earning of DM42,326 per employee, we find that women represent 55% of the labor force, and part-time workers 18%. For hospitals, the percentages are 78% female and 27% part-time employment, with an average salary of DM37,128 per annum. In contrast, jobs in kindergartens carry an average salary of DM24,299 per year; they are to 95% female employment and to 33% part-time. Finally, for homes for the frail elderly the percentages are 86.9% female and 29% part-time employment; average annual earning for jobs in homes for the frail elderly is DM27,299.

The data suggest that a combination of part-time and female employment seems responsible for the differences between the share in the number of jobs and the wage bill: As the proportion of female employment increases, so does the share of part-time jobs; as both increase, average annual earnings decrease. In other words, females are more likely than men to work in part-time positions; part-time jobs are lower paid, and tend to be more frequent in areas requiring less formal education and qualifications.

---

4   The CWE does not report full-time equivalent employment, which would be needed for a valid comparison of wage levels across industries and sectors; rather the CWE presents the total number of full-time and part-time jobs.

The data allow for partial comparisons between 1970 and 1987. Several areas have enjoyed higher growth, whereas as others grew at a less impressive rate. However, only one relatively small subsector, scientific libraries, suffered absolute decline, which can be explained by sharp cuts in government subsidies to the universities in the 1980's. Other fields show a concentration process, indicated by a decline in the number of establishments and an increase in the number of jobs. This is the case for unions public law business and professional associations, like the chambers of commerce and industries, crafts associations, bar associations etc.

The greatest expansion in both absolute and relative terms took place in the fields of social welfare, health, day care, and education. Nonprofit theatres, a relatively small sub-field of the nonprofit sector (.1% of total nonprofit sector wage bill in 1987), has shown the highest growth with a more than fourfold increase in the number of establishments and a close to tenfold increase in the number of employees. All forms of interest associations expanded less between 1970 and 1987. Unions, political parties, employers associations, business and professional associations, and public law professional associations tend to have below average growth rates. Overall, this seems to reflect a stronger emphasis on service delivery rather than interest mediation.

There are two major reasons for this. First, higher growth of nonprofit industries in the area of service delivery appears as a consequence of demand factors caused by demographic shifts and changes in the labor force. The most important factors are an increase in the number of elderly, which manifests itself in a higher demand for resident and ambulatory care, and an increased female participation in the labor market (a 27% increase between 1970 and 1987), which leads to a greater demand for services such as child day care. Despite a declining and low birth rate throughout this period, the demand for day care seems to have increased substantially.

Second, we should recall that during the 1970's the social democratic version of the welfare state expanded to a very large degree. Within the general political structure of the country, and the embeddedness of the nonprofit sector in the policy process, the welfare state was less a matter of state actions alone; rather, it involved the free welfare associations as implementors of welfare policies. More than in other welfare state countries, Scandinavia in particular, the German welfare state resulted less in an expansion of public service delivery and welfare administration than to an expansion of the nonprofit sector.

Thus, nonprofit organizations in the area of social welfare services expanded alongside increased public social spending and a growth
in entitlement programs. It is a German version of the third party
government thesis (Salamon 1987), by which the state implements
policies through nonprofit organizations. However, there are three
important difference between the German and the American case.
First, in Germany, nonprofits tend to be more integrated into the
policy making function of government than their American counterparts. Second, in the case of the free welfare associations, legal
stipulations based on the principle of subsidiarity tend to protect the
nonprofit organizations from both for-profit and public sector competition, and make it more difficult to shift public funds from nonprofits
to alternative suppliers. Third, the church tax system provides those
parts of the nonprofit sector linked to the churches with a stable
source of income, which makes the organization less dependent on
competitive grants, consumer fees and charges, and which enables
them to engage in long range planning.

5   Share of the Nonprofit Sector in Selected Industries

Table 4 presents the relative shares of employment (Table 4a)
and total industry wage bill (Table 4b) for the forprofit, nonprofit and
the public sector in four industries. Two general results can be obtained from Table 4. First, the nonprofit sector is more prominent in
some areas than others. Prominent nonprofit industries are residential care, and homes for infants, children, youths, elderly, the frail
elderly and the handicapped, kindergartens, and correctional schools
for youths. These tend to be industries in which church-related welfare activities are significantly present, and have been for long periods of time. Industries in which nonprofits dominate are also those in
which the free welfare association enjoy a prominent role, and where
the principle of subsidiarity grants a privileged status to nonprofit
providers.

Nonprofits are less prominent in the area of higher education
(universities), libraries, general schools, and most cultural and artistic fields. In all these cases, it is the public sector which dominates. In
the case of universities, the only full nonprofit university in the
country is related to the Catholic Church; other nonprofit establishments in the field of higher learning tend to be seminaries and similar
church-related institutions sometimes affiliated with public universities. In the case of primary and secondary schools, a major domain for

nonprofits in other countries, we find that nonprofit organizations tend to occupy niches, like religious boarding schools and elite educational institutions.

Second, few fields show a pattern whereby all three sectors are significantly represented. This is the case for retirement homes and homes for the frail elderly, scientific institutions other than universities, vocational schools, correctional schools, educational institutions other than schools, and the health sector. These industries are either located next to an area dominated by the public sector, as is the case for scientific institutions and universities, or they represent fields which have experienced significant demand increases, as in care for the elderly.

In the first case, the nonprofit form is often selected by the public sector as a more flexible organizational form. For example, it is generally easier to establish and finance a new research organization outside regular university structures and budgets. The nonprofit form provides the public sector with degrees of managerial and political flexibility that may be difficult to achieve within the often more rigid structures of the civil service. Examples are the Max-Planck-Institutes and the Fraunhofer Gesellschaft. In the second case, we can assume that demand increases in highly regulated policy fields may nonetheless lead to market segmentation, and a stronger presence by for-profit, nonprofit and public providers.

6   Conclusion

This paper presented a profile of the size of the nonprofit sector in West Germany in terms of number of establishments, employment and earnings. In general it was shown that, depending on the criterion used, the nonprofit sector represents the seventh or eighth largest sector in a ten sector economy classified according to the German SIC (SEA). The nonprofit sector has benefitted from the expansion of the service sector in general. It benefitted also from shifts in the labor market, in particular via increased demand for part-time jobs on one hand and an increased supply of female employees and apprentices about to enter the labor market on the other.

It was further shown that religious institutions occupy a prominent position in the nonprofit sector, and that they continue to outnumber economic and political interest associations. In general, in concordance with the expansion of the welfare state in the 1970's, and its relative stagnation in the 1980's, the nonprofit sector has benefitted substantially. Service provision, as a major aspect of the nonprofit sector activity, grew faster between 1970 and 1987 than political and interest associations. We argued that this development reflects both demand changes, due to demographic shifts and changes in the labor force, and the embeddedness of the nonprofit sector in public social service delivery systems.

REFERENCES

ANHEIER, H.K. and SEIBEL W. (Eds.), 1990, *The Third Sector: Comparative Studies of Nonprofit Organizations*, Berlin/New York, DeGruyter.

BAUER R. and DIESSENBACHER H. (Eds.), 1984, *Organisierte Nächstenliebe: Wohlfahrtsverbände und Selbsthilfe in der Krise des Sozialstaats*, Opladen: Westdeutscher Verlag.

DIMAGGIO P. and ANHEIER H.K., 1990, "The Sociology of Nonprofit Organizations and Sectors", in *Annual Review of Sociology*: 137-159.

HODGKINSON V. and WEITZMAN M., 1986, *Dimensions of the Independent Sector: A Statistical Profile*, Independent Sector, Washington, D.C.

JAMES E. (Ed.), 1989, *The Nonprofit Sector in International Perspective*, Oxford, Oxford University Press.

KATZENSTEIN P. J., 1987, *Policy and Politics in West Germany: The Growth of a Semisovereign State*, Philadelphia, Temple University Press.

RUDNEY G. 1987, "The Scope and Dimensions of Nonprofit Activity", in Walter W. Powell (Ed.), *The Nonprofit Sector: A Research Handbook*, pp. 55-64.

SALAMON L., 1987, "Partners in Public Service: The Scope and Theory of Government-Nonprofit Sector Relations", in Walter W. Powell (Ed.), *The Nonprofit Sector: A Research Handbook*, pp. 99-117.

SALAMON L. and ANHEIER H.K., 1990, "Toward a Common Definition of the Nonprofit Sector", Unpublished Manuscript. The Johns Hopkins Comparative Nonprofit Sector Project, Baltimore.

Statistisches Bundesamt, *Unternehmen und Arbeitsstätten: Arbeitsstättenzählung vom 25.Mai 1987, Heft 1, 2, 4, 11*, Stuttgart: Metzel-Poeschel.

Table 1: Establishments, Employment and Wage Bill by Sectors in West German Economy: 1970-1987

Branch	SCI Code	Establishments 1987	Proportion of Establishments 1970-1987 (%)		% Change 1970-1987	Employment 1987	Proportion of Employment 1970-1987 (%)		% Change 1970-1987	Proportion of Total Wage Bill 1987 (%)
Agriculture	0	28 962	0.8	1.1	52.5	137 226	0.4	0.5	58.0	0.2
Energy/Mining	1	6 325	0.3	0.2	-3.8	401 584	2.0	1.5	-18.0	2.2
Manufacturing	2	360 465	19.3	14.0	-18.3	8 352 548	41.5	31.3	-17.0	37.3
Construction	3	186 342	7.4	7.2	10.0	1 851 652	9.2	6.9	-17.0	6.3
Trade	4	707 121	32.0	27.4	-3.4	4 028 741	15.3	15.0	8.0	11.1
Communications	5	122 092	5.3	4.7	0.3	1 547 283	6.0	5.7	5.0	6.0
Banking/Insurance	6	121 795	3.0	4.7	75.6	965 469	2.7	3.6	46.0	4.5
Services	7	858 666	25.1	33.3	48.8	4 784 493	10.0	17.7	95.0	10.9
Nonprofit Institutions	8	79 420	2.3	3.1	49.4	1 165 655	2.4	4.3	99.0	4.2
Public Sector	9	110 013	4.2	4.3	14.9	3 738 285	10.5	13.9	45.0	17.3
TOTAL ECONOMY	0-9	2 581 201	100.00	100.00	12.9	26 972 936	100.	100.00	10.0	100.00

Source: Statistisches Bundesamt, Arbeitsstättenzählung 1987, Fachserie 2, Heft 5 and 11
* excluding private households

Table 2: The Structure of Employment and the Nonprofit Sector 1970 - 1987

Table 2a: Female Employment

Sectors	SIC Codes	Proportion of Total Employment		Female Employment 1987	% Change 1970-1987
		1970	1987		
Agriculture	0	26.50	31.90	43 762	90.4
Energy/Mining	1	7.36	9.16	36 795	3.0
Manufacturing	2	30.07	27.71	2314 878	-24.0
Construction	3	6.57	10.70	198 145	33.9
Trade	4	49.81	52.47	2114 98	13.9
Communications	5	18.42	24.28	375 727	39.1
Banking/Insurance	6	45.80	48.74	470 636	55.7
Commer. Services	7	56.77	56.86	2720 770	95.9
Nonprofit Institutions	8	67.00	69.00	804 359	96.2
Public Sector	9	39.32	45.48	1700 506	68.8
TOTAL	0-9	34.78	39.96	10779 676	27.0

Table 2b: Part Time Employment

Sectors	SIC Codes	Proportion of Total Employment		Female Employment 1987	% Change 1970-1987
		1970	1987		
Agriculture	0	10.6	17.8	24 501	165.9
Energy/Mining	1	0.2	2.5	10 358	17.7
Manufacturing	2	4.4	7	588 909	31.6
Construction	3	1.9	5.1	95 470	121.4
Trade	4	13.2	24.4	985 414	99.3
Communications	5	7.1	11.8	183 866	76.5
Banking/Insurance	6	8.7	14.4	139 603	141.8
Commer. Services	7	14.8	30.2	1445 260	298.6
Nonprofit Institutions	8	18.9	29.6	345 855	212.4
Public Sector	9	10.5	15.6	584 531	116.3
TOTAL	0-9	7.8	16.3	4403 767	130.8

Table 2c: Composition of Work Force

Organization		Civil Servants	White Collar	Skilled Blue Collar	Unskilled Blue Collar	Apprentices	Total
Agriculture	%	0.0	11.5	22.6	27.4	8.3	137 226
	*	-85.0	96.6	77.8	33.7	304.7	58.2
Energy/Mining	%	0.3	30.3	52.9	10.2	6.1	401 584
	*	-41.3	-6.9	-0.3	-68.8	104.5	-18.0
Manufacturing	%	0.0	28.1	29.7	31.1	6.6	8 352 548
	*	-	3.3	-8.3	-36.8	18.4	-17.5
Construction	%	0.0	16.9	50.8	12.4	9.4	1 851 652
	*	-	25.0	-15.9	-56.9	37.4	-17.7
Trade	%	0.0	55.2	7.6	12.7	7	4 028 741
	*	-	30.6	19.8	-3.7	-13.7	8.0
Communication	%	29.9	20.3	19.1	20.5	4	1 547 283
	*	-4.7	32.9	63.6	-25.3	56	5.5
Banking/Insurance	%	0.9	77.7	0.8	4.7	6.7	965 469
	*	-26.0	46.1	111.2	37.6	19	46
Com. Services	%	0.0	38.7	7.0	26.1	6.6	784
	*	-	140.3	69.3	45.9	100.4	95
Nonprofit Institutions	%	3.4	66.8	3.3	17.7	8.6	165
	*	21.7	117.1	84.1	40.3	296.5	99
Public Sector	%	35.2	41.1	6.7	12.8	4	738
	*	52.6	52.1	49.8	4.6	149.5	45
Total	%	6.8	37.9	18.2	21.2	6.4	972
	*	31.3	41.4	0.4	17.2	36.6	10

legend   % = Distribution of total labor force among the major sectors.
   * = Percentage change in composition of the labor force 1970 - 1987.

Please note that the percentage distribution does not add up to a 100%; percentages in Table 2c are based on the total labor force and do not report data for employers and unpaid family help.

Source: Statistisches Bundesamt, Arbeitsstättenzählung 1987, Fachserie 2, Heft 11, Table 2

Table 3: The Nonprofit Sector: Establishments, Employment, and Wage Bill

Organization		Establishments			Employment			Wage Bill 1987	
		Number of Establish-ments 1987	Percent of Establish-ments 1987	Percent Increase 1970-87	Number of Jobs 1987	Percent of Jobs 1987	Percent Increase 1970-87	In Million DM	Percent of Total
811	churches	25 005	31.5	21.8	116 367	13.4	64.0	4 040	11.2
8121	free welfare	5 127	6.4	153.0	82 308	7.0	187.0	2 416	6.7
8122	free youth welfare	1 311	1.6	6.0	11 193	0.9	20.7	346	1.0
813	education & research	1 861	2.3	229.0	23 971	2.0	215.0	844	2.3
814	sports & health	2 437	3.0	-	17 965	1.5	-	552	1.5
815	unions	1 497	1.8	-2.8	12 178	1.0	29.7	591	1.6
8161	communal associations	61	0.1	-	1 562	0.1	-	62	0.2
8162	social security associations	50	0.1	-	1 887	0.1	-	85	0.2
817	political parties	2 772	3.5	18.0	16 876	1.4	26.0	566	1.5
831	employers associations	354	0.4	16.0	3 762	0.3	82.0	186	0.5
834	business & professional associations	2 924	3.6	3.0	31 431	2.6	47.8	1 330	3.7
837	public law business associations	1 329	1.6	-7.6	32 775	2.8	55.2	1 240	3.4
8..51	hostels	870	1.0	-	9 909	0.8	-	252	0.7
8..53-5	recreational homes	425	0.5	-	2 435	0.2	-	49	0.1
8..57	canteens	251	0.3	93.0	3 263	0.2	157.7	80	0.2
8..61	homes: youths	834	1.0	-	8 126	0.6	-	226	0.6
8..62-3	homes: elderly	1 512	1.9	-	45 394	3.9	-	1 197	3.3
8..64	homes: nec*	455	0.6	-	4 820	0.4	-	149	0.4
8..65	homes: children	587	0.7	-	12 690	1.0	-	409	1.1
8..66-7	homes: handicapped	1 742	2.1	-	80 769	6.9	-	2 100	5.8
8..68	homes: frail elderly	1 778	2.2	-	81 007	6.9	-	2 251	6.3

Table 3 continued

Organization	Establishments			Employment			Wage Bill 1987	
	Number of Establish-ments 1987	Percent of Establish-ments 1987	Percent Increase 1970-87	Number of Jobs 1987	Percent of Jobs 1987	Percent Increase 1970-87	In Million DM	Percent of Total
8.69 day care (non-child)	2 083	2.6	-	10 574	0.9	-	256	0.7
8.71 universities	90	0.1	45.1	2 307	0.1	67.2	104	0.3
8.73 school libraries	56	0.1	86.6	441	0.0	-22.6	15	*
8.74 science institutions nec*	384	0.5	9.0	17 405	1.4	18.8	780	2.2
8.75 general schools	1 101	1.3	17.5	38 115	3.2	69.8	1 461	4.1
8.76 vocational schools	1 738	2.2	116.4	43 546	3.7	221.3	1 095	3.0
8.77 boarding schools	271	0.3	66.2	6 964	0.5	29.0	222	0.6
8.78 kindergartens	14 577	18.3	87.5	97 076	8.3	190.5	2 359	6.6
8.79 educational institutions nec*	486	0.6	-	6 896	0.5	-	151	0.4
8.81 theatre, opera	62	0.1	416.0	1 414	0.1	939.0	41	0.1
8.82 orchestras & choirs	60	0.1	172.7	562	0.0	78.9	30	0.1
8.83 museums & zoos	187	0.2	-	1 604	0.1	-	46	0.1
8.84 adult education	657	0.8	-	9 559	0.8	-	267	0.7
8.85 general libraries	156	0.2	-	821	0.0	-	22	*
8.86 sports institutions	255	0.3	72.2	1 604	0.1	114.2	26	*
8.87 sport academies	48	0.1	-	550	0.0	-	15	*
8.88 gardens & parks	14	0.1	-	56	0.0	-	1	*
8.91 clinics & hospitals	1 016	1.4	-16.9	246 866	21.1	21.1	9 166	25.5
8.99 other health institutions	2 977	4.0	156.0	33 131	2.9	2.9	931	2.6

nec= not elsewhere classified

*= less than .1%

**= errors due to rounding

Source: Statistisches Bundesamt: Arbeitsstättenzählung 1987.

**Table 4a The Share of Nonprofit, For-profit and Public Employment
Sectoral Comparison of Selected Industries**

Industries	For-profit Sector	Nonprofit Sector	Public Sector	Total Employment in Industry
HOMES	%	%	%	Million DM
infants, children	9.4	73.1	17.5	17 368
elderly	17.7	67.6	14.7	67 140
handicapped	9.5	83.7	6.9	96 518
frail elderly	20.2	63.0	16.8	128 510
day care (not child.)	5.4	46.4	48.1	22 766
EDUCATION AND RESEARCH				
universities	0.3	1.2	98.6	198 042
university hospitals	-		100.0	107 797
libraries & archives	4.1	4.1	91.8	10 779
scientific institutions nec*	44.2	20.6	35.3	84 713
general schools	1.7	6.0	92.2	632 106
vocational schools	17.6	21.5	60.9	202 898
correctional schools	11.7	76.2	12.1	9 118
kindergartens	1.0	62.3	36.7	155 874
CULTURE, ART & RECREATION				
theatre, opera	22.9	4.5	72.7	31 602
orchestras & choirs	71.5	9.5	19.0	5 915
museums & zoos	19.2	9.2	71.7	17 490
adult education	-	100.0	-	9 559
general libraries	59.2	2.7	38.1	30 559
sports institutions	52.0	3.1	45.6	63 408
HEALTH				
clinics & hospitals	14.2	34.2	51.0	722 734
other health institutions	47.6	36.2	16.2	91 586

*nec = not elsewhere classified
Source: Statistiches Bundesamt: Arbeitsstättenzählung 1987.

Table 4b The Share of Nonprofit Sector Wage Bills:
Sectoral Comparison of Selected Industries

Industries	For-profit Sector	Nonprofit Sector	Public Sector	Total Wage Bill
HOMES	%	%	%	Million DM
infants, children	6.6	73.3	20.1	558
elderly	14.2	68.9	16.9	1 737
handicapped	8.8	84.0	7.2	2 500
frail elderly	15.9	64.2	19.9	3 507
day care (not child.)	3.5	43.2	53.3	593
EDUCATION AND RESEARCH				
universities	0.3	1.3	98.4	7 806
university hospitals	0.0	0.0	100.0	4 018
libraries & archives	6.3	5.2	88.5	288
scientific institutions nec*	49.4	19.4	31.2	4 019
general schools	1.4	5.1	93.5	28 535
vocational schools	12.9	14.2	72.9	7 691
correctional schools	8.9	76.3	14.8	291
kindergartens	0.7	59.7	39.6	3 951
CULTURE, ART & RECREATION				
theatre, opera	18.7	2.9	78.4	1 422
orchestras & choirs	27.7	20.3	52.0	148
museums & zoos	13.0	8.8	78.2	522
adult education	-	100.0	-	267
general libraries	25.9	4.2	69.9	529
sports institutions	29.1	2.2	68.7	1 160
HEALTH				
clinics & hospitals	14.0	33.9	52.1	27 048
other health institutions	34.6	41.0	22.4	2 273

Source: Statistisches Bundesamt: Arbeitsstättenzählung 1987, Heft 5.

THE ITALIAN NONPROFIT SECTOR
An Overview of an Undervalued Reality

by

Carlo BORZAGA

Department of Economics

University of Trento

Introduction

In Italy, there is very little known about the nonprofit sector's size and importance. Only recently has the concept of "nonprofit" come into use[1]. What previously prevailed was the sociological concept of voluntary action,[2] which has been gradually extended to include organizations using also paid work.

There are three main reasons for the limited interest in the nonprofit sector:

a. the absence of the concept of nonprofit organization in Italian law, economics and politics;

b. the view that nonprofit activities are either connected with the charitable activities of the Catholic Church, which has promoted them since the Middle Ages, or are being used to build political and social consensus[3], and the small size, the considerable in-

---

1   See Bassanini and Ranci (1990) and Borzaga (1991).
2   For a survey see Pasquinelli (1987).
3   The view that the function of nonprofit activities is to stabilize the political system rather than to compensate for the lack of services has predominated in countries, which, like Italy, are characterized by ambiguous legislation concerning the function and organizational ideologies of the nonprofit sector (Seibel, 1988).

formality and the restricted spheres of operations of many nonprofit organizations, in particular those that have developed over the past twenty years.

The scant interest in the nonprofit sector explains the substantial lack of official statistical information on its size (in terms of income and employment) and characteristics (Donati, 1991). Although this lack of information is common to most countries (Anheier and Seibel, 1990), the Italian situation is worse. This paper presents a first and partial quantification of the importance of the sector and an analysis of its evolution over the last twenty years. After a brief summary of the recent development of the nonprofit sector, I discuss briefly the limitations of the legal framework. Next I examine the statistical data on the size of the sector, especially regarding employment and income.

1   Evolution of the Nonprofit Sector and the Political Context

The 1970s represented a turning point in both the quantitative and qualitative dynamics of the Italian nonprofit sector (Pasquinelli, 1989). Until the end of the 1960s, the nonprofit sector coincided in practice with the social institutions of the Catholic Church, which for the most part were run by religious institutions. From the 1970s and throughout the 1980s, a number of spontaneous associations developed, based mainly on the voluntary work of their members. These new groups were generally small and maintained close links with local communities and local public entities.

The growth of the nonprofit sector followed a number of important laws passed in the early 1970s, aimed at reforming and expanding the public welfare system. These reforms were, however, only partially implemented, because of a lack of organization and the public administration's limited capacity for innovation, and also because of the onset of the Italian state's fiscal crisis. This created, therefore, a conflict between the legal system of welfare and the actual system which enabled new nonprofit activities to evolve.

Two factors contributed to this evolution:

a.   the increased social awareness that grew out of the student movement of 1968, the union battles for the reforms that followed the "hot autumn" of 1969, and the Catholic Church's renewed emphasis on social action after the Second Vatican Council, and

b.   the direct action by local public authorities which, being unable to set up new services of their own, decided to promote nonprofit activities, in some cases even with their direct involvement.

As a result, in Italy, as in most other countries (James, 1990), the financial resources for nonprofit organizations are to a great extent provided by the public sector. This has strengthened the nonprofit sector, which has gradually acquired more clearly defined organizational forms and increased the number of paid staff employed.

2   The Legal Framework

The legal framework for nonprofit organizations is still very inadequate. As in all countries with a system of Roman law, in Italy there is no legal definition either of nonprofit organizations or of the nonprofit sector as a whole (Anheier and DiMaggio, 1990).

Italian law attaches no importance to the "non-distribution constraint", but focuses on the goals of organizations, which it divides among public[4], private commercial, and private non-commercial. Non-commercial organizations may adopt the legal forms of the foundation and the association[5]. The "non-distribution constraint" is clearly not defined and enforced for either of the forms. In particular, there are no clear regulations preventing the organization's capital from being shared among its members should it dissolve.

The cooperative form should be mentioned, even though it is not normally classified among nonprofit organizations. In fact, the Italian law imposes a double restriction on the distribution of profit of cooperatives: the remuneration of the registered stock cannot exceed an upper limit (which today stands at about 14%), and of the rest of the

---

4   Even the distinction between public and private is not always clear. See Barbetta and Ranci (1990).

5   The foundation is basically "capital that is bound to a purpose which, immediately and directly, is different from that of a business" (Guarino, 1989). It has a legal personality that is distinct from that of the founders and as such becomes liable with its own wealth. The association is formed by an agreement among members to carry out non commercial activities which may be in the interests of either the members themselves or society in general.

profit, at least 20% must be assigned to a "collective reserve" which cannot be distributed among members. Furthermore, it is possible to stipulate in the cooperative's statute that the entire profit must be assigned to a "collective reserve". The 1970s and 1980s saw the development of the so-called "social solidarity" cooperatives providing services not to members but to a community or to a group of under-privileged people, and which laid down the full non-distributability of the profits in their statute[6]. Thus a *de facto* form of nonprofit organi-zation was created with a clear non-distribution constraint, and mu-tual control and public benefit.

Foundations and associations are exempted from income tax only for those activities that are not commercial, and not because they are nonprofit activities. Cooperatives are instead exempt from income tax for that amount of the profit assigned to the "collective reserve"[7]. Exemption from value-added tax is similarly determined: generally, activities of a social nature are exempt.

Finally, although the Italian fiscal system has no general regula-tion concerning the deductibility of donations from personal or busi-ness income, the principle is gradually gaining ground through spe-cial legislation (Preite, 1990). Donations made to legally-recognized foundations and associations for scientific research are deductible from business income (up to 2%). Donations to institutions devoted to the study and conservation of important art treasures, to the enter-tainment sector, to activities of international cooperation, to the Catholic Church and other churches for the "financial support of clergy" (*sostentamento del clero*), and donations by private individuals to voluntary associations providing social services in a general sense,[8] are also deductible from individual income.

---

6   As early as 1982, a bill regulating social solidarity cooperatives, and in particular their role regarding the public benefit and the non-distribution constraint, was put forward. This, however, has not yet been approved because of the opposition of part of the cooperative movement.

7   Producer cooperatives are totally exempt if the cost of labor is greater than 60% of income and exempt by half if the cost of labor is between 40 and 60% of income.

8   For the last three types of donations deductions are possible up to a maximum limit of 2 million lire yearly per tax-payer.

3   Income, Employment and Quantitative Data on Specific Organizations

The lack of statistical information makes the estimation of income and employment in the nonprofit sector in Italy extremely difficult[9].

Table 1 Employment in private organizations and overall employment in certain types of services based on the 1981 Census

	Total Employed	Employed in private services	Ratio of employed in private services to total employed
Health services (1)	732,860	71,090	9.7
Education services (2)	1,343,232	101,051	7.5
Social services	49,902	20,305	40.7

(1) Including private nursing homes, private hospitals, private hydrotherapy centres, chemical analysis laboratories, and private radiology and radiotherapy centres.

(2) Including all levels of private schools.

Source: ISTAT, Censimento Generale della Popolazione del 1981, Rome, 1985

In order to estimate the quantitative size of the nonprofit sector I shall analyze first information from the 1981 population census and from the national economic accounts. I shall then examine a few industries and the various forms of organization in them. However, for much of the data, it is only possible to distinguish between public and private activities, without further distinction between profit and nonprofit.

On the basis of the 1981 population census data (see Table 1) it is possible to distinguish between public and private services for health, education and welfare. In 1981, 9.7% of those working in the health services were employed in private institutions that were mainly nonprofit. In the same year, private health institutions represented 37.2% of the total member of institutions and provided 14.7% of the total number of beds (Bassanini and Ranci, 1990). In 1986, these percentages had shifted to 36.1% and 16.1%, respectively.

---

9   More information should be available in the future: the Istituto Nazionale di Statistica (National Statistics Institute) intends to include nonprofit organizations in the Census of population and industry in 1991.

In 1981, 7,5% of the education employment was in the private sector. Religious schools, which are certainly nonprofit, represented 13.2% of the total number of schools and 7.9% of students in 1984. Among private schools 7.8% with 3.3% of the students are nonprofit and are run by associations and cooperatives. In addition, most professional training not included in the table 1 is organized by nonprofit organizations.

In the social welfare sector, in 1981, private organizations - again mainly nonprofit - employed 40.7% of the industry's employment.

Table 2 Value added at current prices or employment by category and sector in Italy 1980-1988

Branch and sector	Value added (in billions of lire)			Employment (in thousands)		
	1980	1988	% var.80-88	1980	1988	% var.80-88
Agriculture	22,305	39,432	76.8	3,044	2,423	- 20.4
Industry	151,321	365,485	141.5	7,743	6,879	- 11.2
Serv. for sale	164,780	517,575	214.1	7,259	9,742	34.2
Serv. not for sale	45,730	141,750	210.0	3,595	4,196	16.7
Public admin.	42,791	133,017	210.8	3,161	3,593	13.7
Other services	2,939	8,733	197.1	434	603	38.9
Total	384,136	1,064,242	177.0	21,641	23,240	7.4

Source: ISTAT, Annuario di contabilità nazionale, Rome, various years

The Italian national accounts group together both domestic services and "Private Social Institutions"[10] under the entry "other services not for sale". In 1988, the value added of this entry (see Table 2) was 6.2% of those services not for sale and 0.9% of the national income. Employment in the same year was 14.3% and 2.6% respectively. Between 1980 and 1988, employment in this sector grew by

---

10   This does not, however, correspond to the nonprofit sector. In fact the category "Private Social Institutions" covers only those organizations that produce community services and supply them to consumers, generally free of charge. More concretely, if the organization covers less than 50% of its costs from the sale of its service, it is included in the "Private Social Institutions", otherwise it is included in the private firms sector, even if it is an association or foundation (Barbetta and Ranci, 1990).

38.9% compared with an average increase in employment of 7.4% (16.7% for the total of the services not for sale), while the value added at current prices increased by 197.1% compared with the 177% of the overall GNP and the 210.8% of the value added in the sector of the services not for sale[11].

A further attempt to quantify the size of the nonprofit sector may be made on the basis of the number of different types of nonprofit organizations. In 1972, there were 957 foundations recognized by the State. Of these, 314 operated in the field of educational assistance (Mortara, 1973). Between 1973 and 1988, 239 new foundations were recognized by the various Ministries (Rescigno, 1989). In addition to these, there were the foundations recognized by the regional administrations, about which very little information is available.

The number of associations is larger, but not known with precision. Some studies have tried to estimate the number of associations operating in specific fields: in 1985 in the field of sporting activities alone, there were approximately 112,000 associations, both national and local (Mortara, 1985). A survey of voluntary work in Italy identified about 15,000 associations in health and social welfare services (Colozzi and Rossi, 1985). A survey of the Italian population aged 18 to 74 revealed that 28% are involved in associations with social aims (see Table 3) (Iref, 1990). If we exclude political, trade union and professional associations and limit ourselves to those involved in sporting, recreational, cultural, health, welfare, education, ecological, and consumer protection activities, then we find that the percentage of citizens involved is 12.1% of the population (4,821,000 people). Many of these people work as volunteers. As a whole, volunteers represented 15.4% of the population aged between 18 and 74 in 1989, and were mainly involved in associations providing social services (12.5% of the population). Between 1983 and 1989, the phenomenon increased.

Finally, the social solidarity cooperatives deserve separate mention, and will be examined at a later stage.

---

11   The discrepancy between the growth of the values of income and employment is in part explained by the fact that the sector includes those employed in domestic service, generally with few working hours and lower pay than in other sectors.

Table 3 People aged between 18 and 74 involved in organizations with social goals

Types of organization	% of total population
Political parties	2.0
Trade unions	4.6
Professional groups	5.2
Cooperatives	4.0
Social welfare	12.1
Total	27.9

Source: Iref, 1990

4   Results of Empirical Studies

If we focus on specific subgroups of nonprofit organizations, we find further indications of the size and, in particular, the characteristics and evolution of the nonprofit sector in Italy. I examine below the results of two recent studies of particularly important areas: Christian charities and social solidarity cooperatives.

4.1 Christian Charities

In 1987, the Consulta Nazionale delle Opere Caritative e Assistenziali (National Council of Charity and Security Work), a body belonging to the Catholic Church, carried out a survey of social services dependent on or connected with the Church (Consulta Nazionale delle Opere Caritative ed Assistenziali, 1990). The survey involved a sizable part of the nonprofit activities operating in the social services.

The survey examined 4,099 services, which represented an overall estimated total of 4,600-4,700 units (see Table 4). There were services that mainly catered to the elderly (42.4%), juveniles and youths (33.8%), the handicapped (24.2%) and various groups of the socially marginalized (drug addicts, alcoholics, nomads and foreigners, etc). The overall number of people employed in the services covered, excluding part-time volunteers, was 48,801 (see Table 5). Volunteers made up 30.6% of those working in these services, 56.8% were paid workers (43.6% were employees), while the remaining 12,6% did not provide information on the occupational status.

Table 4 Organizations interviewed divided according to legal form and sector of activity

	Total replies	A	B	C	D	E	F
					Legal form		
Total	4,099	515	324	672	1,417	682	235
	100.0	100.0	100.0	100.0	100.0	100.0	100.0
Percentage	100.0	12.6	7.9	16.4	34.6	16.6	5.7
No reply	9.6	6.0	7.7	7.0	10.2	6.0	14.5
Juveniles at risk	28.6	31.5	21.6	38.4	25.9	28.6	26.0
Handicapped	15.8	9.9	39.8	13.7	17.8	10.5	11.5
Drug addicts	7.4	1.0	20.1	3.1	12.0	2.6	6.4
Prisoners, ex-prisoners	3.3	1.0	5.6	0.9	4.7	2.3	8.9
Homeless foreigners	5.9	1.4	3.4	2.5	7.1	8.8	13.6
Families at risk	7.8	1.9	4.9	3.7	13.6	5.6	11.5
Elderly	36.9	58.6	20.7	40.9	27.1	48.7	30.5
Nomads	1.6	1.0	0.6	1.0	2.0	1.8	3.0
Ill people	4.3	2.1	2.5	1.8	6.0	7.2	2.6

Key: A = Public welfare and charity institutions (IPAB)
B = Cooperatives and joint-stock companies
C = Foundations
D = Associations
E = Religious congregations and ecclesiastical bodies
F = Other legal forms

Source: Consulta Nazionale delle Opere Caritative e Assistenziali (1990)

Regarding the legal status, 23.7% of the services surveyed were foundations, 5.3% were nonprofit bodies[12], 34.6% were *de facto* associations (unrecognized), 16.6% were religious institutes and other ecclesiastical bodies, and 7.4% were cooperatives. Forty-five percent of the associations and 80% of the cooperatives were established after 1978.

12   There is a larger number of foundations here because most of the charity and welfare activities of the Catholic Church existed under this legal form before the sixties.

Table 5 Workers distributed according to nature of employment

	Number	%
Independent collaborators	3,790	7.76
Collaborators by agreement	2,656	5.44
Employees	21,271	43.58
Volunteer workers	14,921	30.57
NR	6,163	12.62
Total	48,801	100.00

Source: see Table 4

The study does not quantify the value added produced by the services surveyed, but gives the break-down of sources of revenue. It confirms the importance of the partnership with the public sector: 45.3% of the services receive systematic financing from public entities and 33.7% receive occasional funding (see Table 6). Contributions and financing from public entities represent over 50% of the income for 22.5% of the services studied. As further confirmation of the close link between services and public entities, 42.7% have contractual agreements with public entities and a high percentage of services (between 70 and 80%) have systematic operating links with local public entities.

Table 6 Percentage of different types of income sources contributing percentage shares of the total income of the organizations interviewed

Share of total income	from 1 to 25%	from 26 to 50%	from 51 to 75%	from 76 to 100%
Type of source of income	% of organizations			
Self-financing, production of goods	5.5	2.3	1.2	2.1
Self-financing through members	10.3	3.0	1.3	2.1
Financial agreements with public entities	11.1	9.0	6.8	11.4
Financial agreements with private entities	1.9	0.8	0.3	0.5
Financing from users	8.9	6.4	6.9	13.2
Income from property	8.2	1.1	0.4	0.6
Contributions from public entities	19.9	4.3	1.8	2.5
Donations from individuals	25.9	6.2	2.5	2.8
Contributions from dioceses	4.1	1.1	0.3	0.4
Contributions from parishes	6.1	1.7	0.4	0.5
Contributions from religious congregations	10.7	4.4	1.0	2.0

Source: see Table 4

4.2 Social Solidarity Cooperatives

Since the mid-seventies, there has been a growing number of cooperatives providing cultural, education and social security services, encouraged by the partial non-distribution constraint to which cooperatives are subject. A distinction has been created between cooperatives that have maintained their original purpose (providing services or work opportunities for their members), and those that have adopted, either in their statutes or in fact, the nonprofit constraint and have chosen to provide services to weak or marginalized individuals, even if not members, as their main aim. The latter are defined as "social solidarity cooperatives". Although this legal form has not yet been ratified by law, it may be included in the nonprofit sector. According to the Ministry of Labor, there were 1,242 social solidarity cooperatives registered at the end of 1988 and 2,598 at the end of 1989; it is likely, however, that some of them are not yet operative. A study carried out in 1987 collected detailed information on 496 cooperatives (Borzaga and Failoni, 1990). The phenomenon is a very recent one: the first cooperatives were established in 1978-79. The cooperatives examined (see Table 7) had a membership of 19,858, of whom 4,265 (21.4%) were volunteers and 4,761 (20.4%) paid workers. In addition, there were 2,277 non-member volunteers and 276 *conscientious objectors*[13].

Of the overall work time utilized by the cooperatives during a standard week, 15.9% was covered by volunteer members, 8.4% by volunteer non-members and 6.4% by conscientious objectors. The volunteer members were mainly male (52.2%), adults (40% over the age of 40), involved on a steady basis (56.2%) and mainly had organizational and administrative functions. They seem to play an entrepreneurial role within the cooperative.

---

13 *Conscientious objectors* are young men who apply to work in public services, managed by public entities or by private organizations, rather than be called up for military service. The option of choosing civilian service has existed since 1972. Nonprofit organizations were the first to take advantage of this system, and they make use of the greatest number of conscientious objectors in Italy.

**Table 7 Distribution of the work force employed as of 31.12.1986
in a sample of social solidarity cooperatives**

	Number of individuals	Number per coop.	Weekly hrs worked	hours worked as % of total hours	Weekly hours per coop	Number of weekly hrs per person
Member volunteers:						
Males	2,228	4.5				
Females	2,037	4.1				
Total	4,265	8.6	32,345	15.9	65.2	7.6
Non-member volunteers:						
Male	975	2.0				
Female	1,302	2.6				
Total	2,277	4.6	17,201	8.4	34.7	7.6
Member workers:						
Male	1,188	2.4				
Female	2,869	5.8				
Total	4,057	8.2	118,436	58.1	238.8	29.2
Employees:						
Male	232	0.5				
Female	472	1.0				
Total	704	1.4	22,806	11.2	45.9	32.4
Conscientious objectors	276	0.6	13,099	6.4	26.4	47.5
Total	11,579	23.3	203,887	100.0	411.0	17.6

Source: Borzaga and Failoni (1990).

During 1986 the activities of the cooperatives reached 35,000 users. Balance sheets data from 1985 point to the close link with public entities in this case, too: of the 66 billion lire of income, 44% came from public contributions, 34.3% from the sale of goods and services on the market and the rest from other sources. The same study also confirms the rapid development of the phenomena: in three years (from 1983 to 1985), income increased by 151.6% and property increased by 105.6%.

5   The Economic Importance of the Nonprofit Sector

The nonprofit sector has grown significantly in Italy since the 1960's. Even though the data are very limited, it is now possible to attempt an aggregated estimate of the size reached at the end of the 1980's.

Excluding nonprofit organizations in agriculture and manufacturing and using the data of the Census, and applying a growth rate of 40% during the ten-year period[14], we estimate that, excluding voluntary work, there are:

a.   50.000 employees or member-workers in about 10.000 nonprofit organizations operating in social services;

b.   150,000 people employed in nonprofit education organizations;

c.   100,000 people employed in nonprofit health organizations;

d.   10,000 people employed in nonprofit cultural and recreational activities.

These four industries alone thus engaged about 310,000 individuals (excluding volunteers) by the end of the 1980s, which represents 1.3% of overall employment and 7.2% of employment in services not for sale.

6   Conclusions

The most significant characteristics of the Italian nonprofit sector include:

a.   the small size of organizations with citizen participation and volunteer members;

b.   the limited importance of individual and corporate donors and the much greater financial contribution of the public sector in support of the nonprofit sector;

c.   evolution alongside of an underdeveloped public welfare system and

d.   gradual specialization in the production of services where government shortcomings are greatest.

---

14   This rate is deduced from the national accounting for "other services" (see Table 2).

The increasing presence of the nonprofit sector clashes with a legal framework which is still anchored in obsolete models. As a consequence the adoption of and adherence to the non-distribution constraint in organizations founded over the past twenty years (associations and cooperatives) is voluntary and depends on the moral probity of the administrators. Moreover, the absence of a general provision of a law governing the tax exemption of donations reduces the opportunities of the nonprofit sector to make use of contributions from private individuals.

The future growth of the nonprofit sector depends therefore on improvements in the legal framework, as well as on a better definition of its role vis-à-vis the public sector.

REFERENCES

ANHEIER H.K. and SEIBEL W., 1990, "Sociological and Political Science Approaches to the Third Sector", in Anheier H.K. and Seibel W., 1990, (eds.), *The Third Sector: Comparative Studies of Nonprofit Organizations*, Berlin, De Gruyter.

ANHEIER H.K. and DIMAGGIO P.J., 1990, "The Sociology of Nonprofit Organizations and Sectors", in *Annu. Rev. Sociol.*, n. 16.

BARBETTA G.B. and RANCI P., 1990, *The Nonprofit Sector in Italy*, paper presented at the 1990 Independent Sector Spring Forum, Boston.

BASSANINI M.G. and RANCI P., 1990, (ed.), *Non per profitto. Il settore dei osggetti che erogano servizi di interesse collettivo senza fine di lucro*, Rome, Fondazione Olivetti.

BORZAGA C. and FAILONI G., 1990, *La cooperazione di solidarietà sociale in Italia*, mimeo, Brescia.

BORZAGA C., 1991, (ed.), *Il Terzo Sistema: una nuova dimensione della complessità economica e sociale*, Padova, Fondazione E. Zancan.

COLOZZI I. and ROSSI G., 1985, "I gruppi di volontariato in Italia: elementi per una classificazione", in Tavazza L., 1985, (ed.), *Volontariato ed enti locali*, Bologna, Dehoniane.

Consulta Nazionale delle Opere Caritative ed Assistenziali, 1990, *Chiesa ed emarginazione in Italia*, Rapporto n. 2, Vol. I, Turin, LDC.

DONATI P., 1991, "L'emergere del privato sociale: declino dello Stato Sociale o novità di uno scenario?", in *Impresa Sociale*, n.2.

GUARINO G., 1989, "Le fondazioni. Alcune considerazioni generali", in Rescigno P., 1989, (ed.), *Le fondazioni in Italia e all'estero*, Padova, Cedam.

Iref, 1990, *Rapporto sull'associazionismo sociale*, Rome, Tecnodip.

JAMES E., 1990, "Economic Theories of the Nonprofit Sector: A Comparative Perspective", in Anheier H.K. and Seibel W., 1990, (eds.), *The Third Sector: Comparative Studies of Nonprofit Organizations*, Berlin, De Gruyter.

MORTARA A., 1973, (ed.), *Le fondazioni italiane*, Milan, F. Angeli.

MORTARA A., 1985, (ed.), *Le associazioni italiane*, Milan, F. Angeli.

PASQUINELLI S., 1987, "Volontariato ed ente pubblico: un primo bilancio delle ricerche", in *Prospettive Sociali e Sanitarie*, 13-14.

PASQUINELLI S., 1989, "Voluntary Action in the Welfare State: The Italian Case", in *Nonprofit and Voluntary Sector Quarterly*, Vol. 18, n. 4.

PREITE D., 1990, "Le caratteristiche essenziali delle iniziative di Terzo Sistema", in Borzaga C., 1991, (ed.), *Il Terzo Sistema: una nuova dimensione della complessità economica e sociale*, Padova, Fondazione E. Zancan.

RESCIGNO P., 1989, *Le fondazioni in Italia e all'estero*, Padua, Cedam.

SEIBEL W., 1988, "The Function of Mellow Weakness: Nonprofit Organizations as Problem Non-Solvers", in James E., 1988, (ed.), *The Nonprofit Sector in International Perspective. Studies in Comparative Culture and Policy*, New York and Oxford, Oxford University Press.

POLICY ISSUES FOR THE UK VOLUNTARY SECTOR IN THE 1990s

Martin KNAPP

and

Jeremy KENDALL*

Personal Social Services Research Unit (PSSRU)

University of Kent at Canterbury

Introduction

The scale, scope and variety of Britain's voluntary (nonprofit) sector are appreciated by few. A majority of the general public could list a number of the largest voluntary organisations, and most participate in the sector by volunteering or by giving money. However, knowledge about what government does and what for-profit businesses look like is not mirrored by any widespread understanding of voluntary organisations. The voluntary sector is associated with fund-raising campaigns, with famine relief, with charity shops in the High Street, with organisations like the Salvation Army and Barnardo's, but because of its very diversity and fragmentation, and because so much of its work goes unnoticed and unheralded, the sector as pioneer, advocate, substitute, champion of the minority interest, quality benchmark, and specialist supplier is rarely recognised.

---

*   Work on this paper was made possible by funding from the UK Department of Health (Knapp) and the Joseph Rowntree Foundation (Kendall), though responsibility for the contents rests with the authors alone.

After a lean period in the 1950s and 1960s, the British voluntary sector has received considerable encouragement from central government, notably from the Conservative administrations since 1979. The relative contribution of the sector to the national product and its "market share" in some parts of the economy have increased significantly, but have also brought problems which raise policy questions still awaiting satisfactory answers. In this paper we examine some of the questions which most concern the UK voluntary sector in the 1990s. We first set out the legal and administrative contexts within which the sector operates, and then describe its broad economic characteristics.

Three complications should be noted. First, there are legal and other differences between England, Scotland, Wales and Northern Ireland. In the interests of brevity and manageability, we concentrate on England and Wales for some purposes, for the data have not yet been gathered which would allow a comprehensive description of all relevant features of the voluntary sector. Second, there is a wider problem of lack of data, certainly by comparison to what is available for the United States or Germany for example, and this limits our discussion somewhat. Third, the definition of the voluntary sector is not straightforward, whether in law, policy or research, though we only touch on the many issues here (Kendall and Knapp, 1990).

1   Defining the Voluntary Sector

A definition of the UK voluntary sector is one of the most pressing requirements for a discussion of policies and trends, but also one of the most elusive. Building a definition from first principles would suggest criteria such as that organisations should be formally constituted, self-governing, private (independent of government), not distributing profits to those who control them, benefiting from voluntarism, and producing some public or external benefits. These criteria are arguably enshrined in the law governing charities in the UK, but there are also very many non-charity organisations which meet all of these criteria and which would be recognised as voluntary bodies pursuing objectives and facing constraints which distinguish them from government and for-profit companies.

In English law, in fact, the key distinction is between organisations which are charities and those which are not. (English law applies in England and Wales; in Scotland and Northern Ireland the law has developed separately, though is not radically different.) Although non-charity organisations which might be thought of as voluntary bodies for some purposes may receive somme favourable treatment for which other private organisations are not eligible (for example, in tax law), this treatment is neither as comprehensive nor as automatic as those constitutional and fiscal privileges enjoyed by charities. A body may only qualify as a charity if its purposes are exclusively charitable. The situation is complicated by the fact that there is no statutory definition of what constitutes a charitable purpose, for this is dependent on judicial interpretation, "systematically defined by (literally) thousands of precedents, laid down over the centuries by the decisions of generations of judges" (Gladstone, 1982, p.40).

The single most important listing of organisational objectives which are perceived as legally charitable, the so-called Romilly-McNaghten classification, dates from 1891. It largely superseded the famous 1601 catalogue of charitable activities as "the relief of poverty; ... the advancement of education; ... the advancement of religion; and ... other purposes beneficial to the community, not falling under any of the preceding heads" (Income Tax Special Purposes Commissioners v. Pemsel [1891] AC 531). Under the relief of poverty head, an organisation can be charitable if its benefits accrue only to a small group of people (National Council for Voluntary Organisations, 1990a, p.1); for the others, the organisation's purposes must be of actual benefit to the public as a whole, or a sufficient section of the public for it to achieve charitable status in law. The body largely responsible for deciding whether or not an organisation qualifies for charitable status has indicated that "it is not possible to define precisely what amounts to actual benefit or what forms a sufficient section of the public; cases must largely be considered on their merits" (Charity Commission, 1989, p.3). A large proportion of the active charities today are recognised in law under the fourth head in the Romilly-McNaghten classification. Care and protection of the sick, the young, the old and the disabled have legally been recognised as being beneficial to the public, with the caveat that these purposes be pursued to the exclusion of private gain.

Acts of Parliament relating to English law have been remedial, and have *not* aimed to change the content of the law, or offer a statutory definition of charity; the object has been to provide an enabling framework in which private property can be devoted effectively to public purposes. The most significant recent piece of legislation is the Charities Act 1960 which, building on previous statutes, established the Charity Commission in its present form and provided for the compulsory registration of most charities. Technically, the Charity Commissioners' role is to act on behalf of the Crown which, as *parens patriae*, safeguards the interests of "the public" for whose benefit the charity operates (by definition), together with the Crown's principal legal agent, the Attorney-General. To fulfil this function, it has a number of supervisory, administrative and quasi-judicial powers.

If the Commissioners' controlling powers are regarded as a drawback, the advantages of a good public image, and eligibility for financial help from other charities will usually be enough to encourage organisations to seek charitable status, except perhaps the very smallest and most informally constituted. Another important benefit of charitable status is eligibility for tax breaks. Charities are exempt from most forms of direct taxation, including income and corporation tax, provided the tax collection agency, the Inland Revenue, is satisfied that the income on which relief is sought has been applied for charitable purposes. Relief of 80 per cent on local property tax is mandatory (whereas for non-charity voluntary bodies it is discretionary), and charities also qualify for tax deductibility on certain transfers from individuals or companies. Only registered charities can be certain of their eligibility to receive grants from trusts and foundations. (See the section on sources of income below, and Kendall and Knapp, 1990, for a fuller account.)

2   Income, Expenditure and Employment

With currently available data it is far from straightforward to measure income or expenditure for the UK voluntary sector, and almost impossible to measure employment. As in many countries, the task is dogged by difficulties of definition and legal imprecision, and hampered by a reluctance among government statisticians to accord the sector sufficient status to warrant the collection of reliable data. We can therefore paint only an incomplete picture of the sector's activity.

2.1   The Sources of Income

The National Council for Voluntary Organisations estimates there to be about 350,000 voluntary bodies in the UK, but there is no single register for these, and the most complete picture across all activities relates to registered charities, of which there are now some 175,000. Although they are supposed to lodge copies of their annual accounts with the Charity Commissioners (or with the Inland Revenue in Scotland and Northern Ireland), the majority do not, often because they are moribund. The Charities Aid Foundation annually collects and publishes detailed income and expenditure data for the country's 400 largest charities, with size defined by total voluntary income from covenants, legacies, other gifts and voluntary fundraising. Better estimates come from three sample surveys by Posnett, in 1975, 1980 and 1985, for England and Wales. At 1990-91 prices, Posnett's (1987) estimates would pitch the total income of registered charities at approximately £17 billion, equivalent to more than 4 per cent of Gross National Product. This compares with 3.4 per cent of GNP in 1980-81.

The total and component sources of income from Posnett's samples are given in Table 1. The gross income of registered charities almost doubled in real terms between 1975 and 1985, though growth was slower in the second half of the period. Part of the increase in income was associated with an estimated 27 per cent growth in the number of charities over the ten years, but Posnett (1987) attributes most of the change to increases in government grants and income from fees and charges (some of which are demand-side subsidies from the public sector). The 60 per cent contribution of fees to income in 1985-86 may be exaggerated somewhat by the inclusion of private schools and housing associations (Leat, 1990). Nevertheless, the growing contribution of fee income has been an important feature of recent years. In his 1985 study, Posnett also looked at 1 per cent of all newly registered charities, and found grants from statutory bodies accounted for 44 per cent of their total income, compared with 11 per cent for the full sample, giving further evidence of the growing importance of the public sector to the voluntary, and of the voluntary sector to the public. The main components of voluntary sector income are now described in more detail.

Charitable donations by households reach voluntary organisations along many different routes. Most charitable contributions by individuals whilst alive do not carry tax exemptions, and so there is no comprehensive reporting of donations through tax returns to the Inland Revenue. Only covenants (donations by way of trust of at least four years' duration), payroll donations (up to a maximum of £600 per year) and a recently introduced Gift Aid scheme (for single cash gifts of over £600 per year) carry tax advantages. The impact of the

**Table 1: The Income of Registered Charities
in England and Wales, 1975-76 – 1985-86**

	1985-86 £m	1985–86 %	1980–81 %	1975-76 %	1975-76 / 1985-86 %
Fund raising	1925.3	15.2	12.2	28.4	1.7
Fees and charges	7672.3	60.7	65.9	34.1	237.4
Rents and investment	1398.4	11.1	12.2	21.7	-3.5
Grants from statutory bodies	1375.7	10.9	7.9	7.3	183.7
Commercial activity and other	278.4	100.0	1.8	8.5	-51.0
Total	12650.1	100.0	100.0	100.0	89.7

Sources: Posnett (1987)

introduction and extension of tax changes has probably been muted (see below). Once dead, legacies offer opportunities for giving, and carry tax benefits.

Individual monetary donations represent about 15 per cent of the total annual income of registered charities. The Charity Household Survey for 1989-90 (Halfpenny, 1990) found the median household donation to be just £1.28 per month, less than 0.25 per cent of median gross household income, and a much smaller proportion than the equivalent for the USA (Weber, 1990; Hodgkinson and Weitzman, 1989). As in the US (Auten and Rudney, 1990), the distribution of donations is highly skewed: 49 per cent of the respondents gave £1 per month or less, and 6 per cent gave £30 per month or more. Aggregation, taking account of sampling error, suggests that donations by Britain's households in 1989-90 were between £3.4 billion and £5 billion. Individual donations have grown since the mid 1970s, though the Charity Household Surveys suggest a halt to the growth, and possibly a decline, in the last two years. The share of household donations to total charity sector income has halved in the last decade.

Corporate philanthropy is less common and less generous in the UK than in, for example, Japan or the USA (Flaherty, 1991), though some giving is hidden: financial assistance comprises about 43 per cent of total corporate aid to charities (Saxon-Harrold, 1990b), compared to about 80 per cent in the USA (Cardillo Platzer, 1987). Financial support amounts to less than 2 per cent of total charity sector income (Posnett, 1987). Tax incentives are not as generous as those found in many other countries, which partly explains the level of contributions, but there is also no established (recent) tradition of corporate sector lead in the alleviation of social problems and the promotion of cultural and other activities. The 400 largest corporate donors gave just 0.18 per cent of their pre-tax profits to charity in 1988, no more than the 1977 proportion despite a more favourable tax environment. Since 1986, companies have been able to make one-off donations of up to 3 per cent of annual ordinary dividends, with tax deducted at the standard (basic) rate, currently 25 per cent. The gross payment can be charged against a company's profits before calculation of corporation tax. The Gift Aid scheme is another new concession, available to companies as well as households (see above). In fact, panel data for a subsample of large companies monitored over a few years reveal real increases between 1987 and 1990 in the amounts donated, with no evidence as yet of Britain's current recession reversing this upward trend (Saxon-Harrold, 1990b).

Charitable support from *trusts and foundations* (bodies making grants from an endowment, rather than soliciting contributions) grew particularly after the turn of the Century, with rapid industrialisation enabling some individuals to amass vast personal fortunes. In previous centuries the wealthy had always funded welfare activities, especially churches, schools and hospitals, and some had formed trusts to pursue their philanthropic wishes. A great many trusts were established in the early years of the Twentieth Century to address some of the fundamental social problems of the age and to encourage more systematic giving. At the other end of the Century statistics are available for the 400 largest grant-making trusts (Charities Aid Foundation, 1989). For these top 400, assets and grants made have both been growing in recent years, partly a result of inflated property values and rents; the recent property market slump may now put a brake on these trends. However, to put these transfers in perspective, the overall scale of "intra-sectoral" grant-making is very limited: trusts accounted for only 1.5 per cent of the charitable income of registered charities in 1985 (Saxon-Harrold, 1990a).

Income from *commercial activities* takes three forms: (a) service charges, payments by or on behalf of users, such as for the care provided by voluntary residential or nursing homes, or membership subscriptions; (b) contract fees paid on behalf of users by government agencies; and (c) venturing, diversification into other markets in order to cross-subsidise charitable activities. It is not possible to separate with available aggregate data (such as in Table 1), but it is clear that commercial income as a whole has become increasingly important to the voluntary sector – household purchases of goods and services from charities account for more than 45 per cent of total household transfers to the sector (Saxon-Harrold, 1990a) – and venturing has grown fast from a low base (Leat, 1990), though lags behind parallel developments in the US (Perlmutter and Adams, 1989). Current public policy trends should bring about a major growth in government contracting with the sector (Gutch, Kunz and Spencer, 1990).

Government support for the voluntary sector is now very influential (see Table 2). Support is of three kinds. *Direct* support, such as via grants or contracts, comprised about 11 per cent of total sector income in 1985-86 (from grants) plus sizeable chunks of the 61 per cent recorded as "fee income" (Table 1). Total government funding of the voluntary sector (the charity sector plus non-charity voluntaries) amounted to some £2 billion in 1989. This direct funding grew substantially for some years, but then appeared to plateau in the late 1980s. Local authority funding of the voluntary sector has fallen, despite legislation to encourage or mandate a "more mixed economy". *Indirect* support through demand-side subsidies (such as social security payments), are of unknown magnitude, routed as they are through individual purchases of services, and not necessarily targeted solely at the voluntary sector. The largest of these subsidies are currently the social security supports to people with long-term needs for residential or nursing home care, totalling more than £1 billion per annum (though substantially less than half goes to the voluntary sector), and housing benefit for low income families. *Hidden* support is in the form of tax exemptions or benefits in kind. Tax exemptions are an obvious benefit of charitable status: registered charities are partially or fully exempt from taxation on capital gains, retained earnings generated by charitable activities, investment income and dividends, some income from trading, and some proportion of local property tax, and are also able to receive tax-deductible donations. Non-charity voluntary organisations enjoy fewer and often discretionary tax advantages. In 1988, tax concessions amounted to around £639 million from central government and £150 million in property tax relief from local authorities (Charities Aid Foundation, 1989). About 1 per cent of the total tax bill of charities is given in charitable

Table 2: Government Support for Voluntary Organisations[1]

Funding Agency	1986-87 £m
Central government departments	279.5
Non-departmental public bodies	1668.3
Local authorities	402.1
Health authorities	25.2
Total direct support	2375.1
Tax exemptions[2]	800.0
Support «in kind»[3]	213.7
Total indirect support	1013.7
Total government support	3388.8

1. Excludes demand-side subsidies.
2. This an estimate by Maslen (1988). Property tax exemptions, where appropriate, are included under support in kind.
3. Calculated as 50 per cent of direct grant aid from local and health authorities. See Leat et al. (1986). This support in kind comes from health and local authorities.

relief. Support in kind from local authorities has been estimated to be as much as 50 per cent of their total grant aid (Leat, Tester and Unell, 1986).

2.2   Expenditure

Data on expenditure are available for only the largest registered charities, and there is no published equivalent to Posnett's (1987) representative sample estimates for income. For the largest 200 charities, total expenditure grew annually in real terms between 1981-82 and 1987-88 by between 6 and 10 per cent (and in 1984-85 it reached 17 per cent), but in 1987-88 and 1988-89 a fall in expenditure of 2 per cent was registered. The component shares of expenditure for these large charities remained relatively stable over the period. Spending on the principle charitable cause accounted for just over four-fifths of the total, and fund-raising administration accounted for around 7 per cent (Charities Aid Foundation, *Charity Trends,* various years).

2.3   Employment

The most glaring gap in knowledge about the sector relates to employment. Ashworth (1985) reported that the largest 200 registered charities were employing the equivalent of 47,500 full-time workers in 1984. For the sector as a whole we must currently rely on informed guesswork. In the late 1980s there were at least 250,000 full-time equivalent employees in the sector (National Council for Voluntary Organisation, 1990b), and maybe as many as 500,000 or more (Keynote Report, 1990), which would have represented 1 or 2 per cent of the employed workforce in 1988. The main source of UK employment data is the triennial Census of Employment which classifies reporting units according to their Standard Industrial Classification code only, not distinguishing ownership types within each industry. The only attempt to estimate employment in the sector from this census (Ashworth, 1984), again more guesswork than scientific inference, suggested a range of between 100,000 and 200,000 full-time equivalent employees in the sector in 1981, broadly agreeing with an estimate obtained by Gerard (1983) based on a Gallup survey of 298 charities in 1978.

More is known about volunteering – freely supplied labour – than paid employment in the voluntary sector, though again the data are some way short of the ideal. A poll conducted in March 1990 found that 39 per cent of people had undertaken voluntary work in the previous year, and 16 per cent in the previous week (Volunteer Centre, 1990). The proportions in 1981 were 44 per cent and 18 per cent (Humble, 1982), though based on slightly different questions. The Charity Household Survey of 1988-89 reported that 30 per cent of respondents had undertaken at least one volunteering activity in the last month (Halfpenny, 1990). It is clear that most people give a relatively small amount of time (the most recently estimated average is 40 minutes a month), concentrate on just a few activities, and volunteer infrequently (of those who volunteer, about half do so only once a year). We will not attempt to put a monetary value on volunteer inputs, but the total contribution of time and money is clearly vast (Knapp, 1990).

3   Policy Issues for the 1990s

A variety of challenges face the UK voluntary sector during the 1990s and beyond, and here we can only consider a few. We will concentrate on four: (a) trust, and the part it plays in encouraging people to support charitable causes, linked to the issue of whether tightening the regulatory controls of organisations can raise public confidence; (b) the factors associated with donations in Britain; (c) changes currently underway in the balance of government support away from grants in favour of contracts; and (d) the replacement of some supply-side subsidies with demand-side payments.

3.1 Trust and Charity

Contract failure theory highlights the importance of trust in transactions involving charities (Hansmann, 1980, 1987). Several informational difficulties arise with donative voluntary organisations, so that trust in the supplier from actual and potential donors becomes crucial. The single most important problem is the separation of the donor from the "cause" or recipient, with the consequences that outputs are unobservable and the donor is open to exploitation. Trust is then an efficient mechanism for economising on the uncertainty costs of the transfers transactions. Charitable activities particularly susceptible to this form of contract failure, and therefore more likely to be buffetted by shifts in public perceptions and prejudices, include international relief efforts, disaster funds, animal welfare organisations and medical research. The crucial distinction is between organisations operating under a nondistribution constraint and profit-distributing organisations, the former being perceived to be more trustworthy. However, there is an informational problem within the voluntary sector which arises because of another incentive: the fiscal privileges available to organisations which obtain entry into the sector, and which are not available to profit-distributing companies. These create a financial incentive for for-profit suppliers to try to assume the guise of charities or non-charity voluntary bodies. The effective monitoring of the nondistribution constraint is critical, and in the UK is carried out by the Charity Commission and the Inland Revenue.

The role of law is therefore pivotal in generating trust among donors that their charitable contributions are put to appropriate use. The Charity Commission's central role as watchdog has been widely recognised, and there has been almost unanimous approval of reforms which would give the Commission more teeth. Government proposals were recently detailed, "designed to produce a stronger and more modern framework of supervision which will equip the Charity Commission for a more active role, narrow the scope for abuse, encourage trustees to shoulder their responsibilities, and ensure continuing public confidence in the sector" (Cm 694, 1989, paragraph 1.18). Among the measures suggested are stricter monitoring of accounts, disqualification of trustees in certain circumstances (such as conviction for fraud), and the exchange of information between the Commission and other government bodies. The fact that the Parliamentary

Bill needed to implement many of these proposals has not yet been enacted is causing concern, for trust, as a "moral resource", both grows with use and decays with disuse (Hirschman, 1984).

Over and above legislative controls, the voluntary sector can itself contribute to the generation of greater trust. Indicating to the general public that voluntary contributions are honestly and efficiently used for charitable purposes, and that impropriety is not tolerated, is a common aim. Examples of collective action from within the sector are voluntary codes of practice to curb malpractice in the sector's fundraising activities (National Council for Voluntary Organisation, 1986; Woodfield et al., 1987; Cm 694, 1989, chapter 10). Making actual and potential donors aware of such self-regulation is an important complement to the external regulation from the government or its appointees.

3.2 Barriers to Giving

Perceptions of voluntary organisations play a major part in influencing the amount and direction of philanthropy, along with income levels and variability, taxation and the "price" of giving, government action and roles, and administrative and fund-raising costs. There is limited UK evidence on these influences (reviewed in Knapp and Kendall, 1991a). Three cross-section studies have addressed the income effect on monetary donations; they suggest that increases in donations of between 4 and 6 per cent will result from a 10 per cent increase in income (Jones and Posnett, 1991). Income levels are related to both the amount donated and philanthropic participation in the first place, whilst factors such as level of education, housing and employment status appear only to influence participation and not the amount donated. A worrying implication of the UK income elasticity estimates is that, as aggregate income rises, so the proportion donated to charity will probably fall, other things being equal, whereas the demand for the kinds of product supplied by voluntary organisations is unlikely to fall. Organisations must either increase fund-raising expenditure or improve the returns from it.

For covenanted giving, the response to a 10 per cent increase in income lies somewhere between 7 per cent and 12 per cent. As a proportion of income, donating via covenants is lower among higher income groups (Jones and Posnett, 1990). The variability of giving over time by individuals has not been studied (compare Auten and Rudney, 1990). If giving responds to expected or permanent income, as well as actual income, the anticipation and subsequent realisation of an economic recession in the UK would help to explain the fall in household charitable donations since 1988-89.

The "price" of a donation takes on at least two meanings: one related to the marginal tax deduction, and the other to the amount of administrative expenditure incurred by a voluntary organisation (diverting funds away from the targets of charity). The outputs of most voluntary organisations are "normal" goods for which the price elasticity is expected to be negative, so theory would suggest that a lower marginal tax rate raises the price of donations and reduces giving. (It does not matter if the donor gets no tax relief on a donation; the marginal tax rate determines the price of giving so long as the donor realises that the charity can claim the taxes paid from the government.) UK evidence on the impact of tax changes and income levels on donations implies that an increase in the (after-tax) income of higher rate tax payers has a smaller effect on total donations than an equal increase in the income of lower-rate taxpayers. This means that a tax cut at the top end of the range (such as the reduction from 60 to 40 per cent a few years ago), which is made possible at the expense of those on lower incomes, will reduce the overall amount contributed to charity (Jones and Posnett, 1991). Like the best of the most recent US evidence, information on the UK does not offer much support for treasury efficiency (Steinberg, 1990). Marginal tax rates do not influence individual covenanted giving (Jones and Posnett, 1990).

A fundamental problem for UK voluntary organisations is that large sections of the population know little about the mechanisms for giving. Only 29 per cent of respondents in a recent household survey knew about the tax advantages associated with charitable status, less than half had heard of giving to charity via covenant, and almost half of those eligible to participate in payroll donations schemes were unaware of them (Halfpenny, 1990). 19 per cent of respondents had never thought of making bequests in their wills. In addition to this ignorance among the general public about the means by which voluntary organisations may be supported, there are major misconceptions about administrative and fund-raising activities. The same survey found that 45 per cent of British people agreed with the statement that "there is no point giving money to the bigger charities because so little of the money actually gets to the cause", and 67 per cent were of the view that most charities waste too much in administration costs. The median estimate of the proportion spent on administration was 51 per cent for UK-focussed charities and 60 per cent for those helping the Third World, when the real figure is around 16 per cent. The "conventional wisdom", as Weisbrod (1988, chapter 5) puts it, is that people regard a larger fund-raising percentage as objectionable, and leads them to donate less. Posnett and Sandler (1989) reached the same conclusion from their analysis of the 300 largest UK charities (in 1985-86), with all charitable subsectors suffering in this regard, but overseas and social welfare charities probably suffering more than health and religion charities. Legacies appeared not to be responsive to the proportion of expenditure allocated to fund-raising and administration.

3.3 Replacing Grants with Contracts

Government agencies fund voluntary bodies for a host of admirable and other reasons, the rationales including the promotion of choice, the development of specialised services, the pursuit of cost-effectiveness, the encouragement of innovation through flexibility, the facilitation of participative benefits, and so on (see, for example, Kramer, 1981; Knapp, Robertson and Thomason, 1990). These are long-standing justifications for government support in the UK (Webb and Webb, 1912; Judge and Smith, 1983), but recent policy initiatives have sought to formalise them. For example, radical reforms to health and social care include promotion of a mixed economy, with emphasis on the roles to be played by the voluntary sector. Choice, cost-effectiveness, flexibility and innovativeness are at the forefront of these reforms. At the same time, central government is urging local and health authorities to move away from general grant-funding to more tightly specified contracts. Many undesirable consequences may follow from this change in the balance of government funding, with voluntary agencies fearing that competition could reduce choice, encourage commercialisation at the cost of loss of mission, inflate administrative costs for both voluntary and government sectors, and constrain autonomy and flexibility.

As the contractual links between voluntary and government agencies become more formal they will impose on all parties various monitoring conditions, as well as penalties for non-compliance. Contract monitoring requires "relevant, accurate and complete information ... to judge costs, performance and effectiveness" (DeHoog, 1984, p.244), and appears to threaten the autonomy and fundamental character of the sector. As James (1987, p.409) argues, from a normative standpoint society has a right and a duty to exercise some control over how public funds are spent, whilst from a positive perspective, "politicians have the power to demand *a quid pro quo,* and they use this power to establish rules and standards that gain them goodwill from diverse constituencies". The difficulty is that voluntary bodies may find they cannot afford to refuse government money, but in accepting it they must acquiesce too much. Unable to "exit", to use Hirschman's (1970) model and terminology, "they may try to change existing conditions (... "voice" ...) or to nestle closer to authorities in hope of reward [loyalty]" (Lipsky and Smith, 1990, p.645). Kramer, however, concluded that fears about losses of autonomy had been exaggerated (Kramer, 1981, 1990), with various factors working together to protect the sector's independence. These included a multiplicity of funding sources, the protection of traditional values and practices afforded by some contractual forms and countervailing oligopsony power. The current tension has resulted, not because UK voluntary organisations have never faced monitoring restrictions or experienced the joys of contractual links, but because the climate of policy and opinion in the 1990s is now more strongly interventionist and dirigiste. Available UK research evidence has not been gathered in such a climate and cannot yet say much about the consequences for voluntary sector suppliers, government funders or clients of the replacement of grants by contracts.

3.4 The Shift to Demand-Side Subsidies

The second major shift in public sector support for the voluntary sector in recent years has been a growth in demand-side subsidies at the expense of supply-side payments. In areas such as housing and residential and nursing home care, central government has encouraged the use of "vouchers". For example, the proportion of all residents in voluntary sector residential homes for elderly people supported by local authorities under supply-side payments fell from 65 per cent in 1975 to 17 per cent in 1988, whilst the proportion supported by the social security system through what amount to demand-side subsidies grew from close to zero to 48 per cent by 1986-87 (Darton and Wright, 1990).

The putative advantages of such a shift include the hope that consumer choice will be enhanced, that suppliers will be forced to respond more readily and rapidly to the preferences of service users, and that the discipline of the market will improve the efficiency of service delivery. These will not be easily achieved, if US experience is any indication (see, for example, Kramer, 1987; Lipsky and Smith, 1990), and there are also countervailing disadvantages. Choice may not easily be extended in service areas where, through ill-health, frailty, lack of knowledge, information or expertise, users are in a weak position vis-à-vis suppliers, or where the threat of exit (switching suppliers) is not credible. In addition, there are supply side characteristics such as product complexity and the presence of economies of scale pushing markets naturally towards monopoly or oligopoly, also militating against competition. These features of certain markets, coupled with the trend in public policy towards closer scrutiny of performance when government money is involved, could increase rather than reduce regulatory intervention and increase the risk of "coercive isomorphism" (DiMaggio and Powell, 1983), forcing voluntary sector suppliers to increasingly resemble the public sector agencies. The result could be less choice rather than more.

The other concern in the voluntary sector about the move towards demand-side subsidies is the fear that it cannot compete on equal terms with for-profit agencies. In the case of residential care for elderly people, for example, constraints faced by the voluntary but not the for-profit sector allowed the latter to expand rapidly in response to a considerable growth in publicly-subsidised demand. (Demographic shifts and increases in the wealth holdings of elderly people were partly responsible, but the primary cause was liberalisation of the social security system.) The voluntary sector's market share fell from 20 per cent of beds in 1975 to 13 per cent in 1988, while the for-profit sector's share grew from 15 per cent to 44 per cent. There was probably a labour supply constraint: volunteer or low-paid staff will have found other voluntary activities to be more attractive than residential care of elderly people (a long-standing problem for this sector), and those seeking a career in this service area may have been attracted by public sector salary levels. Of more importance was the capital constraint. Voluntary bodies have generally found it harder to raise new capital revenue, being unable to offer dividends to attract investors, and so respond more slowly than the for-profit sector to rapid increases in demand. This restraint on voluntary sector responsiveness is not insurmountable, for demand-side subsidies could be accompanied by government supply-side support, as the rented housing market illustrates. In the case of housing, generous government capital grants (introduced in 1974) allowed the voluntary sector to increase its market share from 1.9 per cent in 1971 to 8.2 per cent in 1988 (Hills, 1989).

4   Conclusion

The voluntary sector's contribution to British society and to the British economy is substantial, yet relatively little is known about its broad magnitudes, or about how to address those issues which appear to be uppermost in the minds of actors in the sector itself and in government. There is, in fact, a very important parallel between the state of research knowledge about the voluntary sector and the impact of government policy. Both appear to have some of their greatest effects through indirect and often unintended routes. Some of the most useful research did not set out to study the voluntary sector but something broader, and fortuitously chanced upon it along the way. Equally, some of the policy changes of recent years which have had the biggest impact on the British voluntary sector have been addressing other concerns, such as the promotion of choice and cost-effectiveness in social care, the expansion of pre-school day care, the development of housing for people with special needs, or the encouragement of training schemes for the unemployed. Policies in these areas have done much more to shape the income, expenditure and employment profiles of voluntary organisations than legislation or fiscal reforms specifically directed at the sector itself, although we have seen that the latter are likely to be important factors in determining the public's perceptions of, and responses to, the sector. It must be of concern that the sector can be so influenced by unintended or residual consequences, and a further item for the agenda for the 1990s should be a more consolidated, purposive public policy framework for the sector. Such a framework should be enabling rather than dirigiste, within which the special qualities of the sector can be preserved and enhanced rather than stifled. Above all, the policy framework must avoid rupturing the delicate balance between, on the one hand, the need for trust and the valued independence with which it is intimately linked, and, on the other, the need for public accountability and control through regulation to ensure that the privileges extended to the voluntary sector are not abused.

REFERENCES

ASHWORTH M., 1984, Employment in the voluntary sector, unpublished paper, Institute of Fiscal Studies, London.

ASHWORTH M., 1985, "The Charity Financial Survey", in *Charity Statistics*, 10, 76-80.

AUTEN G. and RUDNEY G., 1990, "The variability of individual charitable giving in the US", in *Voluntas*, 1, 80-97.

CARDILLO PLATZER L., 1987, *Annual Survey of Corporate Contributions*, Conference Board.

Charities Aid Foundation, various years, *Charity Trends*, Charities Aid Foundation, Tonbridge.

Charity Commission, 1989, *Starting a Charity*, CC21, Charity Commissioners for England and Wales, London.

Cm 694, 1989, *Charities: A Framework for the Future*, HMSO, London.

DARTON R.A. and WRIGHT K.G., 1990, "The characteristics of non-statutory residential and nursing homes", in R. Parry (ed.) *Research Highlights in Social Work 18: Privatisation*, Jessica Kingsley, London.

DEHOOG R.H., 1984, "Theoretical perspectives on contracting out for services: implementation problems and possibilities of privatizing public services", in G.C. Edwards III (ed.) *Public Policy Implementation*, JAI Press., Greenwich, Connecticut.

DIMAGGIO P. and POWELL W.W., 1983, "Institutional isomorphism", in *American Sociological Review*, 48, 147-160.

FLAHERTY S., 1991, "The voluntary sector and corporate citizenship in the United States and Japan", in *Voluntas*, 2, 58-78.

GERARD D., 1983, *Charities in Britain: Conservatism or Change?*, Bedford Square Press, London.

GLADSTONE F., 1982, *Charity, Law and Social Justice*, Bedford Square Press, London.

GUTCH R., KUNZ C. and SPENCER K., 1990, *Partners or Agents?*, National Council for Voluntary Organisations, London.

HALFPENNY P., 1990, *The Charity Household Survey 1988-89*, Charities Aid Foundation, Tonbridge.

HANSMANN H., 1980, "The role of nonprofit enterprise",in *Yale Law Journal*, 89, 835-901.

HANSMANN H., 1987, "Economic theories of nonprofit organisation", in W.W. Powell (ed.) *The Nonprofit Sector: A Research Handbook*, Yale University Press, New Haven.

HILLS J., 1989, "The Voluntary Sector in Housing: The Role of British Housing Associations", in E. James (ed.) *The Nonprofit Sector in International Perspective*, Oxford University Press, Oxford.

HIRSCHMAN A.O., 1970, *Exit, Voice and Loyalty*, Harvard University Press, London.

HIRSCHMAN A.O., 1984, "Against parsimony: three easy ways of complicating some categories of economic discourse", in *American Economic Review*, Proceedings, 74, 88-96.

HODGKINSON V. and WEITZMAN M., 1989, *Dimensions of the Independent Sector*, Independent Sector, Washington.

HUMBLE, 1982, *Voluntary Action in the 1980s*, The Volunteer Centre, Berkhamsted.

JAMES E., 1987, "The nonprofit sector in comparative perspective", in W.W.Powell (ed.) *The Nonprofit Sector: A Research Handbook*, Yale University Press, New Haven.

JONES A. and POSNETT J., 1990, "Giving by covenant in the UK", in *Charity Trends*, 13, 41-44.

JONES A. and POSNETT J., 1991, "Charitable Giving by UK Households: Evidence from the family expenditure survey", in *Applied Economics*, 23, 343-351.

JUDGE K. and SMITH J., 1983, "Purchase of service in England", in *Social Services Review*, 57, 209-233.

KENDALL J. and KNAPP M.R.J., 1990, The UK voluntary sector: terminology, definitions and data, Discussion Paper 712/3, Personal Social Services Research Unit, University of Kent at Canterbury.

Keynote Report (1990), *Charities: An Industry Sector Overview*, Key Note Publications Limited, Hampton.

KNAPP M.R.J., 1990, *Time is Money: The Cost of Volunteering in Britain Today,* The Volunteer Centre, Berkhamsted.

KNAPP M.R.J., ROBERTSON E. and THOMASON C., 1990, "Public money, voluntary action: whose welfare?", in H. Anheier and W. Seibel (eds) *The Third Sector: Nonprofit Organisations in Comparative and International Perspective,* De Gruyter, Berlin.

KNAPP M.R.J. and KENDALL J., 1991, Barriers to giving, Discussion Paper 741, Personal Social Services Research Unit, University of Kent at Canterbury.

KRAMER R.M., 1981, *Voluntary Agencies in the Welfare State,* University of California Press, Berkeley.

KRAMER R.M., 1990, "Change and continuity in British voluntary organisations", in *Voluntas,* 1, 33-60.

LEAT D., 1990, *Charities and Charging: Who Pays?,* Charities Aid Foundation, London.

LEAT D., TESTER S. and UNELL J., 1986, *A Price Worth Paying?,* Policy Studies Institute, London.

LIPSKY M. and SMITH S.R., 1990, "Nonprofit organisations, government, and the welfare state", in *Political Science Quarterly,* 104, 625-648.

MASLEN P., 1988, "The effects on charities from recent tax changes", in *Charity Trends,* 11, 34-35.

National Council for Voluntary Organisations, 1986, *Malpractice in Fundraising,* National Council for Voluntary Organisations, London.

National Council for Voluntary Organisations, 1990a, What is a charity? Charity law and formation of charities, in *National Council for Voluntary Organisations Information sheet No 20,* National Council for Voluntary Organisations, London.

National Council for Voluntary Organisations, 1990b, Dimensions of the voluntary sector, in *National Council for Voluntary Organisations Information Sheet No 6a,* National Council for Voluntary Organisations, London.

PERLMUTTER F. and ADAMS C., 1989, "The voluntary sector and for-profit ventures", in *Administration in Social Work,* 14, 1-13.

POSNETT J., 1987, "Trends in the income of registered charities, 1980-1985", in *Charity Trends,* 10, 6-10.

POSNETT J. and SANDLER T., 1989, "Demand for charity donations in private nonprofit markets", in *Journal of Public Economics*, 40, 187-200.

SAXON-HARROLD S.K.E., 1990a, The voluntary sector in Britain: a statistical overview 1975-1989, paper presented at the Independent Sector Spring Research Forum, Boston.

SAXON-HARROLD S.K.E., 1990b, "Corporate support of the voluntary sector", in *Charity Trends*, 13, 9-16.

STEINBERG R., 1990, "Taxes and giving: new findings", in *Voluntas*, 1, 61-79.

Volunteer Centre, 1990, *Voluntary Action: A Survey of Public Attitudes*, The Volunteer Centre, Berkhamsted.

WEBB S. and WEBB B., 1912, *The Prevention of Destitution*, Longmans, London.

WEBER N., ed., 1990, *Giving USA '90*, AARFRC Trust for Philanthropy, New York.

WEISBROD B.A., 1988, *The Nonprofit Economy*, Harvard University Press, Cambridge.

WOODFIELD P., BINNS G., HIRST R. and NEAL, D., 1987, *Efficiency Scrutiny of the Supervision of Charities*, HMSO, London.

A PORTRAIT OF THE NONPROFIT SECTOR IN THE MIXED ECONOMY: NEW YORK, 1981–1987

Avner BEN-NER

Industrial Relations Center

University of Minnesota–Twin Cities

and

Theresa VAN HOOMISSEN*

Humphrey Institute for Public Affairs

University of Minnesota–Twin Cities

Introduction

This paper provides basic quantitative information about the economic dimensions of the United States nonprofit sector in comparison with the for-profit and government sectors. The economic portrait of the nonprofit sector in the mixed economy is drawn by employing a rich data set on New York State for the period 1981–1987.[1] The objective of the paper is thus narrowly focused on impart-

---

* John Bonin, Jeryl Mumpower, Jerald Schiff, Richard Steinberg and Dennis Young provided helpful comments on earlier drafts of this paper.
1   The data are described briefly in the Appendix. For further details, see Ben-Ner and Van Hoomissen (1989). The sectoral distribution of employment in New York closely resembles that of the rest of the northeastern United States (see Weisbrod, 1988 and Wilson, 1991). The most comprehensive national picture of the nonprofit sector available to date is presented by Weisbrod (1988). Other studies include Rudney (1987) and Hodgkinson and Weitzman (1989).

ing factual information, rather than providing an analysis of this information.[2]

Section 1 describes the legal environment in which the nonprofit sector operates and the major governmental policies that affect the sector. Section 2 examines the sectoral distributions of employment, size and wages across industries and regions in 1985. Section 3 outlines the main sectoral changes between 1981 and 1987. Section 4 characterizes the revenues and expenditures of nonprofit organizations. Section 5 concludes the paper.

1   The Nonprofit Sector: Legal and Policy Environment

In the United States, federal policies, implemented primarily through the Internal Revenue Code (IRC), establish the nonprofit organization as a legal form of incorporation. Approval of legal non-profit status is conditioned on 1) the type of activity in which the organization is engaged, and 2) the assumption of a nondistribution-of-net-earnings constraint. In order to retain the nonprofit status, members of the board of directors must direct net earnings toward enhanced service or reduced price and cannot distribute profit to owners, employees or others associated with them. Such organizations are then exempt from paying federal income taxes and many state and local taxes as well. Figure 1 provides a classification of nonprofit organizations based on the Internal Revenue Code, and Figure 2 illustrates the types of activities in which each class of nonprofit organization is permitted to engage.[3]

As Figure 1 shows, federal policy divides nonprofit organizations into two major classes: charitable and noncharitable. Charitable non-profit organizations are governed by IRC section 501(c)(3); they must serve a religious, charitable, scientific, testing for public safety, literary, or educational purpose. Noncharitable nonprofit organizations are governed (mainly) by IRC sections 501(c)(4)-(21) and

---

2   Empirical analysis of the data presented in this paper can be found in Ben-Ner and Van Hoomissen (1990 and 1992). Weisbrod (1988) provides a detailed analysis of the nonprofit sector in the United States mixed economy.
3   The classification in Figures 1 and 2 is based largely on the excellent and very detailed article by Simon (1987).

Figure 1. The Nonprofit Sector
A Conceptual Breakdown and Internal Revenue Service
Rules and Definitions

Nonprofit Organizations

Organizations exempt from federal income taxes. Net earnings may not inure to the benefit of any private shareholder or individual.

Noncharitables

Mutual benefit associations. §501(c)(4)-(21): contributions not tax-deductible (except as marked * in Figure 2).

Charitables

Public benefit associations. §501(c)(3): serve religious, charitable, scientific, testing for public safety, literary or educational purposes. Contributions tax deductible.

Other

§521, §527, other.

Public Charities

Schools, churches, hospitals, hospital-related research groups and certain publicly supported organizations which meet one of several conditions specified in §509.

Private Foundations

All §501(c)(3) organizations that are not public charities (see §509). Subject to 2% tax on investment income; complex rules regarding administration, grantmaking, etc.

Operating Foundations

Less than 15% of income to grants [see §4942(j)(3) and (5)]. Income tax deductions for cash gifts up to 50% of adj. gross income, 30% for gifts of appreciated property.

Nonoperating Foundations

Grant-making organizations: more than 15% of income to grants. Income tax deductions up to 20% of adj. gross income for cash gifts and gifts of appreciated property.

Exempt Operating Foundations	Nonexempt Operating Foundations	Independent Foundations	Company Sponsored Foundations
Publicly supported, board broadly represents the general public, not donor controlled.		Assets derived mainly from gift of an individual or family.	Derives funds from a profit making firm to make grants on a broad basis but with regard for the interests of the firm.

Note: § refers to sections of the Internal Revenue Code.
Source: Adapted from Simon (1987).

Figure 2. The Nonprofit Sector
Major Examples of Types of Nonprofit Organizations by Category

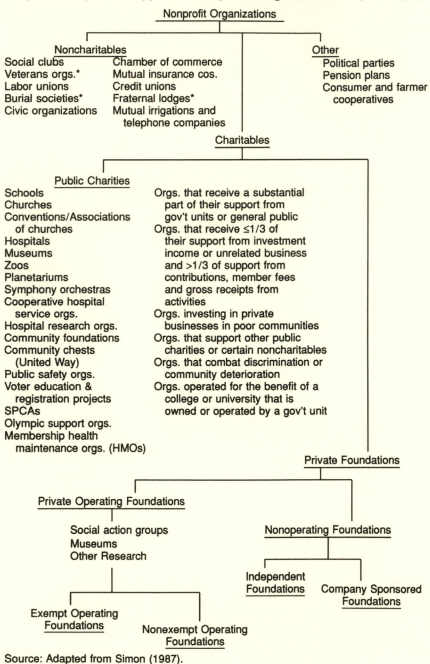

Source: Adapted from Simon (1987).

either pursue activities that primarily benefit their own members or serve the public benefit according to 501(c)(3) criteria but engage in a substantial amount of legislative lobbying (for examples, see Simon, 1987).

This classification is not entirely consistent nor is it theoretically fully justifiable, since many 501(c)(3) organizations are in fact, partly or primarily, mutual benefit, club-like organizations (see Hansmann, 1980, Weisbrod, 1988, and Ben-Ner and Van Hoomissen, 1991, this volume; see also Ben-Ner and Van Hoomissen, 1992 for empirical support of this theoretical view). The data on nonprofit organizations presented in this paper (described in the Appendix) concern only (501)(c)(3) organizations. However, the omission of the "noncharitable" segment, which is lumped here with the for-profit sector, has little quantitative importance because it employs less than 5% of the entire nonprofit sector (see Rudney, 1987, and footnote 4, below).

2   The Nonprofit Sector in the Multisector Economy, 1985

In 1985 there were 14,033 nonprofit organizations in New York State as compared to 419,931 private for-profit establishments. The nonprofit sector employed 753,108 people,[4] or slightly more than one tenth of the state's nonagricultural employment, and paid total wages of $36.5 billion (in 1985 prices) or 7.6% of the total state wage bill. The average wage rate in the nonprofit sector was about 70% of the average wage in the other sectors combined.

2.1 Industrial Distribution

The industrial distribution of nonprofit organizations differs dramatically from that of for-profit firms, but much less so from that of government.[5] As Table 1 indicates, the nonprofit sector is only barely present outside of services, where the for-profit sector is predomi-

---

4   The 3,993 "noncharitable" nonprofit organizations (found in SICs 8611-8699, 6131, 8922 and 6732) employ together 33,142 employees.

5   The comparison with government agencies is complicated by the Standard Industrial Classification system. The system unfortunately separates the provision of government services from their administration, which it does not do for other sectors.

Table 1: Sector Employment Shares by Industry Group, in percent, 1985*

Industry Group	Nonprofit	For-Profit	Gov't	Standard Industrial Code
Agriculture	2.1	97.8	0.0	0000-0999
Mining	.	100.0	.	1000-1499
Construction	0.0	99.7	0.2	1500-1799
Manufacturing	0.0	99.7	0.2	2000-2699, 2800-3999
Transportation	0.0	78.5	21.4	4000-4230, 4400-4799
US Postal Service	.	.	100.0	4300-4399
Communications	1.0	98.9	.	4800-4899
NON-SERVICES	0.1	92.8	6.9	
Financial Services	0.9	96.1	2.9	6000-6999
Personal and Business Services	0.5	99.3	0.0	7000-7699
Amusement & Recreation	7.9	80.1	11.9	7800-7999
Health Services	48.3	29.3	22.3	8000-8099
Legal Services	3.3	96.6	.	8100-8199
Education & Libraries	31.9	2.7	65.3	8200-8299, 8920-8929
Social Services	85.5	11.0	3.3	8320-8399
Museums, Bot. & Zoo. Gardens	91.3	1.1	7.5	8400-8499
Membership Organizations	61.2	38.7	.	8600-8699
Other Services (prof., etc.)	0.3	98.1	1.5	8810-8919, 8930-8999
Government	.	.	100.0	9110-9729
SERVICES	20.3	51.3	28.2	
Commerce	0.1	99.6	0.1	5000-5999
Printing & Publishing	1.0	98.9	0.0	2700-2799
Electricity, Gas & Sanitation	.	76.9	23.0	4910-4999
OTHER	0.2	98.7	1.0	
TOTAL	10.1	73.7	16.1	

*Rows may not total 100 due to rounding.
Source: For this and all other tables, see Ben-Ner and Van Hoomissen (1989).

nant. In services, however, nonprofits provide 20.3% of total employment while the for-profit and government sectors provide 51.3% and 28.2%, respectively.

Within services, the nonprofit sector employs a majority of those working in museums and botanical and zoological gardens, social services, and membership organizations,[6] just under half of those working in the health industry, and nearly a third of those working in education and libraries. In other service industries the presence of the nonprofit sector is small. With minor exceptions, the above picture is reproduced in the state's 10 economic development regions

---

6 All "membership organizations" are 501(c) organizations, but many are not charitable as defined by IRC 501(c)(3) and therefore appear in the data for the for-profit sector.

Table 2: Industries in which the Nonprofit Share of Total Employment Exceeds 25%, 1985*

Industry SIC and name	Sector Share			Standard Employment
	Nonprofit	For-Profit	Gov't	
866: Religious Organizations	99.7	0.3	0.0	28,198
842: Arboreta, Botanical & Zoological Gardens	97.7	2.3	0.0	1,343
892: Noncommercial Research, Ed., and Sci. Orgs.	97.7	2.2	0.1	24,294
833: Job Training & Vocation Rehabilitation Services	93.4	5.5	1.1	20,160
832: Individual & Family Social Services	92.1	7.9	0.0	68,700
841: Museums & Art Galleries	90.2	0.9	8.9	7,017
839: Social Services NEC**	84.4	4.0	11.6	30,651
808: Outpatient Care Facilities	79.7	18.9	1.4	21,260
835: Child Day Care Services	76.5	23.5	0.0	21,682
836: Residential Care	76.0	18.0	6.0	38,551
673: Trusts	74.5	25.1	0.4	3,124
097: Hunting & Trapping & Game Propagation	70.1	29.9	0.0	67
806: Hospitals	67.1	3.3	29.6	393,895
864: Civic, Social & Fraternal Associations	65.4	34.6	0.0	28,010
823: Libraries & Information Centers	60.3	0.4	39.3	14,089
869: Membership Organizations NEC**	54.3	45.7	0.0	3,261
822: Colleges, Universities, & Professional Schools	53.8	0.7	45.5	189,894
862: Professional Membership Organizations	36.1	63.9	0.0	4,672
703: Camps & Trailering Parks	34.3	65.7	0.0	1,146
792: Theatres, Orchestras, Bands & Entertainers	33.4	66.5	0.1	22,512
829: Schools & Educational Services, NEC**	31.4	52.3	16.3	8,467
805: Nursing and Personal Care Facilities	30.6	40.9	28.5	118,052
809: Health and Allied Services, NEC**	26.7	0.0	73.3	31,013

*Rows may not total 100 due to rounding.
**NEC = not elsewhere classified

(with the exception of New York City's disproportionate share in education and entertainment).

More insight about the industrial distribution of the three sectors can be gleaned from an examination of 3-digit SIC level industries in which the nonprofit sector has a significant presence (employing more than 25% of workers). The nonprofit, for-profit, and government sectors in the 23 industries listed in Table 2 jointly employ over one million of New York's workers,[7] of which about two-thirds work in the nonprofit sector. All but four of these industries belong to either the health, education, or social services industry groups. In only three industries does the nonprofit sector stand virtually alone: (1) religious organizations, (2) arboreta, botanical and zoological gardens, and (3) noncommercial research, education and science organizations. Elsewhere nonprofit organizations typically coexist with either for-profits or government, but not both.

Thus there appear to be two kinds of nonprofit organizations: those that coexist with for-profit firms and those that coexist with government firms. This observation bears on theoretical issues concerning the relationship between the nonprofit sector and the for-profit and government sectors discussed in this volume and elsewhere in the literature.

2.2 Industrial Concentration

Almost all nonprofit sector employment (99%) is concentrated in services (Table 3). Organizations in health, education and social services jointly dominate the nonprofit sector, employing 43.3%, 24.6% and 20.4% of all nonprofit workers, respectively. The industrial concentration of nonprofit organizations differs from that of for-profit organizations, but resembles that of government. For-profit sector employment is almost equally divided among the three activity classes ("services," "nonservices," and "other"); within services, for-profit employment is proportionately small in industry groups where nonprofit employment is relatively important (and vice versa). Government employment, like nonprofit employment, is concentrated in services, primarily in education and health.

2.3 Size Distribution

Nonprofit organizations are strikingly larger on average in terms of employees per firm than their counterparts in the for-profit sector.[8] The difference in size is greatest in health services; in only one broad industry group—financial services—are nonprofit organizations smaller on average (Table 4). Systematic differences in firm size are found also in narrowly defined industries (Table 5). Of the 32

---

7   Nonprofits have some presence in 48 other industries, and there are 30 service industries in which nonprofits have no presence at all.

8   Comparison with government is not feasible because the "enterprise" unit used by the New York State Labor Department is overly inclusive (e.g., a municipality, state agency, or functional district).

Table 3: Industry Distribution of the Nonprofit, For-Profit and Government Sectors, in percent, 1985*

Industry Group	Nonprofit	For-Profit	Government
Agriculture	0.1	0.7	0.0
Mining	.	0.1	.
Construction	0.0	4.4	0.0
Manufacturing	0.0	20.9	0.2
Transportation	0.0	3.8	4.8
US Postal Service	.	.	6.0
Communications	0.1	2.4	.
NON-SERVICES	0.3	32.5	11.2
Financial Services	0.9	12.7	1.7
Personal and Business Services	0.4	11.8	0.0
Amusement & Recreation	1.0	1.5	1.0
Health Services	43.3	3.6	12.6
Legal Services	0.3	1.4	.
Education & Libraries	24.6	0.2	31.8
Social Services	20.4	0.3	0.5
Museums, Botanical & Zoo. Gardens	1.0	0.0	0.0
Membership Organizations	6.7	0.5	.
Other Services (professional, etc.)	0.0	1.9	0.1
Government	.	.	38.9
SERVICES	99.1	34.4	87.1
Commerce	0.2	2.9	0.0
Printing & Publishing	.	1.0	1.4
Electricity, Gas & Sanitation	0.3	29.0	0.2
OTHER	0.6	33.0	1.6
TOTAL EMPLOYMENT	753,108	5,453,491	1,187,748

*Columns may not total 100 due to rounding.

Table 4: Average Number of Employees per Establishment in the Nonprofit (NP) and For-Profit (FP) Sectors by Industry Group, 1985

	Average Number of Employees per Establishment			Number of Establishments	
Industry Group	NP	FP	NP/FP Ratio*	NP	FP
Financial Services	11.45	16.90	0.68	628	41249
Personal and Business Services	14.31	10.96	1.31	249	58733
Amusement & Recreation	16.93	9.56	1.77	487	8744
Health Services	407.06	7.01	58.04	802	28269
Legal Services	35.15	7.04	4.99	81	11543
Education & Libraries	64.71	14.07	4.60	2864	1122
Social Services	34.50	13.56	2.54	4459	1462
Museums, Botanical & Zoo. Gardens	37.08	6.13	6.05	206	15
Membership Organizations	12.93	8.34	1.55	3937	3856
Other Services (professional, etc.)	19.94	4.30	4.64	17	24930

*Ratio of average number of employees per nonprofit establishment to the average number of employees per for-profit establishment.

Table 5: Average Number of Employees per Establishment in the Nonprofit (NP) and For-Profit (FP) Sectors in Industries in Which There are at Least 5 Firms and Where Each Sector Employs More than 500 Workers, 1985*

SIC	Industry Name	Average Number of Employees per Establishment			Number of Establishments	
		NP	FP	Ratio**	NP	FP
2721:	Periodicals: Publishing and printing	24.32	45.84	0.53	40	676
4833:	Television broadcasting	91.21	257.40	0.35	14	99
5812:	Eating places	53.03	13.14	4.04	31	23122
6513:	Operators of apartment buildings	7.21	4.06	1.77	86	13488
6553:	Cemetery subdividers and developers	5.68	4.14	1.37	162	497
7392:	Management and public relations	16.00	6.43	2.49	47	7404
7922:	Theatrical producers and misc. theatrical services	21.56	8.83	2.44	258	1341
7929:	Bands, orchestras, actors, and other entertainers	25.36	3.99	6.36	77	784
8051:	Skilled nursing care facilities	218.06	139.98	1.56	134	299
8059:	Nursing and personal care facilities, NEC‡	112.61	57.31	1.96	61	112
8062:	General medical and surgical hospitals	1122.72	397.23	2.83	223	26
8063:	Psychiatric hospitals	511.60	158.79	3.22	5	14
8069:	Specialty hospitals, except psychiatric	669.18	116.20	5.76	17	5
8081:	Outpatient care facilities	62.29	28.85	2.16	272	139
8091:	Home health care, and health and allied services, NEC‡	137.90	75.05	1.84	60	303
8111:	Legal services	35.15	7.04	4.99	81	11543
8211:	Elementary and secondary schools	31.26	16.65	1.88	1512	124
8221:	Colleges, universities and professional schools	615.59	106.88	5.76	163	8
8249:	Vocational schools, NEC‡	17.79	18.69	0.95	52	139
8299:	Schools and educational services, NEC‡	12.91	7.06	1.83	206	627
8321:	Individual and family services (social services)	50.88	28.57	1.78	1243	191
8331:	Job training and vocational rehabilitation services	46.16	30.03	1.54	408	37
8351:	Child day care services	17.97	7.08	2.54	923	720
8361:	Residential care (social services)	57.69	21.23	2.72	508	326
8399:	Individual and family services, NEC‡	18.78	6.56	2.86	1377	188
8611:	Business associations	22.11	7.69	2.87	45	815
8621:	Professional membership organizations	18.96	15.15	1.25	89	197
8641:	Civic, social, and fraternal associations	33.61	7.58	4.43	545	1279
8699:	Membership organizations, NEC‡	8.95	11.45	0.78	198	130
8922:	Noncommercial research organizations	38.71	6.49	5.96	613	83

*The restriction on firm number caused the exclusion of two industries, in both of which nonprofits are larger than for-profits.
**Ratio of average number of employees per nonprofit establishment to the average number of employees per for-profit establishment.
‡NEC = not elsewhere classified

4-digit SIC level industries where the nonprofit and for-profit sectors each hire at least 500 employees statewide, the average nonprofit is larger than the average for-profit in 28 industries. Whatever the reasons for this difference might be, it suggests that these two types of organization produce different services, or at the very least produce the same services differently.[9] While the observation that nonprofit and for-profit organizations produce different variants of the same service has been made (e.g., Ben-Ner and Van Hoomissen, this volume), the larger size of nonprofit organizations relative to for-profit firms has received little attention in the literature.

2.4 Wages

The average monthly wage rate paid by the nonprofit sector in 1985 was $1,347, or roughly 74% of the average wage rate paid by the for-profit sector and 68% of the average wage paid by the government sector. The same ratios are replicated in the service industries class. This conforms with the widely-held view that nonprofit workers are underpaid. Wage differentials are somewhat smaller within the service industries group, and in education and social services, the nonprofit sector leads other sectors, whereas in financial services the average wage rate in the three sectors is about the same. Elsewhere, employees in the nonprofit sector receive lower wages, sometimes by a large margin. Thus nonprofit–for-profit average wage differentials are due, at least in part, to different industrial concentrations: nonprofits concentrate more heavily in low wage industries, although within these industries they often pay better than their nonprofit counterparts.

Indeed, in the more narrowly defined 3-digit SIC industries, where the nonprofit sector employs at least one-quarter of all industry workers, nonprofit organizations pay higher wages than for-profit firms in 12 of 23 industries, but in only 3 out of 13 industries does it pay higher wages than government (Table 6). Further reducing the potential heterogeneity in the service produced by a given industry by focusing on 4-digit SIC level industries (Table 7), we note that nonprofit organizations pay higher wages in 13 of the 29 industries. In most cases, the wage differential between the two sectors is sizable: in only 5 of the 29 industries is the wage differential less than 5%. (An analysis of wage dispersion within and across sectors confirms this

---

9   The differences in services may be reflected in more personal attention accorded to customers in smaller organizations, in the availability of more diverse equipment in larger organizations, and so forth.

Table 6: Wage Rages in the Nonprofit Sector, as a Percentage of Wage Rates in the For-Profit and Government Sectors, in Industries in which the Nonprofit Sector's Share of Total Employment Exceeds 25%, 1985

Industry SIC and name	Nonprofit/ For-Profit	Nonprofit/ Government
866: Religious Organizations	116.6	.
842: Arboreta, Botanical & Zoo. Gardens	124.3	.
892: Noncommercial Research, Ed., and Sci. Orgs.	67.2	189.7
833: Job Training & Vocation Rehabilitation Services	133.4	44.9
832: Individual & Family Social Services	101.0	.
841: Museums & Art Galleries	90.2	78.2
839: Social Services NEC*	94.4	74.1
808: Outpatient Care Facilities	73.8	73.2
835: Child Day Care Services	133.7	.
836: Residential Care	149.2	56.3
673: Trusts	99.4	92.4
097: Hunting & Trapping & Game Propagation	200.3	.
806: Hospitals	96.8	93.5
864: Civic, Social & Fraternal Associations	78.4	.
823: Libraries & Information Centers	101.7	151.1
869: Membership Organizations NEC*	68.7	.
822: Colleges, Universities, & Professional Schools	142.3	95.1
862: Professional Membership Organizations	99.9	.
703: Camps & Trailering Parks	107.4	.
792: Theatres, Orchestras, Bands & Entertainers	63.5	147.4
829: Schools & Educational Services, NEC*	87.5	79.0
805: Nursing and Personal Care Facilities	102.4	76.2
809: Health and Allied Services, NEC*	185.2	.

*NEC = not elsewhere classified

result.) In almost all industries, nonprofit organizations pay less than government (Table 8).

The nonprofit sector tends to pay higher wages in industries where it employs a large proportion of workers,[10] suggesting that when nonprofits are subject to less product market competition some profits are distributed to employees. In general, the wage differen-

---

10 Let vector $W(i,j)$ contain the ratio of sector i to sector j wage rates in each industry k (4-digit SIC), and let vector $E(i)$ contain sector i's share in each industry k's employment, where i = (NP, FP, G), and NP, FP and G denote the nonprofit, for-profit and government sectors, respectively. The correlation between $W(NP,FP)$ and $E(NP)$ is 43%, and the correlation between $W(NP,FP)$ and $E(FP)$ is –38%. Likewise, the correlations between $W(NP,G)$ and $E(NP)$ and between $W(NP,G)$ and $E(G)$ are 39% and –20%, respectively.

Table 7: Nonprofit Wage Rates as a Percentage of For-Profit Wage Rates in Industries Where Each Sector Employs More than 500 Workers, 1985

SIC	Industry Name	Nonprofit wage/ For-profit wage	Share in Total Employment*	
			Nonprofit	For-profit
8091:	Home health care, and health and allied services, NEC#	185.2	0.27	0.73
8221:	Colleges, universities and professional schools	167.5	0.63	0.01
8361:	Residential care (social services)	149.2	0.76	0.18
8069:	Specialty hospitals, except psychiatric	148.4	0.73	0.04
8351:	Child day care services	133.7	0.76	0.24
8331:	Job training and vocational rehabilitation services	133.4	0.93	0.06
8063:	Psychiatric hospitals	121.8	0.06	0.05
6311:	Life insurance carriers	112.7	0.04	0.95
7397:	Commercial testing laboratories	111.3	0.24	0.75
8051:	Skilled nursing care facilities	106.9	0.38	0.55
8211:	Elementary and secondary schools	103.5	0.14	0.01
6553:	Cemetery subdividers and developers	103.1	0.30	0.67
8321:	Individual and family services (social services)	101.0	0.60	0.00
8621:	Professional membership organizations	99.9	0.37	0.63
8249:	Vocational schools, NEC#	95.4	0.27	0.73
8399:	Individual and family services, NEC#	94.4	0.87	0.04
8062:	General medical and surgical hospitals	92.4	0.74	0.03
8299:	Schools and educational services, NEC#	87.5	0.31	0.52
8611:	Business associations	87.1	0.14	0.86
8111:	Legal services	86.3	0.04	0.96
8059:	Nursing and personal care facilities, NEC#	82.4	0.16	0.15
6513:	Operators of apartment buildings	81.2	0.01	0.76
7392:	Management and public relations	80.0	0.02	0.98
8641:	Civic, social, and fraternal associations	78.4	0.65	0.35
8081:	Outpatient care facilities	73.7	0.79	0.19
8699:	Membership organizations, NEC#	68.7	0.54	0.46
7929:	Bands, orchestras, actors, and other entertainers	68.0	0.38	0.62
8922:	Noncommercial research organizations	67.3	0.97	0.03
7922:	Theatrical producers and misc. theatrical services	66.2	0.32	0.68

*Employment shares do not add up to 1 in industries with some government presence.
#NEC = not elsewhere classified

Table 8: Nonprofit Wage Rages as a Percentage of Government Wage Rates in Industries Where Each Sector Employs More than 500 Workers, 1985

SIC	Industry Name	Nonprofit wage/ Government wage	Share in Total Employment	
			Nonprofit	Government
8231:	Libraries	151.1	0.60	0.39
8051:	Skilled nursing care facilities	114.2	0.39	0.06
8063:	Psychiatric hospitals	97.3	0.06	0.89
8062:	General medical and surgical hospitals	96.5	0.75	0.22
8069:	Specialty hospitals, except psychiatric	91.0	0.74	0.23
8221:	Colleges, universities and professional schools	88.1	0.64	0.35
8411:	Museums and art galleries	86.9	0.90	0.09
8299:	Schools and educational services, NEC*	79.0	0.31	0.16
8399:	Individual and family services, NEC*	74.1	0.87	0.09
8222:	Junior colleges and technical institutes	64.2	0.06	0.93
8059:	Nursing and personal care facilities	62.7	0.16	0.69
8361:	Residential care (social services)	56.3	0.76	0.06
6513:	Operators of apartment buildings	55.1	0.01	0.23
8211:	Elementary & secondary schools	43.1	0.14	0.85

*NEC = not elsewhere classified

tials between nonprofit organizations and for-profit firms suggests again the possibility that nonprofit, for-profit and government organizations provide different types of services or produce differently the same services, and thus hire different types of workers (and in different proportions) and pay different wages.[11]

3   Sectoral Changes, 1981–1987

The number of nonprofit organizations in New York State grew from 12,973 in 1981 to 14,450 in 1987, whereas the number of for-profit firms rose from 391,673 to 433,271. While these numbers represent similar growth rates, employment and wage trends in the two sectors differed substantially.[12] Nonprofit employment grew by

---

11   Note that our data do not contain information about individual workers or occupations, hence we cannot make inferences about wages across sectors in specific occupations. For explanations why there might be differences in the wages of nonprofit and for-profit employees, see Preston (1989 and 1990).
12   The data set on which this paper is based focuses only on insured employment, which excludes the self-employed and lumps together part- and full-time employment. If the trends in self-employment differ from those in insured employment, or if the trends in part-time employment vary across sectors, then the analysis here will be biased in an unknown direction.

18.3%, more than twice as fast as employment in the for-profit sector (7.9%) and more than three times as fast as employment in the government sector (5.1%). (Within government, federal employment in New York grew only about 1% while state and local government employment each grew about 5.8%.) As a consequence of these changes, the share of the nonprofit sector in New York State's employment grew between 1981 and 1987 from 9.6% to 10.5%, whereas the for-profit sector declined from 73.5% to 73.2%. The share of government declined from 16.9% to 16.4% (with federal government declining from 2.3% to 2.1%, state government from 3.4% to 3.3%, and local government from 11.2% to 11.0%).

The differences in the growth rates of the nonprofit and for-profit sectors are grounded in changes in the industries in which they operate. The 1980s were a period of decline for manufacturing, where the for-profit sector is prominent, and rapid growth in services. Indeed, the for-profit *service* sector grew at nearly the same rate (17%) as did the nonprofit sector.

The patterns of growth differed considerably between the nonprofit and for-profit sectors. As shown in Ben-Ner and Van Hoomissen (1990), the nonprofit sector grew at a steady pace over this period, while the for-profit sector experienced wide fluctuations. The nonprofit sector thus appears to grow with the rest of the economy, but not to decline along with it: although all sectors grew after 1983, the for-profit and government sectors declined during the 1981–83 recession while the nonprofit sector held steady.[13]

The industrial concentration of the nonprofit sector changed little during this period. Most notably, the weight of the social welfare industry in total nonprofit employment grew from 17.8% to 21.6%. The proportion of nonprofit sector employees working in the health industry fluctuated slightly around the 43% mark and the proportion working in the education sector fell from 25.8% to 24.4%. While there was almost no rearrangement of the distribution of government employment, the for-profit sector was in flux, with the manufacturing industry declining sharply (going from 24.7% of total for-profit employment to 19.1%).

---

13 The patterns described above apply, more or less, to the various regions of New York State. In New York City, the share of the nonprofit sector in employment grew from 10.6% in 1981 to 12.3% in 1987, whereas the share of the for-profit sector—and even its absolute size—declined. Thus, the decline in New York City's unemployment rate from 9.0% in 1981 to 7.4% in 1987 was the consequence of growth of the nonprofit and government sectors only.

In the nonprofit sector the average real wage rate was 12.7% higher in 1987 than in 1981, or slightly better than the 12.5% increase in the for-profit sector as a whole. However, government wage rates grew 18.7% over this period and in the for-profit *services* sector wage rates grew more than 20%.

Within services, the average for-profit sector wage was 20.0% higher in 1987 than it was in 1981, while the growth was only 18.7% in government and 13.0% in the nonprofit sector. In industry groups where the nonprofit sector employs a significant share of workers (such as health and social services), wage increases were only slightly lower (1.1%) than those of the for-profit sector. Nonetheless, the fact that wage growth has been on the average much slower in the non-profit sector than in the for-profit service sector indicates not only that nonprofit employment is concentrated in lower-paying industries, but also that it is concentrated in low-wage *growth* industries (at least during the 1980s). One clear example is social services, where more than one-fifth of nonprofit employees are concentrated and where employment growth has been strongest, but where wage growth has also been much slower (7.9% in the nonprofit sector) than in other industries.

4   Revenue Sources and Spending Patterns in the Nonprofit Sector

Financial information about the New York State nonprofit sector is available for the period 1982–1985.[14] We do not have comparable financial information for the other sectors, hence this section focuses only on the nonprofit sector.

The average revenue of the nonprofit organizations in our data set was about $2 million in 1985. The highest revenue per organization was in hospitals, with an average of nearly $24 million, followed by organizations in foreign relations with almost $7 million on aver-

---

14 The number of nonprofits which report financial information to the Department of Charities Registration (9,250 in 1985) is smaller than the number of nonprofits which report employment and wage data to the Labor Department (14,033 in 1985). This is so because certain categories of non-profit organizations are not requested to report to the Department of Charities Registration but have to report to the Labor Department (see Appendix). Not all reporting organizations provide all pertinent financial information. In addition, the classification of industries followed by the two departments is not comparable.

age. The lowest average revenue was raised by social, fraternal, and professional organizations, with $336 thousand, followed by cultural and educational organizations with approximately three quarters of a million in average revenues. (Colleges and universities, with much higher revenues, are excluded from this data set.)

A nonprofit organization has five different sources of revenues: direct contributions from individuals or other organizations; contributions from federated fundraising organizations (e.g., United Way); grants from various government agencies; program revenue (consisting of fees for services); and membership dues, interest on endowments, and income from business activities and special events.

Table 9 shows that, on average, nonprofit organizations receive more than half (58%) of their revenues from program services revenues. This share of essentially market revenue is by far the largest single category, followed by individual contributions (16% in 1985), and government contributions (12% in 1985). Dues from members, endowment income, and other types of income combine just 10% of the nonprofit sector's income. Interestingly, the shares of various sources in total revenue remained remarkably stable over the period 1982–1985.

There exists considerable variation in revenue sources across industries. Nonprofit hospitals receive 90% of their income from the sale of their services, whereas other health and rehabilitation services receive only about 40% from this source. In other industries, the proportion of income from sale of services is even lower: about one-third for cultural and educational, social and professional, and civic organizations, a little less than that for social welfare organizations, and much less in other organizations, which instead rely for up to a half of their revenues on contributions by individuals. Government contributions figure prominently in the income of foreign relations organizations (58%) and social welfare organizations (about 40%). Hospitals receive very small amounts of government contributions, and other nonprofit organizations rely on government contributions for about one-tenth to one-fifth of their total revenues.

For hospitals, the second most important source of income is endowments. Membership fees and endowments are important for "mutual" types of organizations, for which they account between one-fifth and one-third of their total revenues. Finally, united fundraising organizations contribute almost nothing toward hospitals' budgets, but help out with about one-tenth of health organizations' revenues, and around 5% elsewhere.

Table 9: Nonprofit Organizations' Revenues and Expenditures by Category as Percent of Total, by Activity Type, 1982–1985

Activity	Year	Revenues					Expenditures						N
		CONTR	UNTD	GOV	PROG	OTHR	PROG	GRNT	MGT	FNDR	AFF	COLL	
Animal Welfare & Env. Preservation	1982	42	3	13	22	20	74	1	17	8	0	58	128
	1985	47	2	10	18	23	70	1	19	10	0	59	155
Civic Organizations	1982	16	7	20	35	21	80	4	14	2	1	43	613
	1985	28	6	13	31	21	78	2	14	6	0	47	724
Cultural & Educational Organizations	1982	28	4	17	36	16	78	4	15	3	0	49	2107
	1985	22	3	15	40	20	79	3	15	3	0	45	2467
Fundraising & Support Orgs.	1982	52	8	15	8	17	55	33	5	4	4	75	813
	1985	56	8	5	10	21	54	35	5	4	2	69	914
Foreign Relations Organizations	1982	34	1	58	5	2	93	1	3	3	0	93	62
	1985	35	1	58	5	2	92	2	3	3	0	93	80
Health & Rehab. Organizations	1982	23	10	19	38	9	74	9	11	5	1	52	858
	1985	20	9	19	43	9	76	8	12	4	2	48	989
Hospitals & Related Facilities	1982	2	0	3	87	8	82	0	16	1	0	5	326
	1985	3	1	2	90	5	81	0	18	1	0	6	321
Public Policy Ed. Orgs.	1982	49	3	6	11	31	68	2	17	10	3	59	217
	1985	35	1	13	30	21	75	5	12	6	2	49	249
Social Welfare Organizations	1982	16	6	41	27	10	81	4	13	2	1	63	1408
	1985	15	5	40	28	12	80	4	14	2	0	60	1754
Social, Frat. & Prof. Orgs.	1982	23	5	11	33	28	65	10	16	8	1	39	289
	1985	22	3	7	34	33	65	8	18	8	1	32	307
All Organizations	1982	15	3	13	58	10	78	5	14	2	1	31	6865
	1985	16	3	12	58	10	77	5	14	2	0	31	8010

DEFINITIONS

N = the number of organizations for which information was available.

REVENUES

CONTR = Direct contributions from individuals/organizations to individual organizations.

UNTD = Indirect contributions received through federated fundraising organizations (e.g., United Way).

GOV = Government grants.

PROG = Program service revenue.

OTHR = Other revenue including membership dues, interest, dividends, rental income, capital gains, special fundraising event revenue, and inventory sales.

COLL = the 'collectivity index' developed by Weisbrod (1988). It consists of the combined share of individual, federated fundraising and government contributions in nonprofit organizations' total revenues.

EXPENDITURES

PROG = Program service expenditures.

GRNT = Grants and allocations made to individuals and organizations.

MGT = Management and general expenditures.

FUNDR = Fundraising expenditures.

AFF = Payments to affiliates (see Appendix).

Consider now the expenditures of nonprofit organizations. The direct costs of production of services—program expenditures— constitute the major share (slightly above three-quarters on average) of nonprofit organizations' expenditures (see Table 9).[15] This includes even those organizations that are primarily dedicated to raising funds for distribution to other organizations. Such organizations spend a little more than half of their income on programs and only a little more than one-third on obtaining contributions.

On average, nonprofit organizations spend about 15 cents on fundraising to raise one dollar in contributions (and only 13 cents per dollar if contributions from federated fundraising organizations are included). The "cost" of contributions varies, with the lowest cost being in organizations that collect money for further distribution (fundraising and support organizations, and foreign relations organizations); such organizations spend less than 9 cents per contributed dollar. The highest cost of contributions is in hospitals, which spend almost 40 cents per contributed dollar. However, this figure is misleading since hospitals raise money mostly for capital investments which are not included in their annual revenues.[16]

Management and general expenditures consume about 15% of the income of most organizations, with the notable exceptions of fundraising and foreign affairs organizations, where the proportion is

---

15 Program expenditure is much larger than program revenue for essentially all nonprofit organizations.

16 Correlation coefficients between individual contributions and fundraising costs are quite high for civic organizations (.99), social, fraternal and professional organizations (.97), health and rehabilitation organizations (.96), cultural and educational organizations (.94), organizations in animal welfare and environmental preservation (.82), and public policy education organizations (.77). For these organizations, a dollar of contributions costs about 18 cents in fundraising expenditure, with the exception of social, fraternal and professional organizations where a contributed dollar costs 30 cents in fundraising. (The reason might be that many of these organizations solicit memberships in addition to contributions, and these are recorded under the revenue category 'other.') Lower correlation coefficients between contributions and fundraising expenditures exist for social welfare organizations (.59), fundraising and support organizations (.57), and foreign relations organizations (.56). For these organizations the cost of one dollar in individual contributions is only 9 to 11 cents. Finally, hospitals enjoy very little revenue in individual contributions and the correlation coefficient is very low (.10). It is interesting to note that the more "collective" the services of a nonprofit organization (the higher the COLL index), the higher the correlation between fundraising costs and individual contributions.

only about 5% or less. These organizations have few employees and most of their activities consist of transferring funds to other organizations.

Finally, it appears that while organizations are allowed to make a profit (but are barred from distributing it), they make very little profit. For most nonprofit organizations the difference between total revenues and expenditures is very small and positive. For 1985, the 8,010 nonprofit organizations in our data set had total revenues of $2,026.6 million, just $2.6 million over their combined expenditures.

5   Conclusions

This paper has drawn a portrait of the nonprofit sector in the mixed economy of New York State during the 1980s. The main findings of this paper are:

1.   The nonprofit sector employs about one-tenth of the workforce.

2.   The nonprofit sector is concentrated almost entirely in services industries, where it dominates the museum, botanical and zoological industry as well as social services, and employs almost one-half of all health services employees and nearly one-third of education workers.

3.   Nonprofit employment, like government employment, is concentrated in services most heavily within education and health. For-profit sector employment is almost equally divided among the three activity classes (nonservices, services, and other) and within services for-profit employment is proportionately small in industry groups where nonprofit employment is relatively important (and vice versa).

4.   Employment in the nonprofit sector grew more than twice as fast as employment in the for-profit sector between 1981 and 1987 and more than three times as fast as government employment. The for-profit *service* sector, however, grew at roughly the same rate as the nonprofit sector.

5.   Overall, nonprofit sector wage rates are lower than in the other sectors. However, in many industries with high nonprofit concentration, nonprofit organizations pay higher wages. Still, nonprofits concentrate much more heavily in low-wage industries than do for-profits.

6. Nonprofit wage rates have grown at about the same pace as average for-profit wage rates, but significantly slower than for-profit *service* sector and government wage rages.

7. Nonprofits tend to be significantly larger than for-profit firms within the same industries.

8. More than half of the average nonprofit organization's revenues stem from sale of their services, with hospitals raising 90% in this way. However, most organizations obtain only between one-fifth and one-third of their revenues from fees. The rest of their revenue comes from individual contributions, various business ventures and membership fees, government contributions, and, in very small part, from federated fundraising agencies such as United Way.

9. Nearly three-quarters of nonprofit organizations' expenditures are dedicated directly to the provision of their services, with management expenses consuming about another one-sixth.

10. Fundraising expenses represent on average about 2% of nonprofit organizations' expenditures. It costs on average 15 cents in fundraising expenses to raise one dollar of direct contributions.

11. Nonprofit organizations approximately break even: most nonprofit organizations' revenues exceed expenditures, but only by a minute margin.

APPENDIX

A. Employment and Wage Data

The data set was provided by the New York State Department of Labor, which collects information from employers about employment and wages in establishments for the purpose of state unemployment insurance. The coverage is quite comprehensive, with few exclusions: the self-employed and family members working with them, many agricultural workers, clergy, and those who work "off the books." Volunteers are also excluded. For the remainder of the workforce the coverage is essentially complete. For further information, see New York State Department of Labor, "Employer's Guide to Unemployment Insurance," IA318.1, June 1987, and other pertinent forms.

The data are by county (where an establishment operates), 4-digit Standard Industrial Classification (SIC) code, and sector (for-profit, nonprofit, federal government, state government, and local government). Nonprofit organizations are organizations with 501(c)(3) status, i.e., charitable organizations. Employers must report monthly the number of employees and total wages. Our data are for the first quarter of the year, for each of the years 1981–1987. The variables include (1) **employment,** the number of full and part-time employees (we used the first quarter employment as the un-seasonalized average annual employment); (2) **wages** paid to all employees, not including most fringe benefits (real wages were com-puted by deflating by the January, February and March Consumer Price Indexes); and (3) **establishment** (no firm data were available). The average wage is computed by dividing the wage bill by the number of employees.

B. Financial Data

The data set was provided by the New York State Department of Charities Registration, which collects information from 501(c)(3) non-profit organizations. Charitable organizations which intend to solicit contributions (from persons or governmental agencies in New York) must register and report financial data. However, charitable non-profit organizations that meet one of the following conditions are not required to register or report. These include (1) religious organiza-tions and charities they operate or supervise; (2) educational institu-tions that confine their solicitation to their own student bodies, alumni, faculty and trustees and their families, or which file annual financial reports with the Regents of the University of the State of New York; (3) libraries that file annual financial reports as required by the State Department of Education; (4) organizations that receive less than $10,000 in contributions during the fiscal year, provided none of their fundraising functions are carried on by professional fundraisers or commercial co-venturers; (5) organizations receiving an allocation from a registered federated fund (and comply with condition (4)); (6) all local units of veterans' organization, volunteer firefighters organizations and volunteer ambulance services; (7) fra-ternal, patriotic, social and alumni organizations, and historical so-cieties chartered by the New York State Board of Regents that confine their solicitation to their own membership.

Registered charities that are parent organizations to one or more affiliates within New York may file a combined written report. The term "affiliate" here includes any chapter, branch, auxiliary, or other subordinate units whose policies, fundraising activities, and expenditures are supervised or controlled by the parent organization.

REFERENCES

BEN-NER A. and VAN HOOMISSEN T., 1989, *A Study of the Nonprofit Sector in New York State: Its Size, Nature, and Economic Impact,* Albany, NY, The Nelson A. Rockefeller Institute of Government.

————, 1990, "The Nonprofit Sector's Growth in the 1980s: Facts and Interpretation," *Nonprofit Management and Leadership,* 1 (Winter), 99–116.

————, 1991, "Nonprofit Organizations in the Mixed Economy: A Demand and Supply Analysis," *Annals of Public and Cooperative Economics,* 62(4), 469–500.

————, 1992, "An Empirical Investigation of the Joint Determination of the Size of For-Profit, Nonprofit and Government Sectors," *Annals of Public and Cooperative Economics,* 63 (3), 392–415.

HANSMANN H., 1980, "The Role of Nonprofit Enterprise," *Yale Law Journal,* 89, 835–98.

HODGKINSON V., and WEITZMAN M., 1989, *Dimensions of the Independent Sector: A Statistical Profile,* The Independent Sector, Washington DC.

PRESTON A., 1989, "The Nonprofit Worker in a For-Profit World," *Journal of Labor Economics,* 7 (October), 438–63.

————, 1990, "Changing Labor Market Patterns in the Nonprofit and For-Profit Sectors: Implications for Nonprofit Management," *Nonprofit Management and Leadership,* 1 (Fall), 15–28.

RUDNEY G., 1987, "The Scope and Dimensions of Nonprofit Activity," in W. W. Powell (ed.) *The Nonprofit Sector: A Research Handbook,* Yale University Press, New Haven.

SIMON J.G., 1987, "The Tax Treatment of Nonprofit Organizations: A Review of Federal and State Policies," in *The Nonprofit Sector: A Research Handbook,* W. W. Powell (ed.) Yale University Press, New Haven.

WEISBROD B.A., 1988, *The Nonprofit Economy,* Harvard University Press, Cambridge, MA.

WILSON M.I., 1991, *The State of Nonprofit Michigan 1991,* mimeo, Institute for Public Policy and Social Research, Michigan State University, Lansing, MI.

CONTRIBUTORS

The Editors

Avner Ben-Ner, Professor, Industrial Relations Center, University of Minnesota, Minneapolis, Minnesota

Benedetto Gui, Associate Professor, Department of Economic Sciences, University of Venezia, Venezia, Italy

The Authors

Helmut K. Anheier, Assistant Professor, Department of Sociology, Rutgers University, New Brunswick, New Jersey; and Institute for Policy Studies, The Johns Hopkins University, Baltimore, Maryland

Carlo Borzaga, Associate Professor, Department of Economics, University of Trento, Trento, Italy

Cyril F. Chang, Professor, Department of Economics, The Fogelman College of Business and Economics, Memphis State University, Memphis, Tennessee

Alphonse G. Holtmann, Professor, Department of Economics, University of Miami, Coral Gables, Florida

Dennis A. Kaufman, Assistant Professor, Department of Economics, University of Wisconsin-Parkside, Kenosha, Wisconsin

Jeremy Kendall, Research Fellow, The University of Kent, Canterbury, Kent, United Kingdom

Martin Knapp, Professor, The University of Kent, Canterbury, Kent, United Kingdom

Jerald Schiff, Economist, Fiscal Affairs Department, International Monetary Fund, Washington, D.C.

Richard Steinberg, Associate Professor, Department of Economics and Philanthropic Studies, Indiana University and Purdue University, Indianapolis, Indiana

Howard P. Tuckman, Distinguished Professor, Department of Economics, The Fogelman College of Business and Economics, Memphis State University, Memphis, Tennessee

Steven G. Ullmann, Professor, Department of Economics, University of Miami, Coral Gables, Florida

Theresa Van Hoomissen, Adjunct Assistant Professor, Humphrey Institute for Public Policy, University of Minnesota, Minneapolis, Minnesota

Burton Weisbrod, John Evans Professor, Department of Economics, and Director, Center for Urban Affairs and Policy Research, Northwestern University, Evanston, Illinois

Author Index

Subject Index